The Missionary

THE MISSIONARY

*An Italian Priest's Remarkable Journey of
Faith on the Frontiers of the New World*

Samuel Mazzuchelli
Edited by Paul Dennis Sporer

TARXIEN PRESS

ANZA PUBLISHING, Chester, NY 10918
Tarxien Press is an imprint of Anza Publishing
Copyright © 2005 by Anza Publishing

This work is a new, unabridged edition of a work originally published in 1915: *Memoirs Historical and Edifying of a Missionary Apostolic* by Samuel Charles Mazzuchelli, translated from the Italian by Sister Mary Benedicta Kennedy.

Library of Congress Cataloging-in-Publication Data
Mazzuchelli, Samuel, 1806-1864.
   [Memorie. English.]
   The Missionary / Samuel Mazzuchelli ; editor, Paul D. Sporer.
     p. cm.
   Includes index.
   ISBN 1-932490-10-8 (softcover : alk. paper)
   ISBN 1-932490-23-X (hardcover : alk. paper)
   1. Mazzuchelli, Samuel, 1806-1864.
   2. Missionaries—United States—Biography.
   3. Catholic Church—United States—Clergy—Biography.
   4. Catholic Church—Missions—United States—History—19th century.
I. Sporer, Paul D. II. Title.

BV2765.5.M39A3 2004
266'.2'092—dc22   2004015374

All rights reserved. No part of this publication may be reproduced, stored in a retrieval system, or transmitted, in any form or by any means, electronic, mechanical, photocopying, recording or otherwise, without the prior permission of the copyright holder.

Visit AnzaPublishing.com for more information on outstanding authors and titles. Please support our efforts to restore great literature to a place of prominence in our culture.

ISBN 1-932490-10-8 (softcover : alk. paper)
ISBN 1-932490-23-X (hardcover : alk. paper)

∞ This book is printed on acid-free paper.

Contents

PART I

Editor's Preface   i

Chapter I
THE VOCATION OF THE PRIEST
TO THE PROPAGATION OF THE FAITH.   1

Chapter II
THE DEPARTURE AND VOYAGE OF THE MISSIONARY OF THE ORDER OF PREACHERS FROM ROME TO CINCINNATI IN THE UNITED STATES OF AMERICA.   7

Chapter III
STUDY OF THE ENGLISH LANGUAGE. VISIT TO THE CONVENT OF SAINT ROSE, PREPARATION FOR THE PRIESTHOOD IN THE CONVENT OF SAINT JOSEPH, AND ORDINATION TO THE DEACONSHIP AND PRIESTHOOD.   14

Chapter IV
DEPARTURE FROM CINCINNATI FOR MACKINAC. DESCRIPTION OF THIS ISLAND. FIRST VISIT TO GREEN BAY AND TO THE SAVAGES.   18

Chapter V
THE INFALLIBILITY OF THE CHURCH, THE SUPREMACY OF THE POPE, THE REAL PRESENCE OF CHRIST IN THE HOLY EUCHARIST, CONFESSION, PURGATORY, THE INTERCESSION OF THE SAINTS, THE USE OF HOLY IMAGES, AND ANTI-CHRIST, SUBJECTS OF SIX DISCOURSES DELIVERED BY A CALVINISTIC MINISTER IN 1831.   21

Chapter VI
CONVERSION OF THREE PROTESTANTS TO THE CATHOLIC FAITH, ON THE ISLAND OF MACKINAC, IN 1831.   28

Chapter VII
EXAMPLE OF PUBLIC PENANCE PRACTISED BY A CATHOLIC IN THE YEAR 1831.   34

Chapter VIII
MISSION AT GREEN BAY, CONVERSION OF SAVAGES OF THE TRIBE OF MANOMANIS. BAPTISM, CONFIRMATION AND COMMUNION OF THE SAME DURING THE YEAR 1831.   36

Chapter IX
PHYSICAL AND MORAL CONDITIONS OF THE INDIAN TRIBES OCCUPYING THE TERRITORIES OF MICHIGAN, WISCONSIN AND IOWA.   41

Chapter X
DESCRIPTION OF THE WOODEN CHURCH ERECTED AT GREEN BAY IN 1831.   47

Chapter XI
FIRST VISIT TO THE VILLAGE OF SAINT MARY'S UPON THE RIVER OF THE SAME NAME IN 1831. 49

Chapter XII
THE MISSION OF THE REVEREND F. BARAGA AT ARBRE-CROCHE AMONG THE INDIANS OF THE OTTAWA TRIBE. 51

Chapter XIII
INDIANS CONVERTED AT MACKINAC — CATHOLICS OF POINT SAINT IGNACE — DEATH OF AN OLD MAN — SINCERE CONVERSION OF ANOTHER. 55

Chapter XIV
OTHER SAVAGES BAPTIZED AT GREEN BAY — SPIRITUAL EXERCISES AT MACKINAC — BISHOP FENWICK, HIS FEAR OF GOD'S JUDGMENTS — THIRTY-TWO MARRIAGES SOLEMNIZED AT THE VILLAGE OF SAINTE MARIE. 59

Chapter XV
SIGNS OF WAR WITH THE SAVAGES — MANNER AND DIFFICULTIES OF TRAVELLING IN WISCONSIN TERRITORY IN 1832 — A NIGHT OFF THE RIGHT PATH — THE CATHOLICS OF PRAIRIE DU CHIEN — RETURN TO MACKINAC. 62

Chapter XVI
VISIT TO ARBRE-CROCHE — THE REVEREND FR. BARAGA — SNOW SHOES — OLD ARBRE-CROCHE — LAMENT OF AN OLD INDIAN WOMAN, AND GRIEF OF A YOUNG BRAVE — RETURN TO ISLAND OF MACKINAC. 67

Chapter XVII
ORDINARY DUTIES OF A MISSIONARY — DOGMATIC SERMONS NECESSARY FOR CATHOLICS LIVING AMONG SECTARIANS. 71

Chapter XVIII
FIRST MISSION TO THE TRIBE OF WINNEBAGOS IN 1833 — THEIR VICES ARE OPPOSED TO THE GOSPEL — CONVERSION OF SEVERAL. 73

Chapter XIX
MISSION AT SAINTE MARIE — SECTARIAN OPPOSITION — SALUTARY EFFECTS OF THIS VISIT — A BEAR KILLED AND EATEN. 75

Chapter XX
THE WINNEBAGO INDIANS ARE EVANGELIZED — MANY RECEIVE BAPTISM — PROOFS OF TRUE CONVERSION — A LITTLE PRAYER BOOK IN THEIR OWN LANGUAGE PRINTED IN 1833. 78

Chapter XXI
THE DIOCESE OF CINCINNATI IS DIVIDED — THE MISSIONARY IS SENT TO GREEN BAY — THE INDIANS OF THE MENOMINEE TRIBE AT CHURCH, WHERE THEY SING AND RECEIVE INSTRUCTIONS THROUGH AN INTERPRETER. 81

Chapter XXII
CONFESSIONS THROUGH AN INTERPRETER. 84

Chapter XXIII
HOLY COMMUNION. 88

Chapter XXIV
VISITS TO THE INDIANS ON THEIR FISHING VOYAGES — CIRCUMSTANCES CONNECTED WITH THE CONVERSION OF MANY INDIANS IN 1834. 89

Chapter XXV
VIEW OF A LODGE-CHURCH BUILT OF MATS. 94

Chapter XXVI
THE ANGLICAN MISSION AT GREEN BAY RECEIVES THE SUM OF TWO THOUSAND ONE HUNDRED DOLLARS, IN JUSTICE DUE TO THE CATHOLIC MISSION. 96

Chapter XXVII
FALSE METHODS OF THE PROTESTANTS IN CONVERTING THE SAVAGES. 98

Chapter XXVIII
PROTESTANT MISSIONS AMONG SEVERAL TRIBES OF INDIANS IN WISCONSIN TERRITORY AND VICINITY IN 1834. 100

Chapter XXIX
MISSIONS AMONG THE WINNEBAGO INDIANS IN THE YEAR 1834 — CONVERSION, BAPTISM AND BURIAL OF AN INDIAN WOMAN — AN EXPERIENCE WITH RATTLESNAKES — HOW THE PROGRESS OF THE FAITH WAS IMPEDED. 105

Chapter XXX
MISSION TO PRAIRIE DU CHIEN IN 1835. 112

Chapter XXXI
STATE OF THE MISSIONS AMONG THE TRIBES WHEN THE MISSIONARY LEFT THEM TO THE CARE OF HIS SUCCESSORS. 113

Chapter XXXII
RELIGION IS THE ONLY MEANS OF CIVILIZATION FOR THE INDIAN TRIBES — THE GREAT OBSTACLES IN ITS WAY. 117

PART II

Chapter I
HOW THE MISSIONARY, AFTER HAVING SERVED IN THE PROPAGATION OF THE FAITH AMONG THE INDIANS IS APPOINTED TO THE MISSIONS ABOUT THE HEADWATERS OF THE MISSISSIPPI. 127

Chapter II
THREE CLASSES OF MISSIONS IN AMERICA. 129

Chapter III
ORIGIN OF THE EPISCOPAL CITY OF DUBUQUE IN THE TERRITORY OF IOWA — ITS FIRST CATHOLICS AND PRIESTS — BUILDING OF A CHURCH BEGUN IN 1835. 131

Chapter IV
THE CITY OF GALENA: ITS ORIGIN — THE FIRST PRIESTS WHO VISITED — IN 1835 THE FIRST STONE OF A CHURCH IS LAID.   134

Chapter V
SPIRIT OF THE CIVIL LAWS OF THE UNITED STATES IN THEIR RELATIONS TO THE CATHOLIC RELIGION AND TO ALL THE RELIGIOUS SECTS EXISTING AND TO EXIST.   137

Chapter VI
THE MISSIONARY RARELY HAS THE OPPORTUNITY OF APPROACHING THE SACRAMENT OF PENANCE — ACCOUNT OF HIS MINISTRY UNTIL THE SUMMER OF 1836.   142

Chapter VII
THE CHURCHES OF DUBUQUE AND GALENA.   146

Chapter VIII
THE TERRITORIAL GOVERNMENT OF WISCONSIN IS FORMED — THE PRIEST ATTENDS THE FIRST ASSEMBLY OF LEGISLATURE — HOW CHURCH PROPERTY IS SECURED BY CIVIL LAW.   148

Chapter IX
LONG JOURNEY THROUGH WISCONSIN TERRITORY IN A SLEDGE.   150

Chapter X
DESCRIPTION OF THE BEGINNING OF THE CITY OF DAVENPORT ON THE MISSISSIPPI — HOW CULTURE AND THE ELEGANCIES OF LIFE ARE INTRODUCED INTO THE NEWLY FOUNDED CITY.   152

Chapter XI
THE PROTESTANT MINISTERS IN THE WESTERN STATES AND THEIR PREACHING — EFFECTS OF A RELIGIOUS EXCITEMENT — ADVANTAGES OF THE CATHOLIC PRIEST OVER THE MINISTER IN MISSION WORK.   156

Chapter XII
CREATION OF THE BISHOPRIC OF DUBUQUE IN 1837.   161

Chapter XIII
CAUSES WHICH CHIEFLY CONTRIBUTED TO THE FORMATION OF NEW DIOCESES IN THE UNITED STATES.   163

Chapter XIV
HINTS ON A FEW HARDSHIPS ON THE MISSIONS.   168

Chapter XV
MISSIONS IN WISCONSIN IN FEBRUARY 1838 — THE PRIEST LODGING IN THE CHURCH.   170

Chapter XVI
THE PRIEST IN PERIL OF HIS LIFE ON THE MISSISSIPPI RIVER, IN MARCH 1838.   172

Chapter XVII
THE BUILDING OF THE CHURCH AT GALENA IS RESUMED — SALUTARY EFFECTS OF DISINTERESTEDNESS IN A PRIEST WHO IS ON THE MISSIONS.   174

Chapter XVIII
SERVING THE SICK, IN 1838.   177

Chapter XIX
THE TERRITORY OF IOWA WAS ORGANIZED IN 1838 — ITS PEOPLE,
PRODUCTS, CLIMATE AND CITIES.   179

Chapter XX
HOW THE GOVERNMENT OF THE UNITED STATES CAME INTO
POSSESSION OF THE IMMENSE COUNTRIES ONCE INHABITED BY
INDIAN TRIBES.   181

Chapter XXI
FIRST FOUNDATION OF CATHOLICITY AT SNAKE HOLLOW NOW POTOSI
— THE CHURCH OF SAINT THOMAS IS BUILT HERE.   185

Chapter XXII
THE MISSION: ITS CONDITION PREVIOUS TO THE ARRIVAL OF THE
BISHOP OF DUBUQUE IN 1839.   186

Chapter XXIII
MONSIGNORE MATTHIAS LORAS ARRIVES FROM EUROPE — TAKES
POSSESSION OF HIS CATHEDRAL CHURCH OF DUBUQUE AND VISITS
THE CITY OF GALENA.   188

Chapter XXIV
SPIRITUAL PROGRESS AT DUBUQUE — DEPARTURE AND RETURN OF
THE BISHOP — ILLNESS OF THE MISSIONARY — CONDITION OF THE
EPISCOPATE IN THAT CITY.   192

Chapter XXV
DOGMATIC DISCUSSIONS IN THE CHURCH AT GALENA, DURING THE
AUTUMN OF 1839.   194

Chapter XXVI
CONVERSION OF A LAWYER TO CATHOLICITY — WHY CONVERTS ARE
GIVEN CONDITIONAL BAPTISM.   196

Chapter XXVII
FIRST VISIT TO THE CITY OF BURLINGTON, WHERE SOME
PREPARATIONS FOR WAR DID NOT PERMIT A LONG STAY.   199

Chapter XXVIII
CHURCH OF SAINT PATRICK, AT MAQUOKETA, THE CENTER OF
CATHOLIC EMIGRATION — HOW A CHURCH BECOMES THE SOURCE OF
CHURCH PROPERTY.   200

Chapter XXIX
HOW SETTLERS OBTAIN POSSESSION OF THE LAND FROM THE
GOVERNMENT.   203

Chapter XXX
CONVERSION AND BAPTISM OF A
MOTHER AND HER EIGHT CHILDREN.   205

Chapter XXXI
THE CHURCH OF SAINT GABRIEL THE ARCHANGEL AT PRAIRIE DU
CHIEN, AND THAT OF SAINT PAUL AT BURLINGTON.   208

Chapter XXXII
SEVERAL CONGREGATIONS OF CATHOLICS, VISITED BY THE BISHOP, ACCOMPANIED BY HIS VICAR — THE SENATE OF IOWA IN THE CATHOLIC CHURCH OF BURLINGTON. 210

Chapter XXXIII
PROGRESS OF THE TERRITORY OF IOWA — DIFFERENCES BETWEEN ITS GOVERNMENT AND THAT OF A STATE — ORIGIN OF IOWA CITY — THE COUNTIES, AND THE ORGANIZATION OF THE TERRITORY INTO A SOVEREIGN STATE. 212

Chapter XXXIV
BEGINNING OF CATHOLIC WORSHIP IN IOWA CITY, 1840 — ERECTION OF A CHURCH — CAUSE OF A CONVERSION. 215

Chapter XXXV
CHURCH OF SAINT MATTHEW AT SHULLSBURG IN WISCONSIN — NOTES ON THE LEAD MINES. 218

Chapter XXXVI
FIRST ESTABLISHMENT OF CATHOLIC WORSHIP AT BLOOMINGTON IN IOWA TERRITORY. 220

Chapter XXXVII
THE TEMPERANCE SOCIETY — ITS SALUTARY EFFECTS UPON THE CAUSE OF CATHOLICITY IN AMERICA. 222

Chapter XXXVIII
THE BIBLE, THE PROTESTANT REFORMATION OF THE SIXTEENTH CENTURY, AND THE APOSTOLIC MISSION — SUBJECTS OF MANY DISCOURSES IN DEFENCE OF THE CATHOLIC FAITH, ASSAILED BY THE PROTESTANT MINISTERS OF GALENA. 226

Chapter XXXIX
CONVERSION OF A YOUNG PROTESTANT TO THE CHURCH IN 1842. 230

Chapter XL
MISSIONS AMONG THE INDIANS IN THE DIOCESE OF DUBUQUE. 233

Chapter XLI
CHURCH OF SAINT AUGUSTINE AT SINSINAWA, WISCONSIN — ACCOUNT OF SAINT MICHAEL'S CHURCH, GALENA, 1842. 236

Chapter XLII
THE REASON FOR THE PRIEST'S DECISION TO VISIT HIS NATIVE LAND — PREACHING AND CONVERSIONS IN BURLINGTON IN 1843. 237

Chapter XLIII
THE FALSE PROPHET, JOSEPH SMITH, GOLDEN BOOK OF MORMON — SECT OF THE LATTER-DAY SAINTS AND THEIR ABSURD DOCTRINES. 239

Chapter XLIV
DEPARTURE OF THE MISSIONARY FROM GALENA — HE ASSISTS AT THE COUNCIL OF BALTIMORE — CROSSES THE OCEAN AND FINALLY ARRIVES IN MILAN. 246

PART III

Chapter I
THE SPIRIT OF PROTESTANTISM.   253

Chapter II
PRINCIPAL PROTESTANT SECTS
IN THE UNITED STATES.   256

Chapter III
THE PRESS, PREACHING, EDUCATION OF PROTESTANTS OF THE UNITED STATES IN THEIR RELATION TO THE CATHOLIC CHURCH.   262

Chapter IV
CATHOLIC MISSIONS IN THE UNITED STATES.   266

Chapter V
THE PRIEST IN AMERICA.   271

Chapter VI
RELIGIOUS ORDERS IN THE UNITED STATES.   276

Chapter VII
THE SISTERS OF CHARITY.   280

Chapter VIII
FOUNDATION OF ALL THE DIOCESES OF THE UNITED STATES OF AMERICA — THE SUCCESSION OF THEIR BISHOPS.   284

Chapter IX
PROVINCIAL COUNCILS OF BALTIMORE.   289

Biblical References   291

General Index   293

Editor's Preface

The present memoirs were originally written in 1844 by Samuel Mazzuchelli, while on a yearlong sojourn to Italy, his native country. However, it was more than 60 years before this remarkable account was available in English. Our new edition is based on this translation by Mary Benedicta Kennedy, which was entitled *Memoirs Historical and Edifying of a Missionary Apostolic*, and originally published by W.F. Hall in 1915.

Mazzuchelli performed most of his extraordinary missionary work in the rugged Western part of the United States, especially in Iowa and Wisconsin. He travelled to many places, usually on very poor roads or barely recognizable trails. Yet, Mazzuchelli was urbane, educated, cultured, and took his even tempered sensitive spirit to some of the most wild, unsophisticated parts in the New World. Indeed, the story of the missionary born into wealth and luxury, but spending a large part of his adult life travelling through lands untouched by European sophistication, is one of the most enduringly affecting of any.

There are many examples of Mazzuchelli's optimistic faith and vigour, crisply written, but recounted with great feeling. In one sense, this rare book is a kind of adventurous "folk history" of the West, told from a Christian European perspective. Yet it is significant for the study of religion, because it identifies the diverse types of people who were instrumental in building, or weakening, the structure and dynamics of the Catholic Church in newly settled territories.

The autobiography, for reasons of modesty, was written in the third person. Its translation from the Italian was adequate; however, the English version contained a substantial number of textual errors. We have kept all the original spellings, but we have also provided some clarification to those parts where the author was expressing his most complex ideas. Two elements were added that were lacking in the original: a table of biblical quotations used in the text, and a comprehensive index.

PAUL DENNIS SPORER

Part I

Chapter I

THE VOCATION OF THE PRIEST
TO THE PROPAGATION OF THE FAITH.

If in the world each one is called by Divine Providence to fulfill those duties which constitute the various occupations of life necessary to the formation and progress of human society, it is no less true that among the priests of the Sanctuary of the Living God,—He Himself has distributed the administration of the graces of Redemption which form the Society and Communion of Saints. In the very creation of the heavens, the Omnipotent has ordained that the individual marvelous revolution of each sphere should form but one part of the beautiful universal unity, worthy of the Being, One and Infinite. The spiritual work of Christ is no less grand, no less worthy of Him Who said in the beginning "Be It Made" and all was made, while Saint John declares that all things came to pass through the Word, and without Him was made nothing that was made.

It belonged to Incarnate Wisdom to so order His mercies to provide for the wants of every nation and every grade of human conditions, and to supply the impotence of those who were to be the dispensers of these mercies even to the end of time. Although man may have attained the sight of only a very few of those secret, divine ways, through which the blessing of Redemption is offered to all mankind, what Saint Paul wrote to Timothy is certain, that God our Savior "*will have all men to be saved and to come to the knowledge of the Truth.*"

He who came to save sinners and to provide for all, the means for eternal life, has so ordered the sublime duties of the ministry of His House, that to some He gave Apostolic zeal that they might go forth and bring forth fruit and that their fruit should remain; others He enlightened with Heavenly wisdom against which the enemies of Truth cannot prevail. Many received from the Giver of all good, the power to seal with their blood the divinity of their holy ministry, and they proved that the gates of hell will never prevail against the Faith. Yet others with the gift of miracles have called the nations from the darkness of idolatry to the light of the Gospel. He who has glorified the Heavenly Father with piety and good works, has burned with desire for the salvation of souls; *and they that instruct many to justice shall shine as stars to all eternity.* (Dan XII-3) Many zealous for building churches, can say with David, "I have loved, O Lord, the beauty of Thy house and the place where Thy glory dwelleth." (Psalms XXV-8) Many consecrated to the Sanctuary were called by Divine Providence to the care of the poor, the sick and the ignorant, that they might be the benefactors of suffering humanity. In fine, the needs of individuals, of society and of the entire human race have felt the saving influence of Him Who came for all mankind.

The ministry of Christ our Redeemer is so ordered that the great variety of duties and the distance of time and place instead of keeping souls apart, bind them together yet more closely in the bonds of perfect unity; for those duties are like the waters springing from one and the same divine source, refreshing by their branching streams the aridity of humanity, and leading it on to the ocean of Divinity itself,—its only Good. When the Word Incarnate said: "One is your Master" He suggested the grand Catholic truth that however the operations of the sacerdotal state may be distributed among the many who are called upon to succor this or that particular necessity, yet He Who teaches is One alone, God Himself, from whom spiritual power proceeds. In the Catholic Church the unity of the sacred shines forth like the light of the sun, for there the manifold operations of the Apostolate are stamped with the same visible authority, without which everything would be isolated and powerless. If ignorance, the offspring of vain human learning, did not blind the intelligence, even men of the world at the sight of that apostolate which embraces so many centuries, all societies and all conditions of life, would cry out at least, with the false prophet Balaam: "How beautiful are thy tabernacles, O Jacob, and thy tents, O Israel!" (Numbers XXIV, 5.)

While use of being with Christ in the holy ministry, it is of the highest importance to the Priest to ascertain to what duties he is specially called. The daily happenings of life are the ordinary means which little by little manifest to him His own special mission in the kingdom of Christ on earth. To desire to select absolutely one mode of entrance into the sacerdotal state notwithstanding the lack of those gifts which are required therein would be to call one's self, while our Redeemer

PART ONE

said: "You have not chosen Me; but I have chosen you and have appointed you." (John XV, 16.) He who takes upon himself a holy duty for which his incapacity unfits him, bears the full weight of a divine, eternal responsibility and ordinarily brings forth no fruit which remains. But when Christian prudence permits us to believe ourselves endowed by Almighty God with certain qualities, exalted for the fulfillment of the obligations annexed to the sacerdotal state, then one may reason that he has been called thereto. An upright intention, purity of conduct, docility towards him who has the spiritual direction of our souls, prepare the way for the manifestation of the Will of God, which manifestation if it does not become absolute certainty, is at least that moral probability which can never be accused of imprudence, and which ought to serve as a guide to the most timorous conscience. Absolutely certainty of our vocation has never been granted through ordinary means, although we may be allowed to believe its existence, when time and results have, so to speak, proved the reality of one's election.

Few have that generous disinterestedness in their choice of the varied duties incumbent on the priesthood, which moved Saint Peter and the Apostles to abandon human interests, which often seem determined to oppose the call of Heaven. The sublimity of this career, however, is so great a boon, that the refusal to follow it, on account of any human attachment whatsoever, would render us the objects of those terrible words of Christ: "Every one of you that doth not renounce all that he possesseth, cannot be my disciple. (Luke XIV, 33.)

Of all the duties of the priesthood, that of the Propagation of the Faith among peoples who know nothing of it, is the most excellent and meritorious. He who fulfills this evangelical mission, together with the example of a pure life and good works, and the continual preaching of the mysteries of salvation was expressly commended by the Apostle when he wrote to Timothy: "Let the priest that rule well, be esteemed worthy of double honor; especially they who labor in the word and doctrine." But when a priest is called, as was the Prophet Jeremias by the voice of God Himself, and assured that he has been sanctified and made a prophet unto the nations, he could in truth make the answer: "Ah, ah, Lord God: Behold, I cannot speak, for I am a child." In fact, who will believe himself, I do not say worthy, but even able to be made "a minister according to the dispensation of God, that I may fulfill the word of God. The mystery which hath been hidden from ages and generations." Who will be able to have made "known to him the riches of the glory of this mystery among the Gentiles?" (Col. I.) With the reason then did Jeremias call himself a child at the sight of so great a mission. But the Evangelical word is the work of Christ,—it has naught in common with human ignorance and the wisdom of this world; as the Apostle says: "The foolish things of the world hath God chosen that He may confound the wise; and the weak things of the world hath God chosen that he may confound the strong," (I Cor. I, 27), and he also gives the most convincing reason for this truth when he adds "that no flesh should glory in His sight." (v. 29)

One who is called to the ministry of the word should like the Prophet often humble in the contemplation of his own incapacity and childish ignorance, for even the most profound studies is sacred doctrine become unfruitful in the mouth of the most eloquent, without that divine inspiration of Him Who is the way, the truth and the life. The sublimity of speech and of human wisdom did not accompany the coming of Saint Paul among the people of Corinth, but, as he himself says, the knowledge only of Jesus Christ and Him Crucified, that their "faith might not stand on the wisdom of men but on the power of God." (I Cor. II, 5.) By virtue of the Cross alone ought the Priest Apostle, with the lively faith of Saint Peter let down his net into the troubled sea of this life; sure that sooner or later his Divine Master will make him an instrument of salvation to many. Vainly would one enter upon an apostolic career, even in regions most remote, buried in the darkness of ignorance of Christian truth, or blinded by the errors and extravagances of heresy, unless with an entire self-abandonment to Him Who has said" "Going, therefore, teach ye all nations. Behold I am with you." (Matt. XXVIII, 19). The foolish fear of lacking the necessaries of life would be a want of faith in the Son of God Who gave us this command: "Be not solicitous, therefore, saying What shall we eat or what shall we drink, or wherewithal shall we be clothed?" (Matt. VI, 31.) Amid doubts such as these what would become of the faith of the ambassadors of Christ? The holy Gospel assures us that our Heavenly Father Who feeds the birds of the air and arrays the lilies of the field with a splendor more

PART ONE

dazzling than Solomon's will have a care to give His laborers their hire. Let them seek first the Kingdom of God and His justice and all these things shall be added unto them. This is the promise of our Redeemer to missionaries of the Gospel: whoever doubts it has little faith and in truth is unworthy of the Apostolical ministry.

The comforts and riches of this present life should be despised by one who has left all things, in order to say with Saint Peter to the Divine Master: "Behold we have left all things and have followed Thee." (Matt. XIX, 27.) He Who has promised to give for one such renunciation a hundred-fold in this world and life eternal in the next, will provide for every need. The preacher of the Gospel may apply to himself what Christ declared on this subject to His Apostles: "The laborer is worthy of his hire . . . and into what city soever you enter, and they receive you, eat such things as are set before you." (Luke X, 7-8.) The grace of Providence shall go before him, disposing the hearts of the people in various ways to minister to his needs, that one may recall these words: "When I sent you without purse and scrip and shoes, did you want any thing?" (Luke XX, 35.)

Such should be the mien of him who preaches the truth confirming it with the brightest example: charity, zeal, disinterestedness, piety, modesty and patience should make of him a living image of his Divine Master, Who set example before precept. Then will be verified in him those words of Holy Writ: "How beautiful are the feet of them that preach the Gospel of peace, of them that bring glad tidings of good things!" (Rom. X, 15.)

Placing obstacles to the vocation of a person who is well qualified and desirous of dedicating himself to foreign missions is to oppose one's self to the Divine Mercy of our Saviour, who, "seeing the multitude, had compassion on them; because they were distressed and lying like sheep that have no shepherd. Then he said to his disciples: 'The harvest indeed is great, but the laborers are few'" (Matt. IX, 36, 37.) The consequences of such opposition are dangerous, both for him who hears the call and for him who hinders. For the desire of a close yet brief companionship and the fear of a temporary separation upon this earth might draw down tribulation and chastisements in this present life and everlasting separation in the next; then would be verified that word of Christ: "A man's enemies shall be they of his own household." (Matt. X, 36.)

In place of putting stumbling-blocks in the way, parents and friends ought to glory in seeing their nearest and dearest dedicate themselves so particularly to the propagation of that same Faith which they themselves have received through no merit of their own, and for which they can never sufficiently thank God. It might here be remarked that one of the principal reasons why so few consecrate themselves to the Apostolate is the lack of reflection among the clergy in Catholic countries upon the pitiable condition of those nations who have not received the truth of holy religion. Many priests born and educated in the unity of the Faith have never had the experience of feeling to the quick that anguish of heart inflicted by the sight of the destruction of souls mid the darkness of ignorance and heresy. If they would but know the gift of God, the blessing of being born in the abundance of spiritual riches, of sitting at the Eucharistic Table every day, of frequenting the House of God at their pleasure, of having ever ready to hand the divine remedies for the cure of every spiritual malady, in a word, of enjoying in their degree all the mysteries of the goodness and greatness of our Redeemer, the while nations are yet deprived of these blessings, then would they feel a more efficacious zeal burning within their hearts, and not content with merely being compassionating from afar the miseries of others, would put their hands to the work, mindful of that command of Christ: "Go, teach all nations." God grant that no priest imitates that rich man, who, surrounded by all the good things of this world, contents himself with desiring necessary food for the famished poor, while he himself is too tardy and too avaricious to supply their needs. It should be the glory of Christ's servants not only to hear His call, but to be in reality the instruments for the propagation of the Gospel, the light of the world.

It is almost incredible that the goods of life,—parents, friends, love of country, and worse, love of riches, can be to any a hindrance to the Apostolic vocation. Motives of such a nature would shame even one who is willing to sacrifice the very least of the gifts of Heaven, and would slow a littleness of soul, of which it is better not to speak, that we may disclaim the very supposition that there exist any individuals in the divine career of the Priesthood who are willing by like weaknesses to belittle such career. Preaching the Faith is a work so meritorious, so worthy of the clergy, so like that of the Messias, that it should revive the noblest sentiments of the heart and produce a superabundance of Evangelical laborers, yet Christ tells us the contrary: "The harvest indeed is great, but the laborers are few." (Luke X, 2.) Let us rouse ourselves then, and let us open eyes of Evangelical charity, and if we are called, let us direct our steps wherever the work is great and difficult, but where with the help of Him Who sent us, we shall open the ways for the Gospel and our labors will succeed: "I have planted, Apollo watered: but God gave the increase." (I Cor. III, 6.)

Chapter II.

THE DEPARTURE AND VOYAGE OF THE MISSIONARY OF THE ORDER OF PREACHERS FROM ROME TO CINCINNATI IN THE UNITED STATES OF AMERICA.

Not without difficulty is it for an ecclesiastical departing for the country of his missions, to bid farewell to parent and friends, and native land, and set out towards that region to which the Lord had destined him, for the salvation of others, and for his own sanctification. This material separation does not hinder his bearing with him that sincere filial and fraternal love towards those who have done so much for his education and have a natural claim upon his heart. Yet under such circumstances one ought not to reflect upon the material aspect of the separation from beloved friends and native land, but he ought to have before his eyes the sublime, divine motive which breaks the strongest ties of nature in order to make of them a sacrifice to the will of Heaven. To the flesh such a farewell seems cruel and unjust, but to the spirit of the Christian it becomes sweet and mild, for it is the yoke of Christ. Such was the case of a son, who for the last time embraced a tender father who on every occasion had shown his predilection for him, and who, five years before had besought his son to stay and one day close his eyes. But of what avail could this strong tender love of a father be to one who willed to renounce the world and take upon himself the discipline of a cloister? Could it silence the voice of Heaven and draw aside from his vocation one who felt himself interiorly called to separate from the world, and who believed that he would openly resist the Will of the Lord, if he listened to the allure of flesh and blood? Thanks to the Giver of all good, these whisperings excited by the pleadings of a father's heart were calmed by the words of Christ: "He who renounceth not father, mother, brothers and sisters cannot be my disciple."

In 1828 when obedience destined our missionary for the United States of America, he left Rome, and revisited his native city of Milan after five years absence. Then the farewell to father, beloved sisters and dear brothers was made with all that tranquility, which the certainty of doing the will of God could secure. The affection and the duty towards parents are not all diminished by such occurrences in the life of a Christian; a son fulfilling his mission upon earth, renders to his father that true and just recompense which is due for all the cares and anxieties spent upon his education. A father should consider himself happy to see his sons follow out the career assigned them by divine Providence; since in such case only do they correspond to the purpose of their birth in the world, and recompense the labor spent in forming them to virtue and eternal life.

When the last farewells were over, he left his native land with little hope then of ever seeing it again, and yet without overwhelming grief of heart. In truth we have no lasting home on earth; a Christian's native country is wherever God calls him; therefore for the man called to the Apostolic ministry the fact of leaving the place of his birth to go into missionary countries was rather a setting out in search of his own country. On the other hand he who departs for an object worthy a disciple of Christ, accustoms himself to consider the whole world as his own county because his affections are in no wise circumscribed by the limits of one city or by the boundaries of a kingdom, but more widely do they extend over the vast number of nations, and the boundless seas; so that in this sense also the word of Christ seems to be verified wherein He promises us a hundred fold for what we have given up. Behold, a hundred cities, a hundred nations under different skies become our magnificent fatherland. Oh, how generous is our God! The friends, then, the companions, left behind in that narrow corner of the world which has seen us born into the world and grown to manhood! O, they are not lost, while a sincere affection for them can be and ought to be kept alive; and meanwhile the missionary as he passes on to new lands, goes to find new friends, to increase the number of them and to multiply the consolations of Christian friendship, and because the chains that bind them together in the propagation of the truth of the Gospel are not the work of chance but the fruit of virtue, it follows that such friendships are nobler, more lasting than those of our youth. So does God reward in full, that transitory anguish inflicted by the separation from parents, friends, native country; Almighty God is not outdone in generosity; He never accepts the smallest sacrifice from a human heart without pouring upon it His divine munificence in abundance even in this life.

    The journey of a missionary to the country that Divine Providence has appointed to him is always accompanied by circumstances from which he may derive many experiences useful for the fulfillment of his ministry,—more especially in acquiring that necessary confidence on which he must lean in future needs. Such were the lessons that he learned during his passage from Rome to the city of Cincinnati in the United States of America. The visits made to the churches and sanctuaries of Florence, Bologna, Milan, Genoa, Lyons, Paris, and to the Capital of the Catholic world, monuments which down the ages have been the glory of Religion and Art, had yet more deeply impressed upon him that veneration and spirit of piety which should accompany every act of the Christian, yet more of him who is called to preach the truth of the Gospel.

    Experience has taught us that when God's minister finds himself alone, without a church in the country of the infidel, deprived of all external objects that promote piety, the holy remembrance of things that he has seen in the midst of Catholic surroundings supplies in part the want of such reminders. On such occasions, memory vivified by Faith, bears the lonely spirit into the temples of the Living God, before our tabernacles where, to Jesus in the Blessed Sacrament, are rendered those honors by which man manifest the secret desires of his heart. In truth when he was in the forests and vast solitudes of the heart of North

America often did he imagine himself present at the sacred rites of the European Churches, joining in the solemn canticles of Divine Worship. His imagination of itself turned to those sacred objects, when he was obliged to celebrate the Holy Sacrifice in a log hut, or in the wigwam of a savage, upon an altar not deserving even the name of table, — sometimes constructed of the bark of trees.

Almighty God even made use of the memory of His temples to excite in one an ardent desire to build them wherever the Catholic Faith spread. It was impossible to express in words the holy anxiety which wrung his heart and overcame the great difficulties involved in the building of a Church, an anxiety in great part caused by his having seen in a Catholic countries the vast number of churches and sacred ornaments in all their magnificence. In truth, at times it seemed to him that the things belonging to the service of the Holy Sacrifice were not impartially distributed; he used to say to himself, that in some places, Catholics had a superabundance of everything to be desired and that here where the need is greatest they do not possess even the things most indispensable for Divine worship. Making one's self familiar, therefore, with everything great and sacred in Catholicity will ever be of the greatest advantage to one setting out for distant missions for it will assist his piety when, lonely and derived of the sight of God's temples, the memory of them will fill the void in his heart, in a measure; it will give an impulse to his zeal for the building of churches, notwithstanding the many and serious difficulties to be overcome by one who puts his hand to a work so necessary for extending the Faith and the worship of the true God.

But let us follow our traveler. After making the journey from Rome to Lyons with the Vicar-General of Cincinnati, he was left there alone at the end of July, to make his way towards the new world. Somewhat of fear and doubt made itself felt in such a situation, putting to the proof his vocation and his confidence in Almighty God's disposal of him. The idea of setting out alone for a far-off country, on the other side of the Atlantic, without a knowledge of the language of its inhabitants, to a youth of twenty-two without experience, would have been rather imprudent had it not been justified by religious obedience, that obedience which would be a safe guide in traveling to the end of the world,

PART ONE

if that were necessary. In reality, if a religious man takes holy Obedience as his guide during the great, mysterious journey from this world to the immense eternal regions of God's Kingdom, how can he doubt that Obedience will conduct him safely back and forth to any quarter of this little globe of ours? See how the vow, folly in the eyes of the world, by its power overcomes worldly wisdom itself and inspires that courage and energy of soul that will be sought in vain elsewhere.

The Lord so disposed events that our Ecclesiastic was obliged to prolong his stay in France for two months, in the little Seminary of Said Nicholas, where the charity of the Superiors had offered him an asylum. Such delay was of the greatest advantage, since during that time practising with the good seminarists then enjoying a vacation, he learned the French language, an acquisition which after his ordination to the priesthood became indispensable in the exercise of his ministry. While he was anxious concerning the great loss of time in regard to his long journey, the result convinced him that he could not have spent those two months more profitably. Thus do accidents which seem adverse often co-operate for good and serve to make ready God's ways hidden from us! Moreover this proves that we must always believe there is some design to Providence in the involuntary delays which so often happen in travelling.

On the fifth day of October, 1828, were unfurled the sails of the American ship, the "Edward Quesnel," in which our young Ecclesiastic had secured his passage to New York, and he left the shores of Europe in the firm hope of seeing, when it should so please God, the lands discovered by Columbus. For some days the winds were contrary, and as if jealous of their dominion, refused to permit the ship a peaceful passage across the immensity of the sea. But the fury of the elements calmed down at last, and a favorable breeze from the east sped the barque towards the longed-for harbor. It was a pleasant sight to see on a clear day, all the sails full-spread, the sea peaceful, the sky pure and serene, companions joyous and full of hope, making their calculations on the day in which they flattered themselves they would happily reach port. Like to this is the living, true image of those thoughtless men, who, founding their happiness upon the uncertain things of this world, dream of future pleasures which prove in the event to be naught but shadows and illusions. In fact fleeting was the joy of the sailors; the winds howled both from north and west; the ocean's billows rose threateningly, and the ship was forced to rise and plunge with the troubled foaming waters; the rigging could barely resist the fury of the wind and mitigate the motion of the tempest-tossed craft; then all became silent in the saloon, for he was fortunate who could keep himself steady in his couch. The missionary in spite of the tempest enjoyed the sublime sight of the ocean, when unchained and storm-driven, it seemed to have sworn the destruction of the man who defied its wrath. Clinging to the main-mast he could see the broken, imperious waves venting their wrath upon the ship, often as if striving to engulf it, flooding the deck with their crest, but conquered by man's power, breaking and passing off, the wind howling unceasingly among the masts and cordage seemed to predict death and ruin. The heavens all darkened, crashing with thunder, denied to the gaze of the voyager even the slightest gleam of hope for safety. The missionary's imagination, stirred by this spectacle so really frightful, involuntarily was borne on to meditate on that last catastrophe described by the eloquence of the Son of God:

"And there shall be signs in the sun and in the moon and in the stars, and upon the earth distress of nations, by reason of the confusion of the roaring of the sea and of the waves.

"Men withering away for fear an expectation of what shall come upon the whole world." (Luke XXI, 25, 26.)

A favorable wind succeeded the storm and already on November 17th the sight of land gladdened the hearts of the voyagers, but vainly, for the wind suddenly changed and blew from the west such fury that one might have said the ship had taken flight to Europe; thus for five days she was driven backward over the wide sea, until the Supreme Ruler of the waves set her again upon the right course, and on the morning of the fourteenth she calmly neared the wished-for coast. When men are agitated by stormy passions in the dark night of this vale of tears, if they but knew how to use that tireless industry, perseverance and patience taught us by the mariner! then would all arrive at the port of eternal salvation.

Some days of delay in the great city of New York, convinced our traveler that the grand things of this world are ever in close relationship with the general corruption of morals; thence he passed on to the beautiful, beautifully planned city of Philadelphia, and from there to the Archiepiscopal city of Baltimore. During this short journey, he realized the great inconvenience of not knowing the English language, and of being forced like the Patriarch Joseph in Egypt to hear a language that he understood not. There yet remained about eight hundred miles of a journey, partly by land, partly by water, before reaching Cincinnati, the place of his destination; he was without a companion who spoke one language known to him, and moreover uncertain whether the money at his disposal was sufficient for so long a journey; yet he leaned upon Divine Providence, greater than all treasure. On the first day that he spent in the stage-coach, an American gentleman perceived his extreme embarrassment in the offices and taverns on account of his inability to make himself understood and touched with compassion towards the stranger gave him to understand by signs that he himself would have everything paid for and attended to both by land and by water as far as Cincinnati, and that there the sum expended would be shown to him. In short from that morning the young Ecclesiastic had nothing to do but take his place in the carriage, to go to the steam-boat, or seat himself at the table whenever he was called; so in a few days he reached the place of his destination. His kind protector then wrote upon a card the sum paid out for him on the journey; but perceiving that the poor European had no sufficient money, he smiled and made him a sign just to go to the Catholic Church, which building was seen not far distant. Who would not in such case have given thanks with all his heart to Divine charity for the particular protection under which that charity had so happily led him to the end of his long journey! Had he not reason to say with the holy Tobias: "He conducted me and brought me safe again; we are filled with all good things through him"? (Tob. XII, 3.)

Chapter III.

STUDY OF THE ENGLISH LANGUAGE. VISIT TO THE CONVENT OF SAINT ROSE, PREPARATION FOR THE PRIESTHOOD IN THE CONVENT OF SAINT JOSEPH, AND ORDINATION TO THE DEACONSHIP AND PRIESTHOOD.

Monsignore Edward Fenwick of the Order of Preachers was then the venerable Bishop of Cincinnati; it would not be easy to describe the sweetness with which he welcomed his young brother in the Religious vocation and his kind concern to have him instructed in the language of the country. Our Ecclesiastic devoted the time up to the Feast of Christmas to mastering the principal difficulties of the language, when the Bishop desired him to make a visit to Saint Rose's Convent of the Order of Saint Dominic, in the state of Kentucky, distant about two hundred miles from Cincinnati. Having reached Louisville, a commercial city of that state, he was obliged to continue his journey on horseback, and to travel thus thirty-eight miles without resting. It was the missionary's first riding-lesson, and was so dear a one, that when he finally arrived at Bardstown, then the residence of the Bishop of Kentucky, he was obliged from extreme fatigue to keep his bed for two days. But it was a lesson most necessary for one who was afterwards to undertake long journeys on horseback to places where for many years there was no other means of traversing the country. His strength returning after some days, the Bishop, Right Reverend Benedict Joseph Flaget honored him with the loan of his own horses and a guide to take him the distance of fifteen miles where the convent was situated. This is one of the oldest religious foundations of Kentucky; the first asylum of the Dominicans in the United States, and the first college of the state; there were trained many priests, among them the present Bishop of Tennessee, Monsignore Miles of the Order of Preachers. The Church of Saint Rose is large and much frequented by the surrounding people. The convent is quite large and capable of containing a goodly number of religious. The community derives its subsistence principally from the land which was purchased for that purpose when the Order was first established here. Not far from the convent is found a convent of religious women of the same Order, devoted to the instruction of young girls; in this way the religious are most useful for the propagation of the Faith and cultivation of the mind. When the young ecclesiastic returned as far as Bardstown about the first of February, he was obliged to remain there, for the Ohio River, on account of the ice, was not navigable to Cincinnati. A happy circumstance for one who was glad to profit by such a delay! The gentle, holy companionship of the holy Bishop Flaget was enough to inspire piety and apostolic zeal; ever active, yet kindly with everyone, while he won hearts, he inflamed them with the love of God and of the salvation of souls. Lessons such as these are not easily forgotten.

There lived at that time at Bardstown the very reverend Patrick Kenrick, at present the most worthy and learned Bishop of Philadelphia; he was then professor of theology in the seminary of that diocese. His guest having been present at several of these lessons was not a little surprised at the ease and clearness with which he imparted the truths of holy doctrine to the young; under the priceless mantle of humility, he concealed those superior qualities with which the Almighty had endowed him. The missionary may be permitted to relate this circumstance to the honor of the priesthood and the confusion of modern philanthropists; that one evening on entering the Professor's little room, he had the consoling surprise of finding a suffering beggar occupying the Professor's bed. By what accident this needy one had obtained such a privilege was not known; the fact only remained that the poor creature was occupying the bed by direction of the Professor. Such example of tender charity inspired in the involuntary witness an ardent desire of imitating it.

At the beginning of March our religious returned to Cincinnati where steadily applying himself to the study of English, as also the duties of sacristan, he continued until September of that year. The Reverend J. J. Mullin, an Irishman by birth and a man of great eloquence, at that time occupied the pulpit in the Cathedral. His sermons, enhanced by his zeal and by an elegant style, together with the piety, courtesy and mildness of Bishop Edward Fenwick, O.S.K., were, through the designs of divine mercy, the means by which many were called away from the errors of a many-sided Protestantism to the light of Catholic unity. During this year, 1829, the Sisters of Charity were established in Cincinnati in spite of all the prejudices and hostile harangues of the sects who could not help seeing in their arrival, a precursor of that popularity and wide-spread influence enjoyed at the present time by Catholics. It is but too true that the works of Christian charity even in the very face of their social utility, encounter from the diverse sects opposition and hatred which Almighty God makes use of, however, to render His disciples more conformable to His Divine Son.

The Convent of Saint Joseph of the Order of Saint Dominic, situated in the center of the State of Ohio, was selected by the young ecclesiastic as a place for study and preparation for the priesthood. Arriving there, he was delighted with the pleasant and retired situation of that house, thoroughly adapted to the object of his retirement. Three and sometimes four religious live there, who are however often absent for many days on the various stations attended from the Convent church. Here, as at Saint Rose's, the missionary found that their means of subsistence were derived from the land belonging to the establishment. The congregations of the Catholics to whom these few religious had to administer the consolations of the Faith, were in those days numerous and far apart, so that rarely did it happen that one or another of the religious was not called away. Visits to the sick also rendered their residence always uncertain, for at any moment of the day or night, they might be called upon to carry the Viaticum to the dying, for a distance often of thirty or forty miles or more. It will not be out of place to relate that in March 1830, at nine o'clock at night, while the rain was falling in torrents and the night intensely dark, a man knocks at the door and asks for the priest to carry the Viaticum to a person dangerously ill, who was ninety miles distant from the convent. Father O'Leary, a man simple and of holy life, without being in the least disconcerted by the heavy storm and darkness, made ready to go, mounted his horse and as if under a clear sky and bright sunshine, cheerfully set out to reach the dying bed next morning. Case such as these were then common in the state of Ohio. Would one of our philanthropists have done such a deed for pure love of suffering humanity?

PART ONE

But let us return to our subject. While living in this house for the purpose of preparing better for the Priesthood and the Missions, the neophyte made every effort to acquire by continual study sufficient command of the English language. With the design of exercising himself in the language and in preaching, in the beginning of 1830, he commenced a course of catechetical instructions in the Church of Saint Joseph. The experience convinced him that this first attempt in the preaching of the Word was productive of the happiest results, carrying with it the study of subjects suitable for sermons, the knowledge of a very difficult language, and familiarity with the pulpit.

On the occasion of the coming of the good Bishop of Cincinnati to Saint Joseph's, to visit the Catholic of that part of his diocese, in July, our student was ordained to the Diaconate. By the grace of this degree of the ecclesiastical hierarchy, he was rendered more courageous in the Lord, and by virtue of his office, he began to occupy the pulpit after the Gospel at High Mass, to explain the truths therein contained.

By order of the Bishop he went to Cincinnati, where he was directed to prepare for ordination to the priesthood, to which he was raised on September fifth, 1830. Monsignore Fenwick celebrated pontifically, assisted by the clergy then in the city. The Reverend J.J. Mullen availed himself of that solemn and imposing occasion, with his brilliant eloquence to show forth in its grandeur and glory, the divinity of the Apostolic ministry in the Catholic Church. Oh how clear, how full of power those words of the Messias in St. John's Gospel: "As the Father hath sent Me, I also send you." (John XX, 21). The Protestants of the United States are generally desirous of assisting the ordination of a Priest by a Catholic Bishop. On such occasions, the zealous preacher of the Truth is able always and with much benefit to make known the grand, sublime arguments that prove the necessity of a Divine mission upon earth, by the propagation of the Faith and the distribution of the graces which are the fruit of Christ's redemption, and he can count over, as it were, the sacred links of that golden chain which closely and divinely binds the living Hierarchy of the Catholic Church with that of all the ages past, united indivisibly, to that same Corner Stone, Christ Jesus, who before ascending into heaven, sealed His mission by saying: "Behold I am with you all days, even to the end of the world."

Chapter IV.

DEPARTURE FROM CINCINNATI FOR MACKINAC. DESCRIPTION OF THIS ISLAND. FIRST VISIT TO GREEN BAY AND TO THE SAVAGES.

The newly-ordained priest did not know to what part of that vast diocese he was to be sent, and in truth he neither had nor could have any predilection. The Bishop himself, for several weeks after the ordination was undecided upon this point until the end of the month, when information having been received of the pressing necessity for a priest in the most northern parts of his diocese, he determined to send one where the need seemed most urgent. All the faculties usually accorded to a missionary having been granted, the few matters relating to his departure having been arranged, and the Bishop's blessing having been received, the novice in the apostolic career set out for his destination. It may be well to know that in 1830, the Diocese of Cincinnati comprised not only the state of Ohio, as it now exists, but the state of Michigan and the Territory of Wisconsin, also, which at present form two other Dioceses. The State of Michigan at that time, counted five priests who remained in the southern parts of that region, because the northern part was inhabited only by savages. The Territory, then counting only a very few civilized inhabitants lately settled there, had not thus far had a missionary. Now the first mission of which we are speaking was upon the Island of Mackinac and in the surrounding country, eight hundred miles from Cinicinnati by the common route. Going from this city to the Island of Mackinac one crosses the entire state of Ohio to Lake Erie, thence sailing up its western shore, and passing through the city of Detroit, capital of Michigan, one enters the great Lake Huron, for a voyage of nearly two hundred and fifty miles before landing upon the island.

Mackinac is situated within the strait which separates Lake Huron and Lake Michigan and is not very far from Lake Superior. The geographical position of this island which commands the passage of the

PART ONE

lakes, was at one time of extreme importance to the English and they built fortifications upon its heights during the American War of Independence. The French also, when they masters of Canada, used it as a point of defence. The Republic at present maintains a fort there, for the protection of its citizens against the savage tribes. The real Indian name of the island is Michili-mackinac, that is, Turtle Back, because while only nine miles in circumference, its rises majestically above the water to the height of more than five hundred English feet, and from its summit rules the broad Lakes and vast expanse of land. The great traffic in skins of wild animals, carried on many years in these regions by various companies of traders made this island the market for such merchandise.

In the months of July and August it was swarming with travelers from every quarter, bringing the results of their traffic carried on during the past winter, in the vast regions to the north and west. So great was the number of these precious pelts that they filled immense warehouses, and they were afterwards forwarded in vessels coming from the commercial cities of the east. In this island the fur traders bought various kinds of merchandise which were kept there in immense quantities for the purpose of trading with the savages, and with these purchases they left in August or even before, in their little boats, for their own abodes. Some of these men employed by the Fur Company had to travel two months by land and water before seeing their own poor homes, and this by reason of the mode of travel and the conditions which they are obliged to meet,—the cold and the ice on Lake Superior often putting these poor people to most grievous trials. Those who were inferior employees in the Fur Trade, led a most laborious life in a wild country exposed to all the miseries of travelling, of cold and very often of starvation, while the gentlemen who employed them, were enjoying all the delicacies and luxuries of the beautiful, populous cities of the great Republic. These hints as to the conditions of these countries will serve to throw some light upon what will be recorded later.

Upon Mackinac Island is a little village of about five hundred souls, the greater part Catholics and of Canadian descent; the language usually spoken is French. At least two-thirds of the Catholics had married with the natives, so the youth were of mixed race. There was a little wooden church, erected by the piety of the faithful who were sometimes visited by a priest from Detroit. This served to keep their Faith alive although without the light which make it so rational and attractive. When our missionary had set foot upon this island, it is easy to imagine the consolation of the poor settlers, when they found out that he was to make his principal stay there. On the Lord's Day he gathered the little flock around the sanctuary to praise God and to hear the Divine Word. But in order to visit another of his missions, before the old season, he set out on this first of November in one of the Traders' boats, and after a journey of two hundred miles arrived at Green Bay, situated at the southern extremity of the gulf of the same name, a part of Lake Michigan. The people there were in the same physical and moral condition as those of the Island. For the first time, he celebrated Mass in a garret as there was neither a church there nor a room large enough to accommodate the people. Some of the Catholics profited by that occasion to receive Holy Communion, but the greater number were indifferent and insensible to piety from their lack of instructions, of priests, of a church and of everything that could win them to virtue. One thing, however, consoled the Missionary's heart, and that was the unusually sincere disposition towards holy religion, which was manifested by the Indians of the parts. Very many of these poor children of nature came to see the priest, and accustomed to a sacrifice although a superstitious one, they were delighted to assist at Holy Mass, which they believed to be the Sacrifice in the Christian manner. The priest did not fail to call them around him, and by means of an interpreter, to tell them of his joy at their good will to know the God of the Christians, and after giving them a brief, general idea of the Catholic Faith, he exhorted them to turn to the Great Spirit in order to obtain the grace to know the true religion, and strength necessary for abandoning error and practising virtue, so that they might enjoy after death that happiness that the "Great Spirit" promised to all good Christians. The hope of accomplishing some good in that part of the world, with the help of Divine grace, was so well founded that he planned to make a long and active visit there the next spring.

From his return to Mackinac on November sixteenth the priest was occupied in the instruction and spiritual progress of his little flock. The church was well attended on account of the heavenly word preached to them which produced a beneficial effect upon those who for so many year had had no opportunity to receive the teachings of the church from the mouth of the priest, or even from books, for few knew how to read. The festive days of Christmastide were celebrated with somewhat of solemnity, but the holy sacraments of Penance and the Eucharist were received by only a few people. It is only too true that a long delay in sin makes the human heart insensible. For that reason it was the duty of the minister of the Lord to put into practice on such occasions the advice of Saint Paul to Timothy; "Preach the word, be instant in season, out of season; reprove, entreat, rebuke in all patience and doctrine." (II Tim. IV, 2.) In truth, the young priest was not lacking in that abundance of zeal which is usually the first fruit of ordination. Would to God that he and all priests in the world might persevere and bear with them to the tomb, the holy fervor which animated them when by means of Holy Orders they were raised to the sublime dignity of Ambassadors of Christ.

Chapter V.

THE INFALLIBILITY OF THE CHURCH, THE SUPREMACY OF THE POPE, THE REAL PRESENCE OF CHRIST IN THE HOLY EUCHARIST, CONFESSION, PURGATORY, THE INTERCESSION OF THE SAINTS, THE USE OF HOLY IMAGES, AND ANTI-CHRIST, SUBJECTS OF SIX DISCOURSES DELIVERED BY A CALVINISTIC MINISTER IN 1831.

When the Evil One sees himself in a strait and in danger of losing his dominion over souls, he puts in operation everything to hinder their conversion. There was a proof of this in the violent warfare which he roused in the Island against the Catholic religion during the winter of 1831. A small congregation of Presbyterians had a church in that village and a large school attended also by Catholics, as there was no other school in the place. The minister of that sect, at the suggestion of some of the most zealous of his followers, thought to do a service to God and to his neighbor by inviting the people of the Island to listen to various lectures full of arguments, as he imagined, against the principal dogmas of the holy Catholic church. What the motives were that urged him to begin this warfare and to disturb the peace and concord that reigned in the Island were not unknown to the public. Before this year, the Presbyterian Church although inferior in numbers to that of the Catholics was superior as to the influence and worldly knowledge of its followers to that of the poor Canadians, who without a shepherd were wandering away from the bounden duties of the Christian. But as soon as their little church was attended by a priest and the people began to show signs of a more regular life, then only was it thought necessary to unfurl the banner of religious novelties and to persuade the people that what seemed to be producing a salutary moral effect, was the very society of Lucifer.

A brief digression upon the subjects of the religious controversy held at Mackinac will serve to make clear to the reader the strong opposition against Catholicity which the Protestant pulpits strained every nerve to keep alive.

The determined plan of the Calvinistic minister did not, in the least, intimidate the young Priest who in order to make answer more exactly went in person accompanied by many of his confréres to the Church where his opponent intended to direct all the force of his own wisdom against the Faith of Jesus Christ. On the night of January 9, 1831, the Rev. T. in a discourse of an hour and a half, brought forward all those arguments which the fanatics of the last few centuries have employed to free themselves from the unity of the Church of Christ, accusing her of being fallible and in fact of having erred in many points of doctrine. The Scriptures he pretended to be the sole infallible guide, and, he said, he had vainly searched therein for one proof that our Redeemer had founded one society free from error. How blind is man when abandoned to himself! The minister did not see that, granting his assertion to be true, all Protestant societies were accused of fallibility. He did not think that appealing to the Bible interpreted by private judgment, he was reducing all the religion of Christ to one universal doubt. Destroying the infallibility of the Church, or as some prefer to express it, the infallibility of an interpreter of Holy Scriptures, is the same as destroying the infallibility of every dogma of Christianity, which is equivalent to the total destruction of the Christian Faith; because all dogmatic and moral doctrines of Christianity, are then reduced to a simple chain of arguments founded upon the fallible individual reason which is interpreting the Bible.

In a second discourse the Calvinist vented his spleen upon the Ecclesiastical Hierarchy, openly denying the supremacy of Saint Peter, and, in consequence, that of his successors. In order to bring conviction to his hearers, he deemed it necessary to make a violent attack upon various passages of the Sacred Text and even against good sense, intermingling facts and personal abuses as conclusive proofs against the very dogma of the visible unity of the spiritual power of the Church. Violence, contemptuous language, ever form the ordinary way followed by one who secretly admires and envies in others what he can in no wise himself possess. In fact, the sects, unable to find in history the thread which should unite them with Apostolic times, and seeing themselves condemned by the justice of God to disorder and confusion, like that of the Tower of Babel, dominated against their will by the worst anarchy that ever existed on earth, seek for some retaliation in denying the divinity of that centre of Unity which as a Sun of Truth, vivifies, preserves and illumines for so many ages the kingdom of Christ militant. The ignorance, therefore, or if it may be credited, the malice of the minister did not permit him to see the inexcusable absurdity of using some personal disorders recorded in the histories of the successors of Saint Peter as convincing arguments that the Supremacy of the Bishop of Rome is not the holy work of Christ; thus confounding the divine bestowal of the Keys with the man receiving them, — the character holy and venerable, with the weakness of him invested therewith. Such logic would be condemned by the very Protestant churches themselves, if it were employed against the holy college of Apostles, because one of them betrayed his Divine Master. Strange to hear a citizen of the Republic declaim against a centre of unity of government, in the spiritual commonwealth of Christ, while he as a faithful citizen professed to believe in and submit to the supremacy of a civil magistrate, so necessary, so indispensable to the good order, happiness and union of the states, although independent of one another.

The Real Presence of Christ in the most august Sacrament of the Eucharist gave the Protestant minister the opportunity of seconding the modern mania for denying the existence of everything which cannot be seen with the eyes of the body. His theology upon thus this sublimest of Sacraments consisted in reducing it to a mere figure of Christ, thus lowering the Christian dogma below the beautiful figure employed by the Jews when they celebrated the Pasch, by eating a lamb in the midst of the family. The clear words of our Redeemer in the four Gospels, and of Saint Paul to the Corinthians were rejected by him as bearing a meaning which was not in the words themselves. It seemed impossible to his understanding that such a change could be operated in the Sacrament, and the idea of a man receiving his Creator was altogether unbelievable. Many other vain arguments were suggested by unbelief against the most holy, the most precious, the most exalted of the adorable mysteries of the Redemption, wrought by the same incarnate Wisdom. But who taught a minister that the Sacraments of the Christian Religion did not contain the reality of things? The Messias came not to substitute one figure for another; prophecies and symbols belonged to that imperfect law of which the Apostles writes to the Hebrews: "The law brought nothing to perfection." (Heb. VII, 19.) In the New Testament, the Christian soul lives only upon what is true and real. Christ Himself assured us of this when he says: "My flesh is meat indeed and my blood is drink, indeed." (John VI, 56.) The Scriptures are full of similar expressions. Of what use, then, are the words of Truth itself to him who will not believe in it, and who joins those false disciples who once followed Jesus and strove among themselves saying: "How can this man give us His Flesh to eat?" "This saying is hard and who can hear it?" (John VI.) See how unbelief reasons: it asks Divine Omnipotence, although incomprehensible in its essence and in all its works, in what manner it can give to its own followers the adorable Flesh of the Lamb Immaculate, and when it cannot comprehend the unsearchable ways of Omnipotence, finds his doctrine hard, no longer able to bear the hearing of it, "after this it goes back and walks no more with Him." (John VI, 67.) The blindness of one who lives outside the Church suffers him not to believe that mysterious sentence of Jesus: "Amen, amen, I say unto you: Except you eat the Flesh of the Son of man and drink His Blood, you shall to have life in you." (John VI, 54.) The mysterious, invisible union of the soul with Jesus in the Sacrament of Faith, far from being a strange thing is in truth a simple foretaste of that free, glorious, perfect intercourse which one day will ravish the soul and the body of man away from their present state, to transform them into the very Divinity of God. It is almost useless, however, to speak of these truths to one who rejects the light of Faith and judges according to the flesh as Saint Paul declares, that "the sensual man perceiveth not these things that are of the Spirit of God; for it is foolishness to him and he cannot understand, because it is spiritually examined." (I Cor. II, 14.)

Were Sacramental Confession not of obligation in the true church, the opposition of its enemies would not be so furious, and the Calvinistic minister of Mackinac would have omitted his fourth lecture. The idea of confessing one's own faults to a creature like ourselves was always too humbling to human pride, which found in the enemy of the Catholic Church many excuses for freeing one's self from this cruel torture, as it likes to be called. Among many errors this false theologian denied that Christ had conferred upon the Apostles the power of forgiving and of retaining sins, declaring that these expressions merely signified the power of preaching the Gospel, by means of which sins were pardoned. Then he rambled on to calm the stings of conscience and to claim for his own sect the sublime gift of the Son of the Everlasting God, communicated to His representatives. Nature herself, even without the light of the Gospel, suggests to the man fallen into sin the remedy of a humble confession, and conscience seems to leave him no respite nor to promise him peace of heart except at the cost of a confidential declaration of his own fault. The worldly live slaves to the secret but stern reproaches of a guilty conscience which they cannot hush even in the silence of night, while Christians are called by the Holy Faith to lay down the grievous burden of their sins with their vicious attachment at the feet of him who represents upon the Divine Mercy. There they exchange the restless, cruel, deadly worm of conscience for that peace of soul and of heart that the world could never give. It was for our Redeemer to provide the necessary remedies for the spiritual ills of fallen humanity, and therefore did He speak to His disciples: "Receive ye the Holy Ghost. Whose sins you shall forgive, they are forgiven them; and whose sins you shall retain, they are retained." (John XX, 22, 23.) Why will the Christian deny to his Saviour the power of communicating His graces through the ministry of men? Yet the Calvinistic minister seemed to forget that he himself was preaching, baptizing and distributing his own figurative sacrament, led solely by his persuasion that Christ had authorized these things. And while he was pretending to remit sins by means of preaching and baptism, why then condemn the Catholic minister's doing the same which he believed possible, although in a different manner! The history of error has always been one of contradiction. Good sense leads us to this alternative; the words of Christ above spoken signify precisely the power that is clear and intelligible.

The Presbyterian minister was not content with the attempts he made to destroy the truth last attacked, but through a kind of inborn disposition to protest, he attempted in another lecture to persuade his hearers that there was no place in the life to come for satisfying the penalty due sin not atoned for in this life, that is, — that there was no Purgatory. He inveighed furiously, as he went on, against the pious practice of invoking the intercession of the Saints and declared that the use of sacred images, not even excepting those of Christ Himself, was sinful. These denials cannot surprise one who is acquainted with the real spirit of Protestant theology, which teaches that the Messias has done everything for us, and that corporal penance is, consequently, useless and superstitious, in a word it denies penance for sin. Wherever the word "penance" occurs in the Bible, the English Protestant version has the word "repentance." So, as there are no penances to be performed, Purgatory becomes useless. O how easy and how broad is the way that leads to the Protestant heaven! It was reasonable for one who had no Saints to invoke to deny the Intercession of the Saints; those heroes of all Christian virtues sealed with miracles belong exclusively to the Catholic Church. Here is one of the principal reasons for the invention of so many miserable, absurd and contradictory excuses for abandoning the doctrine and denying the utility of this pious practice. They believe with the Bible that the demon knows our thoughts and is therefore in a state to tempt us, but they refuse to the Angel of God

PART ONE

a like knowledge which permit them to draw us towards good. This of a certainty is an obscure and degrading theology. The minister condemned the use of sacred images as idolatry. His knowledge of the revealed word must have been very limited, since in the Old Testament where idolatry is forbidden, the use of religious images, of angels, for instance, was commanded by Moses and introduced into the Temple by Solomon. But the theologians of the last centuries find it more appropriate to substitute for the representations of holy things those of heroes and friends, but chiefly those of friends. The minister aforesaid had in his room a framed picture of Antichrist surrounded by his satellites; but the Priest without envy of the choice taste of his opponent preferred the image of Christ and His Immaculate Mother.

In his last fiery harangue against the Catholic Religion he displayed all his hatred, contempt and vindictiveness in the supreme effort he made to prove as possible what he desired to be true, namely that the Catholic Church is the true church of Antichrist. The fallen prince of the abyss could not have been able to vomit forth greater contradictions, accusations and blasphemies in order to attain his dark design. By abuse of the Holy Scriptures, especially of the apocalypse of Saint John, without even allowing the supposition of any mysterious meaning therein, he gave to the words of the Beloved Apostle a literal or figurative signification as it suited his fancy, and then, perverting history and the circumstances of the past, he strove to show a perfect analogy between the character of Antichrist and those of the Supreme Pontiff and of the Church. Not content with all that, the minister predicted the ruin of the entire Roman Catholic Church for the year 2000. If our Saviour was accused by the Pharisees of "casting out devils by Beelzebub, the prince of devils" (Luke XI, 15), we need not be at all surprised to see later hypocrites uttering like blasphemies. Because to Lucifer it was denied to make himself like to the Most High, he made war against Heaven; and so do those furiously attack the works of Christ, who are unable to make their won proud and sacrilegious efforts like unto His. Playing the prophet is a thing much in vogue with those who desire to be importance; yet the prophecies against the Catholic Church have been so numerous and so often falsified in the course of time, during the last three centuries, that the minister deemed it prudent to take a hundred and eighty years for the verification his own prediction—that is, when neither he nor his hearers will be here.

Thus the false prophet held forth for six Sundays between eight o'clock and ten in the evening in the fond hope of confirming his own followers in their opposition to the truth, and of creating at least more or less doubt in the hearts of those who possessed the gift of the true Faith. The Catholic Missionary in defense of holy Religion, was obliged to answer to the accusations of his adversary in his won Church and publicly; he chose three o'clock in the afternoon as a convenient time for such a discussion. But this arrangement both Catholic and Protestant had the opportunity of being present on one Sunday, in the evening to hear the accusations and arguments of him who was the aggressor, and on the next Sunday of hearing the answer from the mouth of the Priest. There was, however, a notable difference in that dispute, which was that the aggressor did not give the liberty to his hearers of replying to him in his own Church, while the defendant had publicly offered his hearer the privilege of interrupting him with objections at the very time when he was giving his replies. If the reader of this little history of public religious controversy desires to know anything about the result, he may care to read the next chapter.

Chapter VI.

CONVERSION OF THREE PROTESTANTS TO THE CATHOLIC FAITH, ON THE ISLAND OF MACKINAC, IN 1831.

A public disputation on the dogmas of Christianity in a country where the people are unfortunately divided into so many sects, thus creating confusion and disorder in the minds of men, usually rouses the curiosity of some and the good faith of others. The people of the Island assembled to listen to him who was carrying it on as a true Protestant minister, by proving to the best of his ability his own protestations against the Catholic Faith, and they crowded around him who was to make the defense with the same anxiety. This controversy was carried on in English, as it was the language of the Protestants and was understood by almost all the Catholics. Although the Missionary occupied more than one hour and sometimes two in his replies, he was compelled by the very nature of the subject to divide his arguments into fourteen discourses. Ignorance and unbelief are always made up of negatives, doubts, and bare assertions based upon facts of which they are not the natural and legitimate consequences. Therefore Truth in her manifestation is compelled to take two roads, either over that of her enemies, following the wanderings of their intellects, or over that noble, safe, divine one,—that is of Right Reasoning. The Calvinist did not follow the Priest's example, for he refused to assist in person at his antagonist's lectures as the latter had done; perhaps he feared to be contaminated, in the Catholic Church, by the holy images adorning it, so great was the exterior holiness of his Pharisaical demeanor.

Among those interested in the religious controversy were a certain S.A., member of the Anglican Church; M.G. of the same church; a young girl, A.T., follower of the sect of the Calvinists, and many other individuals of sincere dispositions, as was seen in after years. It will not be out of place to touch lightly upon some of the circumstances which accompanied the conversion of the persons here alluded to, to the True Faith.

When Mr. S.A., through curiosity or some other light motive, first went to the Catholic Church, he stood up during the Holy Sacrifice with his back to the Altar; such was his unbelief in the mysteries of the Faith. Yet he was a just man, according to the world's standard, liberal, loved by his neighbors, a man in easy circumstances and well endowed with talent. He believed, in all good faith, in the truth of that sect in which his parents had trained him, reserving in his heart that aversion to Catholicity which usually distinguishes those who are firm in their own belief. Almighty God Who wills all men to be saved, furnishing sufficient means for persevering in grace or for obtaining it by means of the reading of good books and conversation of good Catholics, aroused in the mind of S.A. doubts which thoroughly disturbed that faith in which he had lived; nor did he slumber when the Voice of the Lord called him secretly unto Himself, but opening his door, so to speak, to the Heavenly Spouse Who knocked he composed a short prayer as he declared after his conversion, a prayer which he recited every day, wherein he implored light and grace to know the truth. This was just like the simple, sincere and fervent prayer of the youthful Prophet Samuel: "Speak, Lord, for Thy servant heareth." If all the sinners of the world, and they who live outside the unity of the Church of Christ, when they are troubled by misfortunes, by bitter remorse and by doubts about the truth of the sects to which they belong would, like that person of whom we speak, with fervent prayers go to the Divine Mercy which calls them to itself by such ways, they would speedily find that peace and that faith which are the solid foundation and the pledge of future happiness. In short, the fruit of that fervent prayer was the compelling force and interest which urged that soul in doubt, to the churches of the Island in the winter of 1831, in order to get explanations regarding the important affair, the knowledge of the true and divine religion. His good will was such that he often visited the Priest for the clearing up of the last difficulties which lingered in his mind upon the last subject discussed. So grace waxed strong, aided by the sincerity of a heart loving and longing for the Way, the Truth and the life.

Lent was already advanced when our neophyte declared his belief that the Catholic Religion was the work of Christ Himself and that the sects separated from her he considered as so many rebellions of various individual among them, devised under specious and vain pretexts. Yet none the less did the life of a true Catholic seem to him difficult and almost impossible and for that reason he feared to take a step followed by too heavy obligations. The greatest of all the obstacles opposed by the enemy of man's salvation, was Sacramental Confession. The idea of making the humble accusation with that sincere grief without which the whole difficult undertaking would be only an insult to the Divinity, so appalled him as almost to make him abandon the way of salvation. Finally, the Missionary weary with hearing from his mouth protestations of Faith in the Church, without seeing him at the feet of Divine Mercy, decided to make known to him, seventeen days before Easter, that if within two weeks he had not complied with that duty which he had already recognized as descending from a divine command, there would be no more response to his religious demands, not any further discourse held with him upon that important subject. This course was

PART ONE

taken through fear of seeing him guilty of resisting divine grace or of falling into final impenitence. But on Good Friday Mr. S.A. presented himself for Sacramental Confession in the tribunal of penance blessed with the heavenly grace granted to the humble and ever denied to the proud. From afar the yoke of Christ seems grievous and insupportable to one who rejects it; but how sweet and light did the tender heart of this man find it, whom we shall now leave to his pious meditations and affections, in his preparation for Holy Communion, that we may speak of two others who were to accompany him to the Holy Table.

A certain Mr. M.G., whom the advanced age of ninety-one years had deprived of sight, was considered the patriarch of the Island, and had been the ocular witness of the various military changes, which in times past had disturbed the peace of his shores. Trained to study the Bible literally, he had acquired in the course of so many years such a knowledge of it that when he was speaking of it, you would have believed that you were listening to him reading from his one infallible guide. Years had more and more made him obdurate in his own mode of understanding the Holy Scriptures, and he defended himself easily from the sectarians who, through curiosity or compassion, took the liberty of opposing his doctrine. The Priest did not pass many days at Mackinac without paying a visit to the blind theologian with some hope in his heart that the Lord in His mercy would not suffer him to go down to the tomb before opening his eyes to the truth. But great was his surprise to find the old gentleman jovial and inclined to talk of the old times, when, strong and robust, he lived in those places still occupied by various savage tribes; he told of their long, bloody and cruel wars, and the reasons for their deadly hatred of the English who in his early years had possession of that country and had carried on there a profitable trade with the tribes. The Missionary, little disposed to talk over such changes, interrupted him to give opportunity for a more serious matter, that is, to ask him if he did not think it better to talk about eternity. The old man became silent to listen to some work of life, but very soon returned to his stories; interrupted again by speaking of his sect, he set to work to defend it with various texts of the sacred page, and to settle all difficulties, he declared his belief that with only faith in his Bible, he could be saved. A second visit found him still more indisposed and averse to religious subjects. However, as our blind theologian had heard of the vigorous controversy between the Missionary and the Minister, he with the help of his niece, placed himself among the number of hearers. A strange thing for him to enter a church! but he corresponded with divine grace, by doing violence to that insensibility in religious matters which would have deprived him of the first step towards the truth. How many are lost by denying to divine mercy that tiny sacrifice which often proves to be the invisible seed of a tree, which is to bear fruit of eternal life. The old gentleman settling himself in the manner of one who did not care whether or not he was seen remained near the speaker and, learned as he was in the sacred text was delighted to hear it so often quoted as a proof of Evangelical and Catholic doctrine. Grace operated little by little in his heart once so indifferent, startled him with the assurance of death so near him, and opened the eyes of his soul to the greatest revealed truths,—so that at the beginning of the season of penance, he asked for a visit from the Priest. His favorite stories of human affairs all forgotten, the old man delighted in learning the holy maxims of Christian piety and the manner in which he was to prepare for his reconciliation with Divine Justice; nor did he delay to lay bare those wounds of his soul which his feeble memory could recall during the course of a long life filled with adventure,—thus doing violence to his own age, to the good opinion of his own knowledge and to self, so that he gladly let himself be led like a little child to the fulfillment of that beautiful word of Christ: "Unless you be converted and become as little children, you shall not enter into the kingdom of Heaven." (Matt. XVIII, 3.) On the eve of the glorious Resurrection of our Lord, as if the eyes of the spirit had opened his bodily eyes, he left his house alone (which he had never done before) and trusting to his sense of feeling by means of his stick, betook himself to the Priest's house in order to seal with his tears that sincere conversion to God, which although coming at the sunset of life was to receive from Divine Munificence a crown incorruptible.

Religious prejudices instilled into the tender mind of youth have always been a fruitful source of error and ruin to the soul who lets herself be guided by them. Such was the ill fortune of the youthful A. T. before her conversion to the holy, apostolic Faith. Left by her father, a Protestant, to the care of a wealthy, distinguished citizen, surrounded by adherents of various sects, who knew little or nothing of Catholic truths, her mind was insensibly filled with strange and immoral beliefs concerning the Faith and practices of the Catholic Church. On her return to the Island from the City of Detroit near the close of 1830, she found her own poor mother already in communion with the Holy Church; but her respect for her mother modified her resentment. She could hardly be induced to visit the House of the Lord or to enter into a conversation with the Priest, who once desired to present her with a little book of controversy. The coolness with which she accepted it plainly enough displayed indifference carried almost to the point of contempt. Curiosity more than anything else led her to take part in the religious dispute which was interesting the entire community of the village. The Lord made use of this means to set her soul free from the prejudices imbibed in infancy, which threatened to leave her to perish in the darkness of false doctrine; and thus rendered somewhat docile, she brought back her little book to the Priest and received two others in its place. Moved by a sincere desire for her own salvation, she devoted herself to the study of the religion that she had despised, and when called by grace she did not remain unbelieving. She finally presented herself to receive those ordinary instructions usually preceding the Sacrament of Baptism; afterwards, contrite and full of faith, she disposed herself to celebrate the holy Feast of Easter which was to purify her soul in the laver of regeneration and present her spotless to the bosom of the Church, beloved spouse of Christ.

She then asked to read the first book received; on being asked her motive, she replied that having taken the book in the first place for politeness, she was so much afraid of awakening doubts in her own heart that she had read no farther than the title-page. Experience has taught us, that very many among Protestants wilfully close their eyes to those means of salvation afforded them by God's infinite bounty; they may not find out that they are in error, and under obligation to bear Christ's yoke—a fear which presses upon them, conquers them and casts them into religious indifference.

The solemnity of the Resurrection of Christ of the year 1831 was, therefore, celebrated together with the spiritual resurrection of young

Mr. S. A., Mr. M. G., and the young girl A. T., who vivified by Faith renounced all error publicly and forever to range themselves under the banner of the Cross. To cement yet more closely their union with their Heavenly Redeemer, they received that Mystic Bread of the Angels which gives life eternal.

It was only too true that the Calvinistic minister after his studied attack upon Catholic doctrine had not the consolation of adding to the number of his follower; while, humanly speaking, the religious contest that he roused was the indirect cause of the conversion of several Protestant, and contributed to render the holy Faith more luminous and manifest to many to whom it had been only imperfectly known. The Church and the Sacraments began to be better attended, Religion brought into greater veneration, the Priesthood more respected. Behold how evil is often wrought in God's hands into an instrument for working good.

To crown the triumph of truth, a plan was devised for enlarging the House of God, by building a new Sanctuary, and enclosing the former one in the body of the Church which was then entirely renovated; besides, a sacristy was built, as also a small wooden house as a dwelling for the Priest. The faithful contributed each according to his means, for paying off the expenses of these improvements.

Chapter VII.

EXAMPLE OF PUBLIC PENANCE PRACTISED BY A CATHOLIC IN THE YEAR 1831.

It will not be unacceptable to the reader to note here a singular proof of true contrition given to the world at the time of which we are writing. There lived on the Island of Mackinac in the service of a Protestant house, a man who, although of honest principles, was drawn by a strong temptation into giving scandal to those who were anxious to find proofs of immorality in Catholics that they might make greater boast of their own Pharisaical conduct. His offence having been made public by the act of civil authority, several among the sectarians laughing him to scorn, said that as he was Catholic, the Priest would pardon him everything. In January the offender presented himself to the Priest that through contrition and the humble confession of his faults, he might obtain that infinite mercy which proceeds from the merits of Christ alone, and which washes away all iniquity in His Blood. Such were the tears, such the tokens or true repentance manifested by this good soul that the Minister of God did not consider it imprudent to exhort him to a public penance and thus repair the scandal given. With all glad good will be accepted the proposal as a befitting means of atonement to the Divine Majesty insulted and for the honor of His Holy Church.

On the next Sunday when the House of the Lord was crowded with people assisting at the Holy Sacrifice of the New Law, the delinquent presented himself at the Sanctuary rail where the Priest explained to the people the object which had called him there. Then he reminded the penitent of the evil consequences of his error, and the immense utility of a public reparation of the scandal, adding a short description of the public penances practised by the early Christians, and ordained by the canons of the Church, but changed as time went on into other works as devotion grew colder. He then directed the penitent to remain at the Church door during the celebration of the Divine Mysteries until Easter Sunday; and having placed around his neck a girdle of coarse rope, a token of grief and of penitence, humbly and with tears in his eyes, the penitent withdrew to take his place kneeling upon the steps which led to the door of the Church. There exposed to the view of passers-by and to the cold of that place and climate, he heard Mass devoutly every Sunday. Such conduct deserved that the Priest should grant him the indulgence merited by true contrition and change of life. On the first Sunday of Lent the penitent was called from his lowly post to the presence of him who well knew his virtuous submission, and from the same place where he had received the public penance, was dispensed from that part which yet remained. Having then commended the reparation made by him who had given the scandal, the missionary took occasion to call the attention of the Catholic people to the fact that if the Church at present dispenses from the long penances of the first centuries, it is not because Divine Justice is more ready to pardon, but by reason of changed circumstances which, however, do not hinder the Divine Justice from being satisfied after our death. He added, besides, that more worthy of honor and more holy were those Christians who choose to manifest their faults by means of public penance than those who studiously conceal their wrongdoings, or reserve the penalty incurred by them for that time when mercy will be superseded by justice.

Chapter VIII.

MISSION AT GREEN BAY, CONVERSION OF SAVAGES OF THE TRIBE OF MANOMANIS. BAPTISM, CONFIRMATION AND COMMUNION OF THE SAME DURING THE YEAR 1831.

The gentle breezes tempered by the rays of the April sun, harbinger of a new life to nature, were beginning to melt and disperse the solid ice, which in winter covers the two Lakes Huron and Michigan for many miles in the strait where the commanding Island of Mackinac rises, and already the sight of a few sails gladdened the eyes of the dwellers and held out hopes to the Priest of being able to go to the place where in the autumn he had sown a few seeds of the Divine Word upon a soil promising abundant harvest. About the beginning of May he left his little flock and went in a trading vessel to Green Bay in the territory of Wisconsin. The village comprised quite a large number of houses scattered here and there on both banks of the Fox River, where it empties into that tributary of Lake Michigan, called in English, Green Bay, from the color of its water. There was a tradition among the old inhabitants that the Jesuits had begun a Mission there in the seventeenth century, of which, however, there were no traces remaining. At this time, the people were in number about a thousand, mainly of Canadian descent and intermarried with the Indians; left without Religious instruction for many years, if they had not given up their Faith, they had at all events forgotten all its works, many aged persons, even, calling themselves Catholic, had not yet received the Sacrament of Baptism; very few were found to have even once received the Sacrament of the Eucharist; to not a few the Sacrament of Matrimony was unknown. The vice of drunkenness, with all its detestable accompaniments, reigned, without a voice lifted to stay the ruinous habit of such long standing.

The trade carried on with the Indian tribes was large, as the country was rich in animals whose furs were of considerable profit. The poor Indians in their dealings with the white man, with the different traders who went there to exchange merchandise for the pelts, had learned all evil habits, theft, vengeance and a consuming desire for strong drink. In short brandy was the universal article of exchange which could buy anything from the savages, even morality, and was the cause of indescribable excesses; in a word that liquor was to them what money is among civilized people.

The reader may imagine the degradation, intellectual, moral and physical of a people, reduced by such disastrous circumstances, to the lowest stage of ignorance and crime. When the loquacious wiseacres of our day, by way of displaying their own talents and affectation of virtue, hint at the uselessness of the clergy, and the possibility of making a people happy without Religion, they forget or rather they choose to ignore those facts which contradict their fantastic notions. The whole world is an unimpeachable witness to the fact that not one of these pretended friends of humanity, or as they are accustomed to style themselves, philanthropists, has ever given up comforts, friends, and native land in order to help one people buried in darkness and evil. Religion alone can lay claim to the glory of breaking the dearest ties and consecrating her followers to the administration of heavenly consolations and effectual remedies to sufferers. The wise one of this world is satisfied with dictating, forming projects, criticising the labors of others. On the contrary, Holy Faith, receiving from Wisdom Incarnate the means wherewith to redeem humanity and snatch it safely away from all evils present and to come, without wasting the precious time of this dark age, bravely gives up all things and puts its hands to the work.

But returning to the simple account of the visit to Green Bay, in May of 1831, it must not be supposed that Almighty God has not His own faithful worshippers even in the midst of the widespread corruption. For the Missionary found in this place not a few pious persons in whose houses he celebrated the Holy Sacrifice. However, on account of the distances between the dwelling-houses, he was compelled to change the place which was to serve as a Church, in order to render the Divine Service more easy of access. Sometimes the Altar was in a garret, at another in a deserted house, from thence it would be transferred to a public hall; in such manner did the Presence of Christ sanctify the places wherein the power of darkness had held sway. Not a day passed without some Religious instructions, either in public or in private. Some individuals were addicted to drunkenness, others to theft, to revenge, or to unlawful business transaction; some scorned Religion, others pretended to associate it with their vicious deeds; all had sore need of the helps of that holy doctrine, which makes ready the saving balm for all mankind,—for every evil and every vicissitude of life. Here it would be needless to say that the Priest found arguments enough for becoming eloquent at the Altar without having acquired the noble science of oratory. Sin by its very excess furnishes the Christian orator with most powerful and irresistible weapons, before which vice shamed and confounded must pronounce its own condemnation by imploring Divine Mercy, or at least overcome by the power of virtue, it must instantly flee away.

Grace did not will that his words should be flung to the winds, but forestalling them with its celestial influence, aroused in many those sentiments of sorrow and devotion that precede the coming of Christ into the soul. Not a few were the Baptisms, the Confessions, the Communions, Divine sources of spiritual regeneration and of the interior peace unknown to the shallow wisdom of the world.

The most visible effects of Divine Mercy were manifested in the almost marvelous conversions of very many of the Indians. These poor children of nature, corrupted by association with Europeans, were specially the object of the Priest's attention and anxious care, for he had devoutly hoped that grace might superabound where sin had once abounded. They had often gathered in great numbers to listen to the instructions imparted through an able and devout interpreter, who had prepared ten of them to receive baptism during the past winter, and the great piety of their behaviour in the place where the meetings were held was a clear testimony that God was speaking to their souls; for which the sincere and universal abandoning of those superstitious practices to which savage tribes are addicted, convinced the Missionary that after a sufficient knowledge of the principal truths of Redemption, he might confer upon them the holy Sacrament of Baptism. In fact, it was not long until, assisted by the interpreter, he implanted in their docile minds, the doctrines of eternal salvation and knew thoroughly the religious sentiments of each one of those who desired to be united with the Christians. So before the end of his visit, the Missionary had the consolation of baptizing twenty-three, thus beginning with the tribe of the Menominees that work of conversion which continued for some years.

The administration of the Sacraments and the preaching of the Word of Truth are not the only duties of one who is spreading Christ's religion: the building of Churches becomes for him a work necessary for the spreading of the Faith, and for fixing firmly in the people's hearts the spirit of true piety. Green Bay more than any other place had need of a House of God, therefore, the Priest, after a suitable site had been selected, held a consultation with the people and with earnest words incited them to the holy enterprise. Then visiting the people personally in their widely scattered homes, according to each one's circumstances, he allotted the kind and the quantity of the material which he ought to contribute for the erection of a frame church of which we shall speak later on.

The venerable and humble bishop, Right Reverend Edward Fenwick, O.P., arrived at Mackinac about the beginning of July, accompanied by Rev. F. Baraga, destined for the missions among the Indian tribes in the northern part of the state of Michigan. Having heard of the successes in the West he set out without delay in order to assist in the labor of conversions. Obtaining the use of a large room for a few days, spiritual exercises were begun for the French inhabitants of Green Bay. It is not easy to describe the earnestness and zeal with which the Bishop and his Priest strove with the help of God to bring about the desired improvement. A proof of this is the indefatigable application which kept both for a week in the confessional; the day was not long enough: it was found necessary to supply by working a good part of the night. Almost all of the confessions covered a space of many years, ten, twenty, or thirty years. The holy Feast of Pentecost saw many approach the most Holy Sacrament who had almost forgotten It: more than forty Indians were regenerated in the waters of holy Baptism. The seven-fold grace of the Holy Ghost, by the imposition of the Bishop's hand in the Sacrament of Confirmation, descended upon many, among whom were numbered not a few of the poor Indians.

The labor corresponded to these Apostolic efforts and the diffusion of Heaven's graces. According as the number of open sins diminished, scandals became less common, and the service of God more vigorous. While being made Christians the Indians were made new men, both in their exterior appearance and in their moral conduct, so that even in the public streets anyone could distinguish at a glance the Christian from the Pagan savage.

In the autumn of that year he spent almost two months in that same place where the harvest has been so abundant, and he continued to instruct and baptize others of the Menominee tribe, many of whom received Holy Communion. The sublime doctrine of this most august Mystery is understood and firmly believed by these Indians with that humble submission which the Word Divine taught us by Faith, merits. Let not the reader imagine that the intelligence of an American Indian is less susceptible perhaps than his own to the comprehension of the truths of our holy Religion. Such a supposition would be extremely erroneous and would incline to the absurdity of believing the Indian incapable of becoming a perfect Christian who lives by Faith. Christ's doctrine is intelligible to all mankind to some degree, and therein differs from human teachings. If this were not true, how could the Messiah command His Apostles to teach all nations, if those very nations were incapable of understanding all the truths of Religion! Besides, the mysteries of Religion are founded on Faith which is a gift of God, and the wisest of mankind cannot take credit to himself of believing more than the simple and unlettered Christian. The Sciences and Arts of the world can be acquired only through the help of certain preliminary studies which for various reasons are not within the reach of every human intelligence, while the sublime science of salvation can neither be taught nor learned by the human intelligence, for it is all divine. God alone teaches it to the soul and He alone disposes the soul to learn it. Many, learned in the Holy Scriptures, in history, both sacred and profane, and in all the paths of human knowledge, are they not unlearned in the science of salvation which was revealed to the simplest of savages and understood by them? The Son of Man was discoursing on this truth when He said: "I confess to Thee, O Father, Lord of Heaven and earth, because Thou hast hid these things from the wise and prudent and hast revealed them to little ones. Yea, Father, for so hath it seemed good in Thy sight." (Matt. XI, 25, 26.)

To consolidate the holy works begun among the Menominees, it was found necessary to establish a school for the religious instruction of those who were already members of the holy Church, and in this way to facilitate the conversion of the pagans who induced by the example which they had before their eyes, were anxious to become acquainted with the Truth. A zealous and prudent person had charge of this, who, mistress of the Menominee language, and familiar with both English and French, rendered a very great service to Religion by calling many to the unity of the Faith. The United States Government subsequently made a small appropriation in money for the maintenance of this school, requiring its superintendent to render a yearly report to the Secretary of Indian Affairs at Washington.

Chapter IX.

PHYSICAL AND MORAL CONDITIONS OF THE INDIAN TRIBES OCCUPYING THE TERRITORIES OF MICHIGAN, WISCONSIN AND IOWA.

The variety of customs, forms of government, modes of living and characters of the various civilized nations of the world, may serve to give an idea of that variety which exists among the different Indian tribes. In the lives and conditions of these, there are some circumstances common to them all, as the lack of the sciences, of the arts, of education, of social order, of conveniences, of luxury, of riches, and of everything else that can distinguish a cultured from a savage people. Besides the privations common to all the tribes, there are other notable differences among them arising from the nature of the country or from other particular circumstances. In the southern regions where winter is unknown, the Indian goes almost naked, while the native of the north finds in the abundance of furs of the wild animals a suitable covering to defend him from the rigors of the long, cold season. The fertility of the soil, with its spontaneous products readily supplies all the needs of the southern native,—the northern native finds his support in hunting and fishing. There are some tribes, warlike and vindictive, who are seldom at peace with their neighbors, while others of milder character are slow to commit murder. There is no little difference between the character of an Indian who holds communication with settlers of European origin, and the haughty, independent savage utterly isolated in his wilderness, forest or mountain fastness who cares naught to behold a white man, and despises his inventions as useless things. Religion with its heavenly power produces such a change in both the moral and physical condition of the Indian that he may be considered as transformed into a new reasonable being. All the mysteries of Faith and the sublime teachings of our Saviour seem to shine forth in full splendor in those souls not yet tainted with the pride of human wisdom, which without Religion has never succeeded in ameliorating the intellectual condition of savage tribes. For these and many other reasons the customs and modes of life of the various native inhabitants of America differ in many respects; and whereas in these Memoirs mention is made only of certain tribes bordering upon white settlements of the United States, we shall merely take some note of their peculiar character.

 The trading which naturally was introduced by European speculators is done by barter; the Indians sell the furs of different animals of the region, and receive in exchange guns, powder and shot, blankets, cloth of various kinds, knives, scissors, rings, ear-rings, handkerchiefs, shirts of bright colored calico, looking glasses, paint for the face, silver ornaments and very many others. Sometimes they take in exchange provisions, but more often brandy, which might well be called the bane of the tribes. Europeans must not take it for granted that commerce is a means of civilizing the Indians, because, in the first place it is for the most part carried on by persons who aim at making a profit enormously out of proportion to the value of the goods; that is, a gain of fifty or a hundred per cent. Moreover, the association with traders only serves to introduce among the red men the vices without teaching them the virtues of civilized nations. The tribes of Michigan, Wisconsin and Iowa are far more demoralized than those who inhabit the vast territory of Missouri and Oregon, This is further proved by the fact that all the tribes who have been for years in the neighborhood of the settled portions of the State are diminished in number, and are now either nearly extinct or in various respects inferior to those distant tribes who still preserve their independence and a more thorough submission to their own chiefs.

The climate of these north-western regions obliges the Indians to be fully clad during six or seven months. In summer, however, the men usually go half clad, but not the women. Ornaments are not as much in vogues among these northern tribes as in the south, and these consist principally of ear-rings, rings, little silver plates about three inches in diameter, chiefly for women's use,—the men often deck their heads with feathers. They paint their faces with red, white, yellow of black; the last on occasions of mourning, for instance the death of one dear, for the manifestation of special grief.

By reason of this mode of trading and of the money received annually from the government by all the tribes near the Northern Mississippi, for the lands ceded by them, agriculture is almost neglected. A few plant corn and raise potatoes in summer. With the money and the furs are bought not only clothing but also provision, corn, flour, and salt, meats; but these serve only to satisfy their needs for a few days at different times in the course of each year. Their wandering life hardly permits families to cultivate, however poorly, even a little piece of ground, and this not protected by fences, is constantly exposed to the ravages of wild animals, so that the people are compelled to live by hunting and fishing the greater part of the year. The use of the gun for shooting the deer, the bear and other game, with the use of iron traps also, is more serviceable in securing a subsistence for these people than the bows and arrows yet in use among the more distant tribes. On account of bad weather in some seasons, it is often impossible for days to go on the hunt; then the most improvident or lazy suffer hunger, in the winter especially, when the snowfall is heaviest; yet Providence preserves life in the them, some way.

A people destitute of the ties most needful for forming society has no permanent or regular abiding-place; the savages have villages of a hundred or two hundred families which remain in one place a few months, that is, in summer. Their dwelling are hits or lodges roughly constructed of the bark of trees, which they call their summer houses; in winter they live in small huts made of mats. There is a great advantage in the second class of dwellings, for they are easily raised and as easily taken to pieces; the women are usually the only workers here, not only making the mats, raising the lodges, but also removing them and carrying them on their backs when they change localities.

Each tribe has its own chief, who is neither wealthier nor more regarded than the others except in case of warfare, emigration, sale of lands of the Government, or some serious trouble in the tribe with neighbors, when these chiefs possess absolute power of legislation. Hence it is that the treaties through which the Government has come into possession of the land once owned by the Indians, were made only with the common consent of their chiefs.

In war the savage is absolutely cruel, without regard to any military discipline; he employs any and every means whatsoever to destroy the enemy; hidden in the grass or behind a tree or in the darkness of night, he takes his foe by surprise and murders him. Vengeance and vainglory often urge him to eat the yet warm heart of an enemy or to put him to death by various modes of torture. The warriors keep as trophies the hair of the conquered which with one blow they cut and tear from the head with scalp all living and agonizing. What makes their warfare yet more horrible is the use of hatchets, the favorite weapons when two tribes are at war against each other. These, almost naked, painted black, glaring ferociously, uttering dreadful yells, spring at each other like famished tigers and lions, and with their hatchets, gash, lacerate, and destroy each other; few of the combatants survive the slaughter which might better be called the human shambles, and very few are they who have not received a mortal blow. The captives are put to death by the victors or ransomed at a great price by their own people. Experience has taught the tribes not to make war upon the United

States citizens, and the Government takes all possible means to prevent like catastrophes among themselves.

Marriages are arranged by the parents or relatives of the girl, and they lead her to the wigwam of the young man, who presents her with some gifts. Those Indians who are considered able to provide for more than one wife, may take two or three; and these are often sisters, "for the sake of keeping peace in the home," as one Indian told the Missionary. Parents are very fond of their children, the number of whom seems to confer importance upon the family. From their tenderest infancy they are the objects of the mother's most tender care, for they are the dearest of all things to the parents, who are ready to make any sacrifice in their behalf. In the lodges where there are many children, one rarely hears them crying aloud, and this is never prolonged beyond two or three minutes. Old age is always treated with respect and cared for in all its needs, by the numerous relatives, who never forget this duty; in this respect they might serve as an example to many of our own race.

This tribe is remarkable for hospitality; any stranger whatever finds among them a kind reception and an edifying generosity, for if they have any food that is needful to him, they offer it with cordiality, and if he needs a place of refuge they assign to him a corner of their own poor dwelling. In time of peace there is not the slightest danger of being molested by these simple children of nature. In character there is much to give them the right to reproach civilized nations,—among whom mine and thine is carried to such a degree as to create the necessity of too many laws, and transform the noblest sentiments of fraternal love into humiliating egotism.

As regards Religion, the Indian of the northern Mississippi could not be considered absolutely idolatrous, but rather superstitious. He has a general idea of God, whom he calls The Great Spirit, "Il Grande Spirito," for such He is in His works and His power. He worships this Spirits with prayer and with sacrifices also, to obtain assistance in the various wants of life over which He is believed to have absolute control. The Indians believe also in the existence of the evil spirit, to whom they attribute power to harm, and on this account have recourse to him with prayers and offerings as propitiation in great calamities. In case of diseases, war, motives of vengeance, strong affections unreciprocated, they put in operation various superstitious rites well known and practised by these savages, who by reason of this knowledge of theirs are called by the Canadians Medicine Men. This Medicine Man is supposed to possess superior power, exercised by means of certain objects of potent charm, generally confined to such as a snake-skin, a bird's beak, a tortoise shell, a night-bird's or an owl's head, a root, a piece of carved wood, and many other things. The sacrifices are performed by boiling the flesh of some animals or the first ripe ears of corn, the people meanwhile dancing around the kettle and chanting during the whole time it is over the fire, after which they make an offering of part of the contents to the good or the bad spirit, and then throw this back into the kettle. During all this the Medicine Man is repeating certain strange meaningless words as an invocation to the spirit.

The principles of the natural law are sufficiently understood by that tribe to make them accountable to their own conscience when they commit faults, for they themselves condemn theft, homicide, immorality of any kind, lying, revenge, etc. The deprivation of the light of the Gospel leaves them in that spiritual darkness, which is the cause of their imperfect idea of the Divinity, and of the means of atoning for their sins, and throws them into that jumble of superstitious practices which constitute their religious system.

Those among them who by Divine appointment have been converted to Catholicity, retain their own peculiar customs, innocent in themselves in which they were trained, while at the same time rejecting every practice whatever not conformable to the truth and sanctity of Christian Faith, that Faith which alone readers them able to improve and civilize themselves. The Christians in general wear a rosary or a cross around the neck, which serves to distinguish them from the pagans. They are well disposed by nature to become followers of Jesus Christ; the greatest hindrances to their conversion arise from their dealings with traders, from whom they usually get those bad examples that repel rather than win them over to the holy Catholic Faith.

Chapter X.

DESCRIPTION OF THE WOODEN CHURCH ERECTED AT GREEN BAY IN 1831.

Because in October 1831, after many journeys to and fro, many fatigues, anxieties and expenses, we had the consolation of seeing Saint John the Evangelist's Church raised as far as the roof, it will be a satisfaction to the reader to know what kind of a church it was, that could be built entirely of wood. We will give a brief description of this structure, for similar ones are very common in America and these Memoirs contain accounts of different styles of wooden churches.

Where the population is scattered and settled only a few years in a country, new, covered with forests, they do not build houses to last a life-time, far less is there thought of building for posterity; money has little opportunity for exchange, because of the distance from trade; workmen are to be found only with difficulty; the restrictions and simplicity of life lessen the wants of the people, their impatience to have a dwelling, the abundance of wood, the facility of working it, the difficulty of hauling stone, or making brick, are the main causes for so many wooden houses seen in all the new portions of the Western States of the great American Republic. There are two modes of building in wood. One is called in America, the Log House, that is Casa di Travi, which is the more rustic, and usually that of the poorer people; the other is rather fine and is called Frame House, or Casa d'ossatura di Travi.

To form an idea of the Church of Green Bay imagine a foundation of rock sunk into the ground a little, and rising from it about three English feet, with a length of eighty and a breadth of thirty-eight feet. Upon this wall are laid oaken beams, a foot and a quarter square, and from thirty to forty feet long, very strongly joined together; into these beams others of lighter weight are fitted, mortised and fastened with nails here and there; these last rise to the height of twenty feet, meeting another frame of long, well-finished beams. In the joists as in the upper beams are made fast the timbers for the flooring and for the ceiling, all put together with skill and proportion by the well-trained American carpenters. At first sight what they call the frame of the house looks like a cage. This is then overlaid on the outside with planks about six English inches wide and half an inch thick, nailed lengthwise to all the upright beams; the upper edge of each plank is overlapped by the lower edge of the one above it, and so on to the top. The wall so the church building are thus formed to protect the interior from the weather. The roof is also of wood converted with shingles an in several places in the Tyrol. Above the centre of the structure is a bell-tower, of the same shape, and connected with the walls from which it rises to a moderate height, so as to withstand the storms. As in nearly all American Churches, above the inner door is a gallery or tribune, to accommodate a number of the people. The finishing of the inner walls is made after the manner of the plafoni of our buildings, that is, with laths, about an inch broad, by which the plaster is held firm. The building is painted with oil paint to preserve it, and this also serves to embellish it. A church of this kind when well built, of good timber; and protected from the weather, may last for centuries. But neglect of little repairs often reduces many of these wooden structures to ruin before their time. Genuine elegance and the following of the various orders of Architecture are readily adapted to these building, and, furthermore, outlay of wealth and elegance are not unknown among many of those families, whose houses are built spacious, of several stories, and embellished with porticoes and lofty pillars. American carpenters are very skilful in constructing these buildings.

To close with our church of Saint John, we will state that it was not completed before the end of 1832, and some time after that was provided with everything needful for the Lord's House. The expense of building was a little less than twenty thousand francs. But what was that sum compared to making so important a step towards the moral and intellectual regeneration of a newly-formed society? The people assisted, some furnishing almost all the material, others money, the poor, any work that they were able to furnish. The church remained, however, with a debt which was paid by the tardy contributions of two years. The society of the Propaganda likewise through Rt. Rev. Bishop

Fenwick made a generous offering, which, in truth, was almost entirely expended in traveling and similar needs.

Almost all the churches of which we shall make mention in time, found benefactors in this way, incited by the diligent persistence of him who was striving to carry on the duties of a disinterested missionary. Experience has taught this lesson, that unless he sacrifices everything, sometimes depriving himself of what might be considered necessaries, he will find it impossible to secure the desired result.

Chapter XI.

FIRST VISIT TO THE VILLAGE OF SAINT MARY'S UPON THE RIVER OF THE SAME NAME IN 1831.

In a country situated to the north, and almost surrounded by water, thus making the summer season the safest and most convenient for traveling, the Priest thought best to take advantage of this, to visit another gathering of his heterogeneous and numerous flock, which was scattered over a vast extent of country. In the middle of August he left Mackinac, his principal abode, in a fragile canoe made of bark, which was to convey him to a village then called Sault Sainte Marie. The distance is about ninety miles by water, for half of which one coasts along the northern shore of the great Lake Huron, and for the rest, sails along the majestic river of Saint Mary's. The Indians served as rowers and after passing the night upon the bank near the mouth of the river, the Priest arrived safe at his destination on the evening of the second day. Consider that during that voyage not the slightest trace of human life was to be seen; the shores of the Lake and River were covered with the densest of forests where Nature showed herself solemn and mysterious in her eloquent silence. The village is situated at the foot of a tumultuous rushing down of the river, cause by a considerable slope of its uneven bed for more than a mile. Beautiful is the sight of the white foaming flood forced to struggle against the obstinate opposition of many enormous rocks strewn from one shore to the other along the whole course of the rapids and seemingly determined to stay the heavy, irresistible onrush of water. These rush down from Lake Superior, so called from its vast extent, which spreads more than four hundred miles towards the west, and contains in its clear depths a prodigious number of excellent fish.

The people who occupy the eastern bank of the river are situated in Canada, under the English government, and those who live on the opposite shore are citizens of the Republic. Their condition, both moral and intellectual, was in a very bad state, and it would not be exaggeration to say that they loved Religion without knowing it; with the exception of the youth, the settlers had been sent there from the thickly settled portions of Canada for the purpose of carrying on the trade with the Indians. For many years deprived of Religious instruction and exposed to numberless occasions of sin, they were living almost without God. As the Missionary had but a few days to spend there, he devoted himself to calling them around him under the shade of a mighty oak and preaching the principal truths of Faith. They listened to him often with great satisfaction, seated upon the grass, near the headlong rushing waters of the river,—a figure of the swift passing of man's life. A few confessions, many children baptized, and a few marriages solemnized, were the scanty fruit of this first visit, which left behind it the hope of a more abundant return when grace should have fructified the scattered seed of the Divine Word. As a courtesy, and on account of a certain idea of honor due the clerical state, he accepted the kind invitation to supper with the Commandant of the American fort which was stationed at Sault Sainte Marie as a protection from Indian uprisings. The military courtesy of the gentleman (although not Catholic) had allowed the Missionary to preach in his apartment to the officer and families, of whom but one was Catholic. A circumstance of this kind deserves to be put on record as a testimony to that docile spirit and sincere inclination towards the knowledge of the Truth which ordinarily precedes the conversion to the Faith of many unbelievers.

PART ONE

Chapter XII.

THE MISSION OF THE REVEREND F. BARAGA AT ARBRE-CROCHE AMONG THE INDIANS OF THE OTTAWA TRIBE.

The brief and cool summer of these regions had passed and the Missionary had retired to his little house just erected near the Church of Mackinac, when he interrupted his ordinary duties towards his flock in order to revive his own devotion during a visit made to the Reverend F. Baraga. This pious and learned Priest exercised his holy ministry among the Indians of the Ottawa tribe at one of their villages called Arbre-Croche, situated on an inlet of Lake Michigan in the extreme northern part of the State of the same name. There still exists at Mackinac an ancient Baptismal Record of 1696 in which are inscribed the names of the First Franciscan Missionaries who traversed this country, and worthy of remembrance is the record of the Baptism of a slave in the College of the Jesuits at Arbre-Croche. This place is not now that of Father Baraga's residence, but is twenty-five miles farther to the east upon a lofty shore of the Lake; there may yet be seen on the surface of the soil, the regular marks of the plough-share where the trees are noticeably smaller than those surrounding the once cultivated space. According to traditions among the Indians the Fathers of this renowned Order were established more than a hundred years ago at Old Arbre-Croche where they unweariedly shed around those rays of the holy Faith which notwithstanding long absence, is not entirely lost, but lives again and buds and blossoms even to our times, yielding fruit to life eternal. The Ottawa had received a visit from a Priest in 1829; then many of them embraced the Religion once professed by their fathers. In 1831 when the Reverend F. Baraga was appointed to spread the truths of the Gospel among them, the Faith revived and with it the practice of all Christian virtues; and in a few years the numerous and frequent conversions made of that tribe a chosen people, with the fervor of the primitive Christians.

At the end of January, 1832, nature in her wondrous power had, as if at one stroke, hardened the surface of the waters which separate the Island from the places where once the good Jesuits were the benefactors of the Ottawas. A solid magnificent bridge thus built over the water, prepared a dry, smooth road for our Missionary, who was traveling accompanied by a few Indians, towards his brother in the holy ministry. Tired after whole day's journey upon ice, frugal repast refreshed him at evening; the Indians sang a few hymns in their own language, then the hard couch of bark received them until morning. He reached Arbre-Croche the following day, after a wretched journey, partly on foot, and partly on horseback, the animal yet unbroken, that as proof of his spirit of independence tried to throw him before night.

There are few who can form a just idea of the emotions of two Priest who after months of such solitude have the consolation of meeting one another. The sacrament of Penance as the primary object of their meeting and of their soul's progress, naturally forms the first care of both. Oh how sublime, how beautiful, is the Religion of Christ! She humbles her child at the feet of one like himself, who, after sitting as judge supreme upon the throne of Divine Mercy and pronouncing over the penitent's soul the sentence from Heaven, comes down at once from that high station, yielding it to him, who contrite, just asked pardon; and thus forgetting what took place a moment before, begins with accents of grief to take the attitude of a criminal and confesses his own faults before a representative of Christ. Who could ever imagine an act more fitted to make atonement to Divine Justice? Where can be found in the annals of history a more efficacious means for humbling man in his faults and rendering him a partaker of the bounty of the Heart of God Himself, leading him to judge one by whom he himself must be judged? Behold how mildness, patience, compassion, true charity for the neighbor and the just knowledge of one's own weakness and his neighbor's, are learned in the school of that Sacrament, which if they were but practised holily, would bring perfect happiness to society, to the family, to each and all men.

The mission at Arbre-Croche had several stations with a few tiny church buildings; the largest of these was in the village where the Reverend Father Baraga was established. It must be noted that in this region there were no oxen nor draught-horses nor any roads by which building materials could be transported thither; so when the Indians set about building the church, after preparing the beams fifty feet in length, in the woods, they were obliged to move them by main strength, thirty or forty joined together for this purpose. A Canadian carpenter with the help of these good people, skillfully laid the beams one above another to the required height of the wall, in which were fitted some windows. The manner of constructing the floor and wooden ceiling was the most laborious possible, for the planks were wrought out and shaped by the axe alone: one huge tree two or three feet in diameter often furnishing a single plank. This immense work distributed among the different families, however, was completed within a few days. Before the church had been built not one even of the Christian Indians had troubled himself to raise a little house of timber for his family; but after that, they built a fine village on this remote, solitary inlet of Lake Michigan, and they called it by the old name of the place where the Jesuits had first diffused the light of Faith. The Ottawas did not allow traders to live in their village, fearing to see the contamination of these men's habits introduced therein; moreover there was a prohibition against bringing their brandy there, for it had been the source of the direst evils among them.

In this happy spot of primitive fervor everyone rose at the sound of the Ave Maria and in a few minutes was ready to repair to the church. There they recited every day morning prayers, then assisted at the Holy Sacrifice of the new Law with the greatest devotion, accompanying their worship with pious canticles in their own language. Before departing to their homes and labors, the holy Priest used to say a few words of instruction through an interpreter, until the time when with indefatigable application, he became able to speak their language himself. At the noon Ave Maria, the poor Indians did not fail to turn hearts and minds to the great mystery of man's Redemption, by reciting the Angelus. Thus did they also at even at the sound of the bell which summoned them to the Church for vesper prayers.

But that the vain philosophers of our own day could but learn from these people, the "poor in spirit"! A Christian savage is far wiser and more far-seeing than that man, who after spending his days in storing his intellect with sciences, divine and human, afterwards forgets his

Creator. The former studies and loves with all his soul the Uncreated Wisdom which communicated itself to his spirit by Faith, and by a life pure and lowly is secured the eternal possession of its Divine Source; the other, insensate and short-sighted, loses himself in the Creator's works but without well comprehending them,—and while refusing his heart's constant homage to God, loses himself in those everlasting shadows which will encompass the spirit which in life loves not and serves not Christ, the true Light of the world.

Religion possesses in the treasury of her graces the efficacious means for the regeneration of humanity, even when fallen into the most deplorable state. The savage owes to the Gospel the amelioration of his physical condition, because this calls upon him to form the society in which he readily finds the means of subsistence. Before he heard the word of truth, the necessities of life were secured almost entirely by the chase, and rarely did he provide in the summer against the cruel needs of a long winter when he was compelled to follow up here and there the forest prey, that he might support life on their flesh. To add to his misfortune, the trading with Europeans taught the savage the vice of drunkenness with its train of all other vices; then famine and homicide decimated the tribes. The Ottawas enlightened by holy Faith, planted the poor homes around the Altar, whereon was offered the Divine Victim for man's salvation, and faithful to common prayer, tasted how sweet a thing it is to dwell in unity. When they advanced thus far, many abandoned hunting to devote themselves to cultivating grain and vegetables; domestic animals and fish supplied them with meat; so the church was frequented, and their own hearth-stone during the long winter, was enjoyed in peace by those who, but a few years before, had to pass days and nights exposed to all inclemencies of the elements to save themselves from perishing from hunger. The necessary arts found some to cherish them in that tribe; the carpenter had his workshop, and blacksmith mad Arbre-Croche ring with the measured strokes of his heavy hammer; the fragile hut had been given up for a solid dwelling of timber, a floor dry and comfortable, with chairs, tables, bedstead, in place of the bare wet earth. The change verified the promises made by Christ to those who "seek first the kingdom of God and His justice," and them will have all things added to them.

Apostolic zeal is not content with doing good only to those around it, but carries its solicitude on wherever its forces can assist it. The Reverend Father Baraga often traversed that northern portion of Michigan inhabited by the Ottawas, and in a few years of toil was gathered there a flock of more than a thousand Christians almost all of whom had been baptized by himself. In four localities he built a plain little church, where the good Indians assembled to recite daily prayers in common, and on Sunday they chanted the Mass prayers and pious hymns. The zealous Priest, did not fear to undertake long voyages upon these immense Lakes in a frail canoe constructed of bark; familiarized with a life destitute of all delicacies and ordinary comforts, everywhere he found wherewith to barely sustain life. Loved and revered by his spiritual children, he found in them his glory and heavenly riches.

They are unjust who seeing not the beam in their own eye, desire to blame the mote in their brother's eye; if they behold or heedlessly believe, that they behold imperfections in some of the Catholic clergy, they condemn the entire body of the Sanctuary. But the holy lives of many Priests, who have forsaken father-land, parents, every friend on earth, and have consecrated their lives to the salvation of wild and savage peoples, ought in justice to be put in the balance on the side of the Sanctuary. But the bad see only the evil which they love, and strangers to the good, they ignore it and pass judgment blindly.

Chapter XIII.

INDIANS CONVERTED AT MACKINAC — CATHOLICS OF POINT SAINT IGNACE—DEATH OF AN OLD MAN—SINCERE CONVERSION OF ANOTHER.

The parish of Mackinac was favorable to the conversion of the savages. Many of these came from its vicinity to hear the Religious instructions given in their own language through an interpreter; in the spring of 1832 were counted more than fifty members of the Catholic Church. This island having been a central trading point, the Indians who had pitched their lodges there, were an intermixture of Chippewas who still occupy the upper portion of Wisconsin Territory, with Ottawas and Menominees. The language of these tribes are almost identical, and are therefore easily understood among them. To facilitate their conversion and invite them to come to the Church on festival days, at Sunday Vespers, they chanted alternately one verse in Latin and the next in Indian; the variety and pleasing effect of this new method of singing psalms, aroused in the heart the sublime emotions suggestive of the grand Catholic unity and universally. The Indians from a small gallery thus chanted the praises of God with the pious affections of King David and mingled voices and languages in the same words which for so many ages resounded in the magnificent Temple of the God of Israel.

It was delightful and consoling to see the humility, modesty and simplicity of the Indians at Sacramental Confession, as they were obliged to use an interpreter in this Sacrament. This mode of Confession will be spoken of in another chapter. The tender devotion which all saw written upon their countenances when they drew near to receive the mysterious Sacrament of the Body of Jesus, was such as to condemn the extreme perversity of many Christians who either refuse to participate in this great Principle of Eternal Life or through want of proper dispositions turn It to their own condemnation. Terrible and irreparable will be the confusion of these false disciples of our Redeemer, when they shall see the living faith and love of the poor savages of many tribes towards the Most Holy Sacrament, crowned with glorious immortality, while their own indifference and negligence shall make their own remorse in the realm of everlasting sorrow.

A part of the population belonging to the parish of Mackinac were living about three miles from the Island upon a tongue of land named Pointe Saint Ignace. Traditions assert that this name was given by the Jesuits in memory of their founder. See how the ancient Religious travelers who first penetrated into the heart of North America, named the various parts of creation; they chose holy names! We have very many proofs of this pious practice in the names of the rivers, especially of southern America. Pointe Saint Ignace was at that epoch inhabited by about two hundred Catholic whites and by many Indians; therefore our Missionary was often obliged to cross the strait which separates them from the Island, sometimes by water, often upon the magnificent bridge of ice which afforded a secure support to the foot of the traveler for about four months in the year. Several aged Canadians, unhappy survivors of many years of trading with the tribes, had been left there, it might be by chance, to end their days in extremest poverty. The voice of the Priest had often fallen upon their ears without reaching the hard heart rendered insensible by twenty, thirty or even forty years of absence from the Sacraments. The infinite goodness of Him Who grants this present life to His enemies that He may save them in the next, wrought their conversion by degrees. The almost unprovided death of a few of the very aged who had conditionally prepared to appear at the judgment seat, startled their companions out of their obstinate lethargy, and, fearful of falling unprepared into the hands of the Living God, they embraced the means of reconciliation and salvation so often offered to them in vain. The holy Feast of Easter, 1832, saw more than a hundred communicants who a few months before, dead to the graces of many years, had coldly pursued the ways of final impenitence.

Persuaded that good example proves a stimulus and encouragement to virtue, a brief mention will be made here of two aged persons; one will serve to make a death-bed conversion dreaded; the other will give edification with its sincere sorrow. A certain N. at the advanced age of more than eighty years was drawing near the close of his career. He did not take kindly to the visits of the Priest for the reason that the latter was young and was presuming to know more than he. His infirmities held him prisoner in his wretched cabin, and death was already knocking at his door. After many attempts to persuade him to the repentance indispensable for an ill-spent life, his nearness to his dissolution and the terrible judgments of the Lord laid before him with the powerful words of Religion at last urged him to promise to make his Confession. But although upon the very brink of hell he kept deferring the fulfillment of his promise from one day to another. The Priest was obliged to use that gentle severity inspired by charity in order to persuade him to begin the humble and penitent self-accusation of his faults; by dint of questioning he obtained from that benumbed soul only a probable disposition to receive a favorable sentence in the Sacrament of Penance which under other circumstances would have been denied. The indifference of the sick man and the Priest's hope of seeing him better disposed to a worthy reception of the Most Holy Eucharist, kept that Bread of the dying away from the old man's house. But one night the Servant of the Altar is called to assist that soul in its passage to Eternity. He enters the cottage, sees the man breathing with such difficulty and so oppressed by his disease as to be absolutely unable to receive Holy Communion, the Sacrament of Extreme Unction is administered, the last prayers are uttered and the old man dies without any sign of Religion. Oh how true that a death-bed conversion itself participates in death! The living nourish fine hopes in like cases, but a secret fear taught us by Divine Justice and by experience makes us tremble for their safety.

Safe and comforting would it be for sinners to imitate the conduct of that aged man who in 1832 went from Pointe Saint Ignace to the Church of Mackinac to lay down the burden upon his conscience; for more than forty years deprived of the Sacramental Grace of Confession, Mr. N. with the intent of ending the gnawing at his heart said with the prodigal son, "I will go to my Heavenly Father's house. Why should I defraud myself of the inheritance of the children of God? The moving words of life which I heard last Sunday from the mouth of the Priest pierced my heart, they seemed to be aimed at me. I am a true son of the Church who made strange misuse of the gifts of Heaven received in my youth. Lo my soul for many years lives in direst poverty and is dying of hunger!" Moved by these thoughts which softened his heart, he makes ready and leaning upon his staff crosses over upon the ice which in winter joins his place of abode to the Island. Like the leper of the Gospel, he shows himself to the Priest manifesting the clearest signs of a true contrition in the accusation of his faults of more than forty years. He blots out his sins with his sobs, he washes them with floods of tears in the merits of Christ, and provides for the welfare of his soul which he wills to save at any cost. Rising then from the tribunal of Penance with a deep sigh from his very heart, he said: "My father, I seem to have laid down from my shoulders the weight of a mountain!" Such was his gratitude to God's Mercy that he could never afterwards speak of his confession without tears of tenderness.

Chapter XIV.

OTHER SAVAGES BAPTIZED AT GREEN BAY — SPIRITUAL EXERCISES AT MACKINAC — BISHOP FENWICK, HIS FEAR OF GOD'S JUDGMENTS — THIRTY-TWO MARRIAGES SOLEMNIZED AT THE VILLAGE OF SAINTE MARIE.

By the first canoe that passed through the Straits of Mackinac in the spring of 1832 when the ice of a long winter had been scattered and melted by sun and wind, our Missionary betook himself to Green Bay where during the preceding winter the conversion of many Indians had been wrought. He spent almost two months to strengthen among the French settlers that piety which may easily grow cold when far removed from the Sacraments. The poor Menominee Indians baptized some months before were awaiting the Black Gown, as they call the Priest, with the greatest impatience, because they longed to receive Holy Communion, and to see others of their tribe received into the bosom of the Church. In fact, more than sixty at that time were judged worthy of receiving the Sacrament of Regeneration. It would be beyond the limits of truth, to consider the Priest as the principal instrument in the Hand of God in this work of conversion; he was but the secondary means, properly speaking. The real reason is that the Indians, once made Christian, feel for the pagans of their nation that Heaven-sent charity that urges them to consecrate themselves with all their might, by force of example and instruction, to gain them over to the same Faith, by which they themselves are animated.

Returning to Mackinac at the beginning of July, the Priest had the exceeding great consolation of finding there his beloved, humbleminded Bishop Fenwick, who had come there from Cincinnati as on the previous year, to pay a visit to the poor dwellers in this country, but especially to the Indians. His health was so feeble, however, that after a visit to Arbre-Croche he fell so ill at the Island that he was unable to go on the Green Bay in Wisconsin as he desired. Recovering somewhat from this extreme debility, near the end of July a course of Spiritual

Exercises was begun for the people of the Island, and for a large number of Canadian traders who at that season came to bring the skins obtained from the savages to procure the provisions needed for the next winter. These traders were then arriving from the north and from the east, some after a journey of six or eight hundred miles, both by land and by water. Nearly all professed the Catholic Faith, but employed many years among pagan tribes without ever seeing Priest or Church, the Faith was nearly dead within them. The Exercises carried on in the Mackinac Church were mainly for the conversion of these. God blessed his people, and for almost two weeks the good Bishop with his Priest were occupied with the confessions of hundreds, who, some for twenty, some for forty years and more, had not approached that Sacrament. The sincerity of repentance at the sacred tribunal raised gladdest hopes that they would bear away to their far-off homes the priceless grace of perseverance.

On this last occasion when the Missionary had the satisfaction of enjoying the companionship of that Prelate who had conferred upon him the Sacrament of Ordination, there was a circumstance that deserved to be transmitted to the remembrance of posterity. The Most Reverend Jean-Jean, having come at the same time as the Bishop, when he saw him stricken with illness showed in a little book the words which he had heard from the Bishop's mouth in Cincinnati, on Pentecost of this year, after the Pontifical High Mass: "This is the last time in my life that I celebrate Mass in this Church." The event verified the prediction. So persuaded was Monsignore Fenwick of his approaching dissolution, that in the Priest's room at Mackinac he often walked back and forth buried in thought, without uttering a word, and without giving any reason for his sorrow. One day the Priest on entering his little house found the Bishop seated and such was the sadness of his heart that his cheeks were bathed in tears; the reader may imagine the feelings this caused in the heart of him who loved the Bishop so tenderly. For some time it was impossible to discover the cause, but overcome by the anxious pleading of his spiritual son, he broke forth in solemn accents expressing the fear which agitated his soul, of appearing soon before the dread tribunal of God; he blamed himself for having accepted the Episcopacy of which he was unworthy and unable to

PART ONE

carry the burden, declaring that he had badly governed his diocese and that he knew nought to answer to the Judge Supreme. Who would not be affected and edified at the profound humility of these laments uttered before one who so tenderly venerated him? Silencing his own sorrow, his disciple set himself to console his afflicted teacher, representing that as he had taken the Vow Obedience in the Order of Saint Dominic, in accepting the Bishopric he had only executed the command of his Superior; and even should he have lacked aught in the solemn duties of the Episcopate, his upright intention and the mercy of Jesus Christ would intercede for him before the just eternal Judge. With such words did the Priest strive to console his humble and holy Bishop whom an interior voice was summoning the life wherein all tears would be wiped away, sorrow changed into joy, and the holy saving fear of Divine Justice recompensed by the assurance of enjoying forever the peace and the glory of the heavenly Jerusalem. The venerable Bishop Fenwick died towards the end of the next September, at Canton, while on his way from Mackinac to Cincinnati. His Memory is yet in benediction among the faithful; his spirit of prayer, of poverty, of humility, of all virtues, enhanced by that charming affability, sweetness and noble bearing can never be forgotten by one who had the good fortune to know him well in life. His last sentiments may well serve not only as salutary advice and instruction to one raised to ecclesiastical dignities but also as just warning to many who, ignoring their tremendous responsibilities, too lightly and eagerly desire them.

Having bade farewell to the good Bishop for the last time, the Missionary set out on the fifteenth of August 1832, for Sault Sainte Marie. The remarkable circumstances of this second visit was the number of marriages solemnized among the Catholics. In a region where there are no clergy, the faithful had contracted the marriage obligations in presence of parents or friends, as witnesses of their solemn promises; and generally they added that of renewing them before a Priest when they had the opportunity, which happened to not a few. They refused to recognize the civil authority in such cases and in the absence of a priest, they did not have recourse to the magistrate to legalize their union. The laws, divine and human, upon this important contract this year were expounded by the Priest with great earnestness during this

Mission; finally, the Catholics consented to prepare worthily for the Sacrament of Matrimony, and in six days thirty-two couples received the nuptial benediction. Among these was a decrepit old man who came with his aged wife to renew the solemn promises,—followed by their sons who had children also. To facilitate these marriages of prime necessity, the offering, even the very least, was refused. Thus many spiritual and temporal woes found a seasonable remedy through the influence of Religion. This short but profitable Mission was also crowned by many baptisms among the Indians, chiefly of the Chippewa tribe.

Chapter XV.

SIGNS OF WAR WITH THE SAVAGES—MANNER AND DIFFICULTIES OF TRAVELLING IN WISCONSIN TERRITORY IN 1832—A NIGHT OFF THE RIGHT PATH—THE CATHOLICS OF PRAIRIE DU CHIEN—RETURN TO MACKINAC.

The crying needs of an old village on the Mississippi River, inhabited at that time by more than six hundred Catholics, for the most part Catholic in name only, called the Missionary to return from Sault Sainte Marie to the Island of Mackinac, and from there after a brief stay to set out for Green Bay; thence he continued his journey as far as Prairie du Chien. The warlike tribes of the Sacs and Foxes, with their stubborn war (Black Hawk War) against the United States Government had in 1832 spread terror and confusion for many months throughout the southern and western parts of Wisconsin Territory. There some of the citizens had been barbarously murdered, but their death was avenged later by the united forces of the settlers who, pursuing the hostile and rebellious tribes, after different bloody encounters, drove the wretched savages to the necessity of swimming across the vast river Mississippi, near Prairie du Chien. How great the slaughter among the Indians it will not be easy to recount, because, forced after useless resistance to save life by getting across the river, many perished in that difficult passage. Not provided with a sufficient number of horses, each

PART ONE

of these carried more than one rider and so their flight was slow and perilous. The white man ceased not pursuing the fugitives by force of arms, killing them in the very act of leaving the bank. Not a few women and children perished in the current, victims of the cruelty of some citizens, or of their own inability to cling to the horse during their dangerous and headlong passage of the River. Peace was made in the autumn between the United States and the savage Sacs and Foxes, rendering traveling safe and secure again, which allowed our Missionary to cross the Territory as far as the great River.

At that period there was no travel possible in that part of the country except on horseback, as there were neither roads nor bridges: a little winding path traced by the feet of the Indians through the woods and over vast natural meadows was the only road. The rivers that were not too broad or deep were crossed on horseback; over the others, the animal was made to swim alone to the opposite bank, and the traveler followed in a little canoe hollowed out of a log; when no ford could be found, a rude and perilous bridge was thrown across by felling a tree tall enough to reach from one bank to the other. Across rivers that are both swift and deep, while one crosses in canoe, he has to make the horse also swim behind him, holding him by the bridle. In this way all the floods are overcome. Not seldom the many swamps formed a most serious obstacle because over these one had to cross on foot to lighten the horse. Notwithstanding all possible precautions, the noble creature often broke through the thin crust covering the underlying soft, watersoaked ground; when such misfortunes happened, it was not easy to get the animal upon its feet, for the very effort made to rise only sank him deeper into the swamp; sometimes the poor creature was lost there. The few wretched log huts found twenty and often forty miles apart were entirely destitute not only of conveniences, but also of the most necessary things. The open air was often preferable to such a hovel, and to carry one's provisions along was the most inconvenient course, but the most secure.

Our Missionary had to encounter these and other inconveniences, when in the middle of September 1832, in company with the judge of the Territory of Wisconsin he left Green Bay in order to visit Prairie du Chien. Eight days of difficult travel on horseback over a crooked route were spent before reaching our destination, having made more than two hundred and twenty-five miles. Whoever undertakes a long march in such countries is provided with a blanket, some meat, cooked or raw, tea, kindling wherewith to make a fire, with some tin kettles. A gun not seldom serves to provide a meal of delicate wild fowl. Twice a day the cooking was done near some clear stream; the ground served as table and comfortable seat, a bit of wood or bark furnished plates; a good piece of meat roasted at the fire, without bread; water or tea made in a tin cup, satisfied the demands of appetite. In fact, such a meal was always more savory than what the rich enjoy, who in abundance have no contentment, and know not what means the blessing of a good appetite. Whenever no house was in view at evening, the horses were tied to a tree, leaving their halters long enough to allow them to graze, and the two wayfarers comfortably passed the night wrapped in their blankets upon the magnificent carpet of nature, the weary limbs enjoying sweet repose under the starry vault of heaven. If Almighty God provides for His servants a room so grand and so vast to contemplate in the silence of the night, who can conceive what He has prepared for their enjoyment in the everlasting, more luminous day of Paradise? Oh, how beautiful, how sublime the idea that silently coursed through the soul of one who on the bosom of the vast prairie, was raised by the countless gleaming stars to meditate the glory of the Blessed!

An example of the difficulty of travel in those days was the unlucky consequence once of deciding to leave the narrow beaten path in order to avoid a swamp. Its breadth of more than half a mile, and the sheet of water over it, intimidated the two travelers, who believed they could find a better and more direct route by making a circuit round it, and after an hour and a half of riding, the swamp was passed to where it was straight and dry. But then neither knew how to find the right path, in fact the only path, and so in their uncertainty they traveled on till night, when tired out and taciturn, the darkness compelled them to defer their search until next day. The judge, without waiting for food, discontentedly took refuge in his blanket; his companion gaily employed himself in playing cook, plucking a pigeon shot that day, which well prepared and roasted at a fire made from an old dead tree, turned out of exquisite flavor. One thing was lacking, that was water; but to quench their burning thirst in the morning, the two friends set to work collecting in their tin cups the dew that bathed the grass. Providence permitted them about nine in the morning to find the right path at last, where their thirst was quenched at a limpid stream.

A useful reflection is here suggested by this unlucky chance. What happened then teaches us the reality of what happens to those who, dreading the difficulties to be surmounted in the narrow path of virtue, seek by vicious circles to reach that happy end which virtue alone points out. But over the wilful ways of human wisdom, they lose the true path without reaching the object of their desires. But when with the help of grace they leave the arid plains and journey towards the path of Religions, then only, drawing near the never failing springs of true happiness, they freely drink of the waters of eternal life and arrive at the longed-for city of the Blessed.

Here we were, at Prairie du Chien by journey over land and water, on September twenty-second. This village, according to an old tradition, bears the name of a chief called "The Dog," whose tribe inhabited that immense prairie which follows the Mississippi for many miles, with a chain of hills to the east. Situated at the mouth of the Wisconsin River, it had been for about a century a post of great importance for the traders in their traffic with the different tribes, and like many other places of this region, inhabited for the most part by Canadians from Quebec and Montreal. It now contains a United States Fort for defence against the savages, who, however, have ceded their lands to the Government and are leaving the vicinity.

The Catholics of Prairie du Chien were visited from time to time by Priests, who used to come from the city of Saint Louis in the state of Missouri by ascending the great river for almost six hundred miles. There was no sign of a Church there in 1832, and the poor people wandering without a shepherd, were dying of that hunger of the soul which destroys its life. The disorders mentioned in the eighth chapter of these Memoirs, in this place, also offered a new proof of the decadence of society, when, lacking the restraints of the Christian Religion, if finds itself at the mercy of its own weakness. A visit of fifteen days gave the Missionary an opportunity of preaching to the Catholics of Prairie du Chien on the supreme importance of turning from the ways of evil to the God of Mercy, and reflecting upon the affair of eternal salvation, he strove to move them to true repentance. The Divine precept of Sacramental Confession was in like manner dwelt upon for the good of those who had opened their hearts to grace. There were added also various familiar instructions upon the principal truths of Faith as contained in the Apostles Creed. The people did not fail to come to hear the words of eternal life — which were announced by the Priest in a large vacant house, wherein the Holy Sacrifice was being offered. But the long delay in sin, which renders the soul deaf to the voice of the Lord suffered only a few to give true signs of contrition; and few presented themselves at the tribunal of Penance, and still fewer had the consolation of receiving the Holy Eucharist. A great many children received the Sacrament of Baptism and a number renewed in the presence of the Priest the solemn promises of matrimony, which they had already contracted according to the civil law.

The Priest had been wishing to make some preparation towards the building of a House of God, but since he was then domiciled at Mackinac, about four hundred miles from Prairie du Chien by the common road it, would have resulted in beginning a work too far away, and too impracticable for him. So he decided to leave the affair to the good pleasure of Divine Providence. Returning in company with some traders to Green Bay, he there found the new church finished and attended by two Priests of the Congregation of the Holy Redeemer, sent by the Vicar General of the Diocese of Cincinnati.

The people were exceedingly glad to hear from these good Priests the Word of Life, which then made much progress among the savages also. In the beginning of November the Priest set sail for the Island, which was to be his dwelling during the winter. But a sudden violent storm rising from the northern part of Lake Michigan, offered such obstinate resistance to the little vessel that the captain was forced to seek refuge in a little inlet of the stormy lake; there it lay anchored for a day and a night, exposed to a storm of wind and snow; at last a favorable breeze arose, and the traveler was able to reach the desired goal.

PART ONE

Chapter XVI.

VISIT TO ARBRE-CROCHE—THE REVEREND FR. BARAGA—SNOW SHOES—OLD ARBRE-CROCHE—LAMENT OF AN OLD INDIAN WOMAN, AND GRIEF OF A YOUNG BRAVE—RETURN TO ISLAND OF MACKINAC.

If the first step of one desiring to teach others the doctrine of Christ is to practice it first himself, it will not surprise the reader to know that the Missionary, although wearied with his late voyages by land and by water and just returned to his island, determined to pay a visit to his spiritual director. Taking advantage of ten Catholic Indians leaving for Arbre-Croche in a bark canoe one evening he crossed the Straits of Mackinac with them, and spent the first night in a dense forest, under a little tent cheered by a crackling fire close by,—which was supplied with fuel by the company. Who will forget the sweet canticles sung in their own native tongue by the pious oarsmen while crossing the Lake? The starry vault above, the calm of the limpid waters, their immensity lost in the western horizon, the pensive stillness of the shores far-off yet barely discernible, all seemed to echo the sweet reverent tones of the simple good Ottawas, who are never weary of celebrating the glories of that Almighty God who had just now called them to the saving light of the Gospel. Sublime picture which floated before the mind of him who sailed in their company! The just man in the dark night of this mortal life traverses the narrow space which leads to eternity,—passes it in the fragile vessel of flesh,—sees beyond this space that eternity which he fears to approach,—and then Faith discloses to him on that other side of the land of salvation near, but all unknown,—then doth the just raise his voice to the heavens, and joining the perseverance in good works to his own timid faltering, yet joyful accents, glides safe to the longed-for shore. Thus did he muse in that narrow bark.

Following the winding curves of the Lake Shore, on the evening of the second day, they landed at the safe port of the new Arbre-Croche. (See Chapter XII.) Our attention was immediately drawn to several

Indians who were in the act of throwing a barrel into the Lake,—while another party of Indians was breaking up another barrel in the middle of the village street. On our asking the reason of this proceeding, we were answered that one of the traders had brought there two barrels of brandy, which was an offense against the laws of the villagers; the Ottawa chief had ordered one of the barrels to be thrown into the lake and the other to be smashed up and as a sign of contempt to be spilled in the street. Religion alone had the power to teach these simple children of nature the hard lesson of fleeing the occasions of sin; their behavior on this occasion might well be an example to be followed by many educated Christians.

The main object of this journey found in the piety and holy learning of Father Baraga, and in the tranquillity and sanctity of the place, that spiritual unction felt to the quick by him who so rarely had the opportunity to look upon the face of a Priest. Among the different trials of a Missionary in distant countries, the privation of the Sacrament of Penance is the most cruel. May God grant that his state of isolation may perfect in him the holy fear of God, that the sincere desire to confess may take the place of the Sacrament.

The devoted Priest of the Ottawas, Father Baraga, had it in mind at that time to transfer his flourishing Mission to the zeal of another, in order to bear the light of the Gospel to the many-peopled tribe of the Chippewas, who occupied the upper portion of Wisconsin Territory near Lake Superior. Holy and salutary was that call to give up the Lord's fair Vineyard to the care another laborer, that he himself might begin the hard toil of planting a second. In this design the favorable opinion of his Society was with Father Baraga. For many years has this holy Father been toiling at the farthest western extremity of Lake Superior, called La Pointe; here far from the world he lives happily among his converted Chippewas speaking their language; in these good people living in evangelical poverty, he holds the pledge of future glory with the holy apostles.

During this visit to Arbre-Croche in the beginning of December, 1832, there was a snow fall to the depth of two feet, and when our Missionary was ready to return to Mackinac, it was necessary to learn to travel with an additional pair of shoes, called "Snow Shoes." These

PART ONE

consist of a network about a foot and a half wide and two feet long, woven of cord, stretched tightly over an oval-shaped wooden rim, terminating at the heel in a point. One desiring to travel easily over deep snow without sinking into it, fastens these frames or snow shoes under his ordinary shoes; he measures his steps so as to avoid setting one of these snowshoes upon the other. With a little practice, they prove most useful for, covering almost four square feet, of snow, a man's weight in distributed over the space covered. With this new mode of locomotion, the Missionary traveled about thirty miles in one day along the shore of Lake Michigan; arriving, weary enough, at old Arbre-Croche, formerly evangelized by the Jesuits, he remained there three days.

He was walking near the Lake one evening, reading his Breviary while the Indians were going up to the little church for evening prayer; a blind woman at the advanced age of ninety or a hundred years[*] was among the number, and on her asking where the Priest was, they answered her that he was walking by the Lake and saying his prayers. "Ah," she rejoined, "I remember in my own youth, the Priest who taught us the Faith, used to do the very same thing in that same place." These simple words confirm the general belief that the Jesuits had planted the Faith in that region. At the foot of a little hill upon which the church now stands, are seen the tips of several cedar posts in a straight line, almost entirely buried under the sand piled up there by the waves of Lake Michigan; tradition has it that this was the old cemetery of the Christians in the time of the Fathers long remembered.

It would be a serious omission to pass over in silence, two edifying circumstances which occurred during these three days which the Minister of the Altar passed with the good Indians of Old Arbre-Croche. Many Ottawas of that village and its vicinity were not yet Christians, so the occasion was propitious for making converts to Christ. Among these an old woman came to the Priest's cabin carrying a rough wooden box about a foot and a half wide, and containing some red feathers and an eagle's beak. These the Priest threw into the fire, along with many other objects of superstition belonging to other pagans who

---

[*] It is almost impossible to find out the age of the old Indians, who were not baptized in infancy or of whom no register was kept.

were asking for Baptism. The old woman wept bitterly at the sight of the destroying flames; the interpreter asked her if she was sorry for having given to the fire these charms once so dear to her. "Oh, no," she answered, "I weep at the knowledge of my past ignorance. See the fire burning up the things in which I used to believe there was a divine power." A good lesson for those carnal minded men who see the pleasures in which they placed their whole hope and happiness destroyed by those same flames to which they furnish fuel. If they would but weep with the old Indian over the ignorance which caused their past wanderings.

Entering an Indian wigwam the Priest noticed a young Indian of melancholy aspect who seemed to have no part in the happy hearts and joyous looks of those around him; fearing that some misfortune had befallen him the interpreter asked the reason of this behaviour. The ready response was to the effect that the deep and constant melancholy of the young Christian arose from the obstinate refusal of all his nearest relatives to be converted to the Divine Faith which he himself was professing. The Lord hearkened to the pious grieving of this tender heart and soon called his beloved parents to the light of Truth. How foolish are those Christians who weep and lament over poverty, misfortunes, sickness, the death of kindred, and never think of sorrowing or sighing over their own sins and obstinate resistance to Divine Grace. The young Ottawa might well teach a lesson to such as those.

A few Indians having been baptized, the Missionary left Old Arbre-Croche the morning of the first Wednesday in Advent, guided by four young Ottawas. The snow was so deep that it was still necessary to use snow-shoes. After traveling some miles along the Lake Shore, a weakness in the knees caused by the use of the indispensable snow-shoes, compelled the Priest to let himself be carried on the shoulders of his traveling companions. It was probably noon when they reached a deserted cabin. The appetite of a fast day strictly observed, in spite of toilsome travel, was satisfied by a few ears of corn roasted at the fire and a porridge made of flour and water, seasoned with sugar. Thus does Divine Providence sometimes will to succor our extreme needs thus meagerly, as penalty, for that original disobedience committed in the midst of plenty, and to try at the same time our humble submission to the Will of an offended God. Resuming our journey, we passed the night at a poor Canadian's house, opposite the Island of Mackinac. We made landing there next morning before day, the lake being smooth, although there was much floating ice. The weather changing that same day, the four Indians remained in the Priest's little house for two weeks, until the surface of the straits was hardened by the cold into a safe and magnificent bridge.

Chapter XVII.

ORDINARY DUTIES OF A MISSIONARY — DOGMATIC SERMONS NECESSARY FOR CATHOLICS LIVING AMONG SECTARIANS.

The life of a Missionary when he is living in any place where there is a Church does not differ greatly from that of a zealous parish Priest who finds himself alone to govern his scattered flock over a vast extent of country. Instructing the children, especially in Advent and in Lent, preaching twice every Sunday and Holy Day, celebrating the Holy Mysteries daily, holding one's self ready at any hour to receive penitents visiting the sick, sometimes twenty or thirty miles from the Church, guarding one's from idleness and from care of temporal things not appertaining to the Church, leading the people in good works, — these are the chief duties of one two in a distant land desires to sanctify the souls committed to his care. The poor Catholic dwellers on the Island of Mackinac not only needed these pastoral cares, but they were to be defended against the repeated assaults of the enemies of the Catholic Faith. We have seen how in the winter of 1831, the Calvinist minister made trial of his knowledge against the truth; the religious war continued yet to give signs of life. It is a truth from the mouth of Truth itself: "He who is not with Me is against Me." So religious hostility can be avoided in no way except by the adoption of the name belief, or by the indifferentism which is a culpable abandonment of every Christian truth.

Quite a number of the soldiers who were stationed at the little fort overlooking the Island were Catholics and until the winter of that year had been allowed to assist at the Divine Service of the Church. A new official took command in 1833 and by an infraction of the general law of the Government he compelled all the soldiers without distinction to attend the Calvinist Church every Sunday at the hour of Divine Service. The Catholic soldiers with their Priest made complaint of this as a tyranny and an injustice, without obtaining liberty of worship, however, before summer. See how far a false belief can blind even a cultured man; the most sacred laws of nations are sometimes trampled under foot by reason of this blindness, even in a Republic.

To keep the Faith, the Missionary was often obliged to take the dogmas of the Church as subjects of his discourses, and sometimes to enter the enemy's camp in order to disclose the absurdity and falsity of their principles. Almighty God, Who makes use of our nothingness to complete His plans, so willed that such discussions should bear fruit of great good, calling not a few people of the Island to the knowledge of the Truth, particularly a number who trained in the Calvinistic school for many years, had forsaken their Faith in early youth. The holy Festival of Easter was celebrated this year by the Reception of the most holy Communion by all the Catholics of Mackinac and its vicinity with the exception of eight who refused to draw near the Table of Angels.

The contemplated incursions into the yet unsettled Territory of Wisconsin, as will be seen later, suggested to the Priest the advisability of learning to sleep upon the ground. To acquire this physical accomplishment it was only necessary to make the experiment in his own soon. The first night of making this test, although two blankets were between him and the floor, he was compelled after many hours to take refuge in his ordinary bed, but on the next night, having finally fallen asleep upon the floor, he continued to find repose there every night for about two months, thus making sure of a couch anywhere without expense.

Chapter XVIII.

FIRST MISSION TO THE TRIBE OF WINNEBAGOS IN 1833 — THEIR VICES ARE OPPOSED TO THE GOSPEL — CONVERSION OF SEVERAL.

The lately deceased Bishop of Cincinnati had expressed his desire some months before his death that the Missionary would go to announce the word of the Gospel to the Winnebago Tribe in Wisconsin Territory. He left the Island April 16th, 1833, and after a few day's sojourn with the good Redemptorist Fathers at Green Bay, he pushed o to the west on horse back for a hundred and ten miles to a place Fort Winnebago, because the Government held a little fort there as defense against the incursions of the Indians. On the western bank of the swift, impetuous Wisconsin River, about eight miles from the Fort, is a village of the tribe, perhaps a hundred families altogether. These Indians are more fierce and evil disposed in character than either the Menominees or Ottawas; their habits were bad, addicted as they were to drunkenness, immorality and homicide. Their language differs entirely from that of the neighboring tribes

The priest was cherishing the fond hope, with the help of Divine Grace, that he might convert some of these. He had the good fortune of finding an excellent interpreter in Mr. P. Paquette, whose mother was a Winnebago. Mr. Paquette was in Government employ, — often engaged to deal with the tribe, on account of his character and influence over the Indians. Many times they were assembled in a cabin to hear the instructions given for their conversion to the Faith; on these occasions, the Priest spoke to them of the Unity of God and of the Three Divine Persons, of the mystery of the Incarnation, how from the Fall of the first man proceeded the poverty, ignorance and slavery to sin of those who, tempted by the Evil Spirit followed their many superstitious practices; then he exhorted them to a change of life, declaring that the Great Spirit had sent his servant to speak to them in His Name; and that whoever would still continue in their ways of evil would after death be punished forever, both in body and in soul, by that same Great Spirit in whom they themselves believed, and by Whom they had been created. These discourses were usually expressed by simple and natural examples suggested by circumstances. The holy Sacrifice of the Mass was also celebrated, for which these Indians have great respect, because they find therein a conformity with their own conceptions of the Divinity, Whom they believe an be propitiated by voluntary sacrifices.

The hardheartedness of the Winnebagos, too sadly known by whoever has lived among them, did not permit these hearts to be penetrated by the power of Truth, still less to be persuaded to a better life. A few responded that the subjects of which the Priest had spoken were of too grave moment to be decided upon at once, and they also alleged as and excuse that as they had lately sold a part of their lands to the Government, they did not yet know to what place they would be assigned. All this did not hinder a few women from presenting their children for Baptism, and within three weeks, twenty-three received that Sacrament, among them eight adults who had been carefully taught the Pater Noster, Ave Maria and Credo, translated into their own dialect. And here must be noted the great help given to the cause of Religion by Catholic women, children of Winnebago mothers married to Canadians. These good women instructed in Christian doctrine and knowing the language of the tribe, would go from house to house to speak of Religion. There was great difficulty, however, in expressing in their dialect, ideas for which they had no corresponding expression, for these religious ideas were entirely new to these people. To supply the deficiency of Religious terms, it was necessary to use compound terms, for instance: The Trinity, Mystery, Altar, were expressed by Three in One, Hidden Truth, Table of Sacrifice, etc.

This visit was made for the sole purpose of finding out the true state of things, and whether or not there was any well-founded probability of establishing the Faith among the Winnebagos. Notwithstanding the very slight success, the Priest still cherished the hope of succeeding better on another occasion, when he could arrange to make a longer stay there and thus might be able to consecrate himself to this mission with yet greater intensity of purpose.

Chapter XIX.

MISSION AT SAINTE MARIE — SECTARIAN OPPOSITION — SALUTARY EFFECTS OF THIS VISIT — A BEAR KILLED AND EATEN.

It ought not to be forgotten by the reader of these memoirs that wherever the Missionary was occupied among the Indians, the other Missions under his spiritual care remained wholly deprived of all spiritual religious help, without the celebration of Mass even on Holy Days, and the sick breathed forth their souls without the consolation of the last Sacraments. This was the reason of the shortness of his stay among the Winnebagos, and of his speedy return to Mackinac at the beginning of June; whence a few days after, he set out by way of Lake Huron and St. Mary's River for the village of Sainte Marie, having thus traveled over more than four hundred miles.

It was on Saturday about sunset, when by dint of rowing across the river in a little bark canoe, the Priest drew near the place, where next morning, for the first time that year, he was to sanctify the Lord's Day by the Unbloody Sacrifice. A Baptist minister saw that the man clad in black in the middle of the little boat was the Catholic Priest; without loss of his precious time he ran to carry the sad tidings to the persons belonging to his mission station. His coadjutresses, believing that they were doing God's service, fearing to be too late, visited the Indian's wigwams in the vicinity, informing them of the Priest's arrival, but that it would be a sin against the Great Spirit to assist at his Sacrifice, because he was not teaching the true doctrine of Christ. The malice, or rather the ignorance of these female apostles, instead of producing the intended effect, served only to give a welcome warning to the people, that the Priest would celebrate Mass the next day.

In fact on Sunday the concourse was so great at the house where Mass was celebrated, and the necessity of conversion to Penance preached, that in the afternoon, in order to accommodate the number of hearers, services were carried on in the open air under the shade of an old oak tree. Many of those who were engaged the day before dissuading the people from assisting at Catholic services, now through curiosity came to listen to the reasoning which proves the unity and perpetuity of the Church and the fallacies of the ever varying sects.

The missionary afterwards reproached the minister for his conduct on the previous Saturday, but while not denying the fact, he excused himself by saying that never in his life had he had the pleasure of speaking with a Catholic Priest. Error is ever dashing itself against the truth, which it does not comprehend; of the same fault are the falsely wise of our own day guilty, who in their profound ignorance blaspheme what they do not understand.

The week was spent in preparing a large number of the poor people to make their Easter duty of the following Sunday, when, too, a great many of the Indians, especially those married to Canadians, were received to the Sacrament of Baptism. The Lord's Day, on the twenty-third of June, was celebrated in a commodious frame house, near the eastern bank of Saint Mary's River, in the Province of Canada, that the people of that part of the country might have the consolation of assembling in Church. Even the windows were occupied by the worshippers, the building not being able to accommodate the great number. Many of the Communicants had been for many years with no knowledge of the duties of a Christian far away from the Blessed Sacrament; for this reason the Missionary considered it a favorable opportunity for preaching upon the spiritual Resurrection of a sinner to a new life of fervor and good works.

Among the blessing bestowed by Divine Grace, that which touched the heart of an aged man, a Canadian, must not be passed over in silence. Since the age of eighteen years, when he left his native city, Montreal, he had not been to confession for sixty-one years; he had passed all that time in distant quarters of the country, among the Indians, and engaged in trading with them. Although confined to the house by his many infirmities, and in danger of death, he had taken no heed of his opportunities of reconciling himself with that God, in Whose Presence he must soon appear. When the Priest visited him in June 1833, he reproved the aged man for his past obstinacy and indifference; the poor old man, impressed by this, with the hope of having a happy death, promised that he would prepare for Confession. Though this conversion perhaps displayed few external signs of grief, yet as a man of keen understanding he realized the great peril in which he had lived, the danger of dying unrepentant, and permeated with gratitude to the Divine Mercy, he kept giving thanks for it, with fervent and repeated pious ejaculations. With such dispositions, while confined to his bed, he received the most Holy Communion on the twenty-third day of the same month, and Almighty God called him home, the next January. He Who willed not his death but his conversion, had detained him on the borders of the grave, until with humility and confidence he had received the Price of man's Redemption. This striking occurrence will help to set forth more resplendently the ways of infinite Mercy.

During this year the spiritual charge of Sainte Marie Parish was given by the Administrator of Cincinnati to a Priest who made his home there permanently.

While going down Saint Mary's River, about ten miles from the village, the Missionary saw a bear swimming across; immediately the two Indians who were rowing left him upon the bank and hurried to overtake the beast. While one was urging the canoe forward, the other was fastening his knife to the end of a pole. The bear was not far from the river bank when his two enemies were upon him and dexterously wounded him with the spear, when the furious animal made many attempts to climb into the little boat, but without succeeding, for they always drew back in good time. Though wounded all over and having lost much blood, the bear at last reached the bank, weak and powerless, tried to crawl forward a few steps, but unable to defend himself, he turned round showing his teeth, with fierce looks, yet pitiful cries at his pursuers, who despatched him by a blow on the head with the gun. The huge carcass was loaded on the boat, the victors crossed the river to the place where the Priest, the only spectator of their exploit, was waiting for them; the skin fell to his share and the delicious flesh to all, and a sumptuous dinner was served of it that very day. The company of three having gone farther into the woods to cook the meat, found a number of Indians hunting; these too shared in the spoils and ate to the full.

It was an odd experience to the European to find himself eating the flesh of a wild bear that was living and swimming not two hours before.

Chapter XX.

THE WINNEBAGO INDIANS ARE EVANGELIZED—MANY RECEIVE BAPTISM—PROOFS OF TRUE CONVERSION—A LITTLE PRAYER BOOK IN THEIR OWN LANGUAGE PRINTED IN 1833.

The Very Reverend Frederic Rèsè at that time Administrator of the diocese,[*] wrote to our Missionary on the twenty-fifth of July 1833, to the effect that as the Mission to the Winnebagos had been entrusted to him by the Right Reverend Edward Fenwick, the lately deceased Bishop of Cincinnati, and as it had already borne some fruit, the mission had been conferred upon him, the Missionary, anew; and that he begged him to devote himself, with all earnestness, to carry on to a successful issue what had been begun by Divine Grace. Accordingly towards the middle of August, when the crowd of traders had left Mackinac for their various posts, the Priest set out on his journey of two hundred miles by boat, and more than one hundred on horseback, to reach the western bank of the Wisconsin River, a second time. The first thing to be done in his estimation was to learn something of the difficult dialect of the Winnebagos, but as his progress was too slow, he secured the assistance of a Catholic Indian, named Michael, and of others who had learned the prayers which Reverend Father Baraga had printed in the Ottawa language. He then applied himself to translating these prayers into the Winnebago dialect. The language of the Ottawas and Chippewas is especially rich in compound words, suitable for expressing Religious ideas and particularly the mysteries of the Faith. This useful labor had been begun by the first missionaries of Canada and continued by the holy Priest of the Chippewas, Father Baraga.

Several of the Winnebagos spoke the Chippewa dialect; so with their assistance, not without much difficulty and various errors, were translated the Acts of Faith, Hope, Charity and Contrition, the Pater, Ave,

---

[*] This was the Diocese of Cincinnati, of which Rev. Frederic Rèsè was appointed administrator on the death of Bishop Edward Fenwick of Cincinnati, September, 1832 (page 83, Memorie). Rev. F. Rèsè was consecrated first Bishop of Detroit, October 6, 1833.

PART ONE

Credo and several hymns. Translating from one Indian language to another is far less difficult than translating from French or English into any Indian dialect; experience proved this fact to him who was making the attempt, for the simple reason that the languages of the various North American tribes, although differing somewhat, are in reality of one family; however, in the orthography of each word the simplest use of the letters was adopted, giving to each, one single and invariable sound and omitting diphthongs entirely. Reading this alphabet correctly is the same as having a sure key to the pronunciation.

The good example given by the few who had been converted during the spring, incited many others to come to the cabin where instructions were given upon the principal truths of Faith. The children were the first to learn the prayers, the Priest repeating each, until the children could say them without help; the adults were present at these meetings, and were delighted to see their children preparing to become Christians, or as they express it, to be consecrated to prayer. As a further means of increasing the spirit of devotion, more and more in their hearts, they remained kneeling while learning their prayers and the Missionary was very often obliged to show them how to kneel down, for they found this an entirely new posture. Those who knew the melodies of the hymns translated from Ottawa into Winnebago, sang them in this language; they were assisted by the young men, highly delighted at finding themselves so soon raised to the rank of choristers to the public. In three weeks, more than fifty Indians were judged to be in suitable dispositions for receiving Baptism. The Sacrament was conferred with great solemnity before Mass on Sunday. On this important occasion Mr. P. Paquette, Government interpreter, translated into the Winnebago language the long instruction made by the Priest to the newly baptized converts.

A few observations upon the new Christians may serve to edify our readers. An Indian chief called Decari, who took the name of John in Baptism, had two wives, polygamy being commonly practised in the tribe. The Priest having taught him that according to the Law of Jesus Christ he could keep but one wife, the husband replied that he was willing to give up one,—but had no choice between the two. The wife who had no children came privately to the Missionary with the proposal that as the other wife was the mother of a little boy, and was of a somewhat dissatisfied temperament, it would be more prudent to leave the latter with the husband so as to put no obstacle in the way of her conversion. So our worthy John was married to the mother, although the other had been his first choice and more worthy of affection. A few months afterwards Providence called the mother out of life; then the husband and son fell as prize to the generous woman who with brave unselfishness had heroically separated herself from her husband for the sake of Religion. This zealous family is still living full of faith and hope in the happiness of the life hereafter.

While the Priest was preparing to administer the Sacrament of Baptism to a great number of Indians, one of them called "The Little Prophet" cast off the woolen blanket in which he had been wrapped and threw it far away; being asked the motive of this singular behaviour, he answered that thus he desired to show his sincerity, in utterly despoiling himself of all his evil ways and becoming a new man. This was the fruit of the familiar instructions. This Indian had comprehended the true meaning of the change which Faith in Christ should operate in the soul, that is, that change which makes us live by the spirit and die to whatever is carnal and sinful. All Christians are acquainted with his doctrine, but few indeed cast far away the mantle of their vices as did this poor savage.

Among the most fervent souls converted to the Faith was the daughter of the chief of the tribe; at Baptism she took the name Agatha. She was a maiden of singular modesty, always occupied with her work; she was the best beloved child of the old chief, her father; she was first in attendance at every Religious duty, and was a model to all the maidens of the tribe. She was afterwards married to a young Canadian, but died soon after in sentiments of true piety, while recommending her soul to Almighty God.

The new Christians had already increased to the number of two hundred when the Missionary left by way of the Wisconsin River for the city of Detroit, about six hundred miles distant. This journey was for the purpose of having the few things printed which had been translated into Winnebago. These form a little work of eighteen pages, in small octavo, containing an Act of Adoration and of Consecration to God, the

Acts of Faith, Hope, Charity and Contrition, the Pater Noster, the Ave Maria, the Credo, Act of Firm Purpose of Amendment, the Ten Commandments, the Precepts of the Church, a Hymn calling the Sinner to Repentance, an Invocation to the Holy Ghost, and an Invocation Jesus; added to these, in a very few words, the principal Truths of Faith in the form of a dialogue, lastly the alphabet, and the mode of reckoning. The little book was entitled "Ocangra Aramee Wawakakara," that is, "Winnebago Prayer Book," Detroit, 1833.

To facilitate the conversion of this tribe the Priest had brought with him to Green Bay, two Winnebago youths. His intention was to have them trained in a Catholic household, to render them able to teach reading and writing in their own language, and in this manner, impart the Truths of Catholicity to their own tribe. But having no means to pay their expenses, he was forced after three months to let them return to their own country. There is no doubt that a few years at school would have produced the excellent results in these two well-disposed youths.

Chapter XXI.

THE DIOCESE OF CINCINNATI IS DIVIDED—THE MISSIONARY IS SENT TO GREEN BAY—THE INDIANS OF THE MENOMINEE TRIBE AT CHURCH, WHERE THEY SING AND RECEIVE INSTRUCTIONS THROUGH AN INTERPRETER.

In the summer of 1833 the immense Diocese of Cincinnati was divided by the Holy See, a new Diocese being created of the Territory of Michigan, which at that time embraced the present Territory of Wisconsin. The thickly settled State of Ohio remained to the Bishop of Cincinnati. The city of Detroit, which counted at that period about six thousand inhabitants, became the Episcopal Seat of Michigan, which the Right Reverend Frederic Rèsè was appointed to occupy. This new order of things led the Vicar Provincial of the Order of Saint Dominic in Ohio, to hope that he might be able to recall our Missionary to that State. The latter having reached Detroit for the purpose of having the prayers printed which had been translated into Winnebago, wished to continue his journey and thus carry out the wishes of his Brother in the Order. But the bishop elect with determined will opposed this plan and desired the Priest to return to his Missions, requiring him besides to preach in his Cathedral every Sunday in October, in the morning to preach in French, at Vespers in English.

On the evening of All Saints Day he left the city of Detroit in a little barque which was to sail for Green Bay, his destination for the winter. The Bishop-elect had arranged that one of the two Redemptorist Fathers of that place should go as Missionary to Arbe-Croche to take the place of the worthy Father Baraga, who had just left for the new Mission on Lake Superior. The other Redemptorist Father had already been appointed as Pastor over the parish of Mackinac. Truly was that a long and tempestuous transit over Lakes Huron and Michigan. Although the Missionary had set sail from Detroit on the first day of November, yet contrary winds, snowfalls and intense cold did not allow his reaching Green Bay until the twenty-second of the month.

Two nuns of the Order of Saint Claire had also gone to that place in order to open a school for girls in a building bought for that purpose by their Order; the example of these Sisters was a source of great edification to the Catholics of the Mission.

In the course of that long winter the Priest devoted himself to the instruction of the French inhabitants, many of whom were still indifferent to the Truth. Services were regularly held in the Church, and since there was but one Priest, he celebrated two Masses every Sunday and Festival Day; this was necessitated by the fact that there was not room enough in the Church to accommodate all the Catholics if they were to come at the same hour.

The holy Festival of Easter was celebrated with the Holy Communion of almost all the Catholics of the place, and also of that of a Protestant young man, who, having become convinced of the obligation of satisfying Divine Justice by works of penance, and particularly by that of fasting, commanded in both the Old Testament and the New, had become a Catholic during Lent.

The principal motive which had determined the Bishop-elect to send our Missionary into that part of his Diocese, was the conversion of the Menominee tribe to the holy Faith; therefore something must be said of what our Lord wrought for their salvation. One of the most efficacious means of inspiring the savages with the truth of Christianity is the Divine Service; children of nature as they are, they believe in the great necessity of a Sacrifice, but deprived of the light of Revelation, in their ignorance they follow many superstitious practices. The Catholic Church with her altar, her Priests, sacred vestments, lights, canticles and all the other appurtenances of external worship, convinces them that all is done for the honor and adoration of the Great Spirit; and then they desire to become acquainted with the Religion which by just such acts speaks to the Deity. To foster these favorable dispositions among the Menominees, the Missionary recommended that the Christians among them should come to the Church on Holy Days, suitably clad, and show by their bearing that they truly believed that they were in the House of God. During the Holy Sacrifice of the Mass they sang hymns in their own tongue to the accompaniment of a small organ played by a Catholic German who was band-master in the United States Fort there stationed. These hymns containing the doctrine of the Most Holy Sacrament and the other Truths of Faith, accompanied by fervent aspirations, did not fail to produce most salutary effects. The psalms for Vespers were chanted, one verse in Latin, the second in the Indian tongue, and so on alternately, like the hymns, and with the organ accompaniment. While the novelty of all this delighted them exceedingly, it roused the devotion of these poor Menominees in a striking manner; they considered it a great happiness to be allowed to sing the praises of the Lord in His own Temple. Vesper Service on Holy Days was especially consecrated to the instruction of the Indians; after an explanation of the Catechism given to the French portion of the congregation, the latter withdrew form the benches, to give place to the Christian Indians, and also to the well disposed pagans who were often in attendance. First came the intoning of a hymn to the Holy Ghost, another, suitable for disposing their hearts for the reception of the Word of Life; and hundred and fifty, often two hundred savages, united in the canticle, imploring the Divine assistance. At the close of the hymn the interpreter took his stand between the Communion rail and the people; the Priest, standing in the Sanctuary, began his instructions. To facilitate the translation of what he wished to say, he expressed but one, perhaps two or three, ideas at once, according to the ability of the interpreter to fully comprehend what had been said in French, and to convey its meaning in the language of the savages. The sermon carried on in this manner occupied a long time, but it attained its object whenever the interpreter understanding fully the subject of discourse communicated it well and zealously to his hearers. Experience has taught that the difficulty of expressing the Truths of Faith in the meagre language of the savages explains the extreme rarity of good interpreters. Long practice alone can secure that necessary facility which can render the very translated word itself eloquent and full of unction. In case of a poor interpreter one can only trust that a yet more abundant gift of grace may supply this deficiency.

Chapter XXII.

CONFESSIONS THROUGH AN INTERPRETER.

In January in the year 1834, the number of the Menominee Indians converted to Christianity, including those received by the two Redemptorist Fathers, was more than six hundred; but not all of these lived in the vicinity of Green Bay, so a number of them could not often come to the Church. About two hundred and fifty of these were regular communicants, who received the Most Blessed Sacrament almost every month. The reader may desire to know how the Priest received the confessions of penitent with whom he could not establish direct communication, from his ignorance of their language.

Although Confession is an inviolable secret for the confessor, it is not so for the penitent who can make use of the services of an interpreter in the accusation of his faults, if there is a necessity. This is the case of an Indian with whose language the Confessor is unacquainted. The interpreter, whether man or woman, is generally selected by the penitent, but must always be a person of piety and mature years as possible. The circumstances of place and of the penitents themselves govern their selection, yet they are often deprived of making a choice, in the event of only one interpreter being at hand, which circumstance, however, proves no obstacle in their eyes.

Many of the poor Canadians employed in the business of trading with the Indians have married with the women of these tribes; the children of these marriages for the most part are better acquainted with the mother's language than with French, and when baptized Catholics, in time serve as good interpreters. The Menominee, of whom in 1833 there were about two thousand five hundred individuals, had contracted many more of these intermarriages with the French of the country than the other tribes, and consequently the influence of Religion of facility in finding interpreters was in proportion. Few, however, possessed the ability and piety indispensable to one who would serve as interpreter in the case of Sacramental Confession and of Religious Instruction.

The Interpreter was under the obligation of holding the secret of the Confessional inviolable and in the same degree as was the Priest. A suitable place for Confessions thus performed was seldom to be found in the Church; so usually a room apart, or the Sacristy, was employed for the purpose. The penitent knelt with his face to wall, between the Confessor and the interpreter, the latter repeating in French what the penitent wished to say, and translating into the penitent's language, as well as he could, what the Priest desired to communicate to him. This mode, as anyone can see, required much time, since everything had to be expressed twice. It belonged to the Missionary, therefore, to instruct the Christians how to make Confession in the simplest, humblest and clearest manner, the most suitable means of rendering the accusation more expeditious, while it is also the most meritorious. So was avoided all that excessive and useless superabundance of words, which not rarely is a culpable abuse of the Sacrament and waste of the precious time of him who is its minister.

Experience of the effects of the holy Sacrament of Penance among the savage tribes has given to one long practiced therein, the conclusive proof that Catholicity can in a very brief time teach them all Christian morality, and that they are not inferior in the least degree to the other nations in the world as to the knowledge of good or of evil. Amid the ignorance of human arts and sciences there is ever in the depth of their hearts that secret, but infallible voice which tells them that they are guilty before God of the evil that they commit, even before becoming Christians. The morality of the Gospel only illumines, enforces, wisely applies that same law already imprinted upon the soul endowed with reason, and by which the pagans themselves shall be judged.

Guided by the dictates of conscience, the Indians recognize Confession as the most natural effect of a true repentance. Confessing to a man holding the place of an offended God was a wise mercy, facilitating the accusation itself, and the healing correction of the fault. But the foolish wisdom of our modern religionaires, with the approbation of false philosophers, adduce a mass of arguments against the practice of acknowledging one's faults; and this very act in which they vaunt themselves as promoters of man's happiness, they teach to reject as useless and superstitious the remedy most efficacious to cure the spiritual which are the primary cause of his unhappiness.

Saturday was the appointed day for Confession among these Indians, and it should be recorded to the honor of Religion, that their general bearing and appearance on such occasions proved that interior penitence and humility, which should accompany the faithful to that throne of Divine Mercy in the Sacrament of Reconciliation. The words of the Priest were heard and received with fullest confidence; to him they expressed every doubt as to an adviser most capable and disinterested, and thus these simple Christians, truly the "poor in spirit," were unable to make use of all the illuminations of the Priesthood, on critical occasions. And this shows forth with greater splendor the superiority and perfections of the true Faith, pouring out the treasures of heavenly wisdom upon the souls of the rudest, and dispelling the darkness of ignorance. When would the wise men of our day devise a means like that of Sacramental Confession so wonderfully adapted to point out to every branch of society and to the barbarians even, the straight path to virtue, to order, to happiness, without the help of book or of that human science of which these poor children of nature are ignorant? Here in Confession is one proof only of the blessed power of Catholic Doctrine above all the inert and clamorous pretensions of so-called philanthropy.

But to make Confession through an interpreter, will be declared a sacrifice too great for the human heart. There are two reasons that persuade the Indians to this; the first is their in the general judgement when the iniquities of the reprobates shall be made known to all men by the just Judge; again to avoid such a misfortune they believe it better to confess one's faults before two persons than to be compelled to make them known to the whole universe. A wise resolution suggested by lively faith. Another reason for the Indian's submission in this case is the benefit derived from the Sacrament itself, and the salutary advice that they desire to receive in doubtful or dangerous crises. Surely it must be that Almighty God grants to these "poor in spirit" a more abundant and special grace, with a forgiveness the more efficacious because preceded by a greater humiliation. The conduct of those who seek the saving Sacrament in the manner of these poor Indians is in striking contrast with that of those delicate, timid, exceedingly cautious Christians, who with great difficulty and after long delays, at last find an "Extraordinary," to whom reluctantly they may make a Confession none too sincere.

Whether the Catholic Indian is rigorously bound to make his private Confession thus through an interpreter, we shall not undertake to discuss here. The fact alone remains that he follows the safest path in his estimation, and so doing feels bound to all this, by submitting with unbounded simplicity and confidence to the Infinite Mercy.

The Missionary did not devote himself exclusively to the study of the Indian dialects for two reasons; one was that he had been assigned to this region only as a provisionary arrangement while waiting until the Bishop could find other Priest who were to devote themselves exclusively to this meritorious work; another reason was the ceaseless labors in the sacred ministry among the Canadians and Americans of English descent scattered over a vast extent of country who had been strictly confided to his pastoral care.

Chapter XXIII.

HOLY COMMUNION.

In order to confound the unbelief of those men who through contempt or pride will not recognize in the Most Holy Sacrament of the Eucharist the hidden Divinity of the Word become incarnate to make us participators in Its own Essence, the Lord revealed to the simple the incomparable Truth of this Institution of the Last Supper. Although the Indian tongue lends itself with difficulty to the expression of the Religious ideas associated with so great a Mystery, yet the light of Faith shines out in them with such radiance that they comprehend the full doctrine of the Real Presence of Christ in the most Blessed Sacrament. Docile to the Divine Word in which they trust, they are not searching out the possibility of the mysterious change with vain questionings; but humbly they adore, because Jesus Christ declared that the bread which He would give as food was truly His Flesh, and the wine which He would give them to drink was in very truth His Blood. Often was the Missionary, seeing the Menominees in great numbers drawing near the Holy Table, constrained to mediate on the Divine Goodness and just predilection of the Messias Who was this manifesting Himself to the poor and simple. The multiple who followed Him into the desert and the children who once proclaimed Him the Son of God at the very time when the learned in the law were plotting His Death, are this day as well, the proof that human wisdom and prudence are insufficient and mistaken; while it pleases the Father Almighty to reveal the sublimest works of Redemption to the weak and the ignorant.

It was a consolation to a Christian heart to see thirty or forty of the poor natives surrounding the Sanctuary, in order to receive at the Banquet of Christ under the Sacramental veil that precious Body and Blood, the Price of man's salvation. The devotion and modesty of exterior which marked their approach to the Eucharistic Feast, might serve as a model to the most fervent of Christians. The frequent reception of the Holy Mysteries, followed as it was by an improvement in general conduct and by a great increased of fervor, clearly manifested the Truth and Divinity of that Bread which produced wondrous fruits of life eternal. It was not easy to explain how a roving savage, addicted to drunkenness and other vices, sunk in superstitious practices without any clear idea of a Deity or of his own nature, could within the space of one or two months, without the assistance of any training except the simple words of a Priest and through the medium of an interpreter, come to believe in all the sublime mysteries of Religion, and to prostrate himself in all humility, adorning His Creator and Redeemer under the appearance of the Eucharistic Bread. Yet this wonderful transformation was wrought among them, under the eyes of many witnesses who could only look upon it as the work of the Most High.

The Missionary on entering the Church one day found there one of the head chiefs of the Menominee tribe, whose name was Ajamitá he was alone, kneeling upright before the Blessed Sacrament, seeming to see nought else but his beloved Jesus. The Priest stood still to watch the venerable old chief, and could not but feel moved not only by his piety but more by the thorough conviction that the Indian felt in his heart that flame of love that Faith enkindles for the Real Presence of Jesus Christ in the Blessed Sacrament. Who at such a moment could refrain from giving thanks to God for this outpouring of Light Divine into the soul of a man whom the world would call rude and ignorant?

Chapter XXIV.

VISITS TO THE INDIANS ON THEIR FISHING VOYAGES—CIRCUMSTANCES CONNECTED WITH THE CONVERSION OF MANY INDIANS IN 1834.

The Church was the appointed place in which the Christians and those preparing for Baptism used to receive instructions, but the Pagans hostile to Religion rarely came there to listen to the Truth. The conversion of these, therefore, had to be wrought in their own wigwams, by means of the presence and exhortations of the Missionary himself; without following this method one sees little inclination in them towards Catholicity. In truth, it is not the lost sheep who runs after the shepherd, it is rather the shepherd who runs to and fro in search of the lost one to bring it back to the fold. Now must be noted many visits made in the neighborhood of Green Bay in the early months of 1834, because they were most efficacious in bringing about many conversions.

The ice had formed a very solid bridge over that inlet of Lake Michigan which also bears the name of Green Bay, and which extends from ten to twenty miles in breadth and ninety in length. The savages occupy themselves in winter, fishing for sturgeon; they make a hole in the ice about a yard across, and let down by a cord a little wooden fish which they keep playing back and forth; stretched at full length with head over the hold and under cover the better to see under the ice, they watch for the sturgeon as he makes for the little fish; then the Indian expertly spears the sturgeon with a barb fastened to a pole. Many derive subsistence almost entirely from this in winter.

The Priest went in a sledge to visit these savages, a very few of whom were Catholics. Going from hut to hut, he exhorted them through the interpreter to become Christians, on the grounds that their faith in sacrifices and superstitious practices should obtain in benefit in this life, and that from these they did not themselves believe they could obtain the least happiness after death. He explained to the simple and well disposed pagans, that Christianity alone gives true consolation in this world, and that its chief object is to enjoy after death the companionship of the Great and Good Spirit to whom they sometimes offered sacrifices. As they have an idea also of the evil spirit, or demon, the Missionary made use of this to convince them of the power of the Christian Religion in overcoming the malice of the evil spirits whom they fear. The example of the Menominee Christians also furnished a very powerful argument in defense of the truth. These poor heathens, reduced to the extremity of misery by trading or by their own profligacy, especially in the winter, often used to envy the lot of the Christians, who were leading more comfortable lives with food to eat, and better protected from the cold. Religion, then, producing such happy effects even in this life, ameliorating their poor condition so greatly, gave the Priest very many proofs that appealed to the simple natures and ended in completely silencing even the most obstinate. Visiting twenty or thirty families in this way, the seeds of conversions were sown; these were not always wrought at once, for many who were persuaded of the truth and contemplated conversion to Christianity, seldom spoke of it on such occasions. But after several weeks or sometimes even months, they used to go to the Christian Indians to learn the catechism, the prayers, and at last would present themselves for Baptism. This was the usual mode of conversion among them. The Christian Indians were in truth better adapted to making converts and more adventurous than the Missionary himself.

The following circumstance is a proof of this; one evening the Priest entered a wigwam not far from the Lake and found there an Indian woman with her four children, whose faces bore the signs of hunger and sadness. A little kettle of water was boiling over the fire and the mother was stirring in it not more than a handful of flour. When asked if she had anything to eat, "No," she answered sadly, "for when my husband catches fish the Whites (that is, people of European descent) buy it from him even against his will, and pay him by giving him brandy, and he is drunk now; we have not seen him for two days, and we are now wasted with hunger; this is our last handful of flour." Our compassion was stirred by such a story and without delay we opened our basket of provisions for the journey and urged its contents upon the poor woman and her children. How sweet is charity! Words could not express the consolation afforded him who had the privilege of feeding the hungry; the most sumptuous banquets could not be compared to that delicious feast enjoyed by the poor. When the hungry had been fed, Religion became the subject of discourse. It found no difficulties in its way, for it had been preceded by charity. A few comforting words touched the tender heart of a mother, who was discovering that the Christians' Religion was the best cure for all ills. On the next Easter, this good woman with her husband and children was baptized in the Church at Green Bay.

A journey round the shores of Lake Winnebago resulted greatly to the advantage of the cause of Religion. This Lake is about thirty miles from the Church, and as it abounds in fish, the Menominees remain in the cold season near the Lake and carry on their sturgeon fishing.

The Missionary reached the Lake after some hindrance and crossing the ice to about its length, which is about thirty miles, came upon the site where many families of the unconverted Indians had pitched their wigwams for the fishing season. One of these, about forty feet in length and containing four fire-places, had been chosen for his occupation; the Indians are full of hospitality, so that the stranger finds there a ready reception. More than thirty persons inhabited this low dwelling, whose walls were formed of mats. His hosts making him welcome, the Priest sat down upon a fine mat, and the exemplary kindness of his entertainers had a splendid sturgeon prepared and served in a few minutes, furnishing a delicious meal. The interpreter explained to the occupants of the wigwam and to many others gathered there from the vicinity through curiosity, the object of the Priest's coming. He then, as usual in like circumstances, with all the simplicity of conversation, seated on the ground near the fire, with various arguments was exhorting them to abandon superstition and profligacy, in order to become Christians and thus secure everlasting happiness. Some of the heathen Indians made objections to Religion and a defense of their mode of propitiating the Great Spirit, of banishing the evil spirit and of curing diseases by religious incantations. It proved an exceedingly easy matter to confute the feeble reasonings of the ignorant, but zealous Menominee convert called Michael, who had come with the Priest, entered upon a hot religious discussion with the heathens. His eloquence did not appear to promise a very speedy termination of the discourse, whereupon the Missionary, tired out with his long journey, stretched on his mat under his blanket, yielded to a sweet sleep, leaving the religious disputants to the heat of their arguments.

Next morning, the Priest was informed that Michael had silenced his opponents, proving to them the nothingness of their superstitions, and the sanctity of the Religion of Christ, but that some of them offered as their excuse for their unwillingness to become Christian that it would oblige them to give up brandy and other pleasures. Here is the true reason openly adduced by poor savages, but even uttered interiorly in the heart of him who follows not the dictates of Religion. Believing the truths of Faith, hoping in the glory to come, and loving the Maker of all that is lovely, are in themselves easy to mankind but they are irreconcilable with affection for sinful passions. They are the two masters whom no one can in any way serve at the same time.

Among the many subjects discussed by the Indians the night before was that of the visit of the Priest to their poor wigwams, as they said. One of them remarked simply that the Missionary had come from Green Bay satisfied to eat what little they had to offer him and to sleep on a mat as they did without any recompense. "The traders when they come among us are looking for gain, buying pelts or what we get at our fishing," added he. The interpreter explained it in this way: "You see him so satisfied with everything, that he may make you children of the Great Spirit. He is not thinking of his own interest, but only desires and longs for your good." To this he added, that the ministers of the other religious did not expose themselves to such privations without some return, while the Priest was living for charity and was ready to deprive himself of what belonged to him rather than to take anything from the Indians whom he was instructing, as was plain to anyone.

For two days more he continued visiting, conversing and reasoning upon Religious subjects with the Indians at their various lodges; many promised to become Christians when spring should come. And Almighty God so blessed this little sojourn, that a few months later than fifty received holy Baptism; on one Sunday twenty-two were drawn up around the altar rail in order to enter the number of the faithful through means of this Sacrament. The necessary instructions, that is, the Catechism and the principal prayers, as told before in this chapter, had been taught to the converts by the fervent Christians who had taken it upon themselves to repeat it until their pupils knew it by heart.

These short visits in the vicinity of the Church were often made not only during the fishing season in winter, but also on other occasions, as when the people were making sugar or cultivating corn in some rich, sheltered patch of land. The Menominees made a great quantity of sugar during February and March when a certain species of trees begin to sprout. Selecting more than a hundred of these trees, they make an incision in the bark in which they insert a slip of wood so as to make the juice run down into a vessel. They take this sweet liquor and boil it down until the water evaporates and the substance becomes thick and syrup-like; this is then stirred constantly until it cools, when it forms sugar in small dark yellow grains. When they cultivate the earth to secure a little corn or vegetables, they have to keep near their little unfenced fields to protect them from harm from the animals, either domestic or wild. At these times it is easy to find many families only a little distance apart; then those who were studying catechism or prayers had a good opportunity for meeting, especially at evening. In the hunting season, as in autumn and part of the winter, the Indians were generally scattered here and there in the woods or along to river-banks, making it exceedingly difficult to visit them. This fact is mentioned only to give an idea not only of the means, but also of the season most favorable for the conversion and instruction of the tribe.

Chapter XXV.

VIEW OF A LODGE-CHURCH BUILT OF MATS.

He Who dwells in the immensity of the Heavens, and delights in the magnificence and splendor of external worship, when it is the sincere expression of man's love for his Creator, with no less delight receives the rude and simple offerings which accompany the adoration given by the poor Indian. The Divine Saviour Who preferred a wretched stable to the palaces of the great is the same Who is often pleased to dwell in a hut. The sublime Sacrifice of the New Law has been many times celebrated on an altar made of bark, within a Church put together with mats in an hour. When the Missionary visited his new Christians, he preferred a house, although it might be small and very poor, of one room rudely constructed of logs, but very often when the savages were busied at the fishing round one of the Lakes, or at the sugar-making in the woods, or far away from their usual habitations for any cause, then some thought had to be given to preparing a suitable shelter upon the very spot, in order to celebrate holy Mass.

The size of the simple improvised Church had to be regulated by the number who were to assist at the holy Sacrifice; it might be from twenty to fifty feet long; along this extent they set firmly in the ground slender poles eight or ten feet long and about four feet apart; the upper ends of these were brought over from the sides and fastened, thus making an arch. The whole was strengthened and held firm by other small poles laid horizontally upon those set in the ground. This structure, which our architects called the "frame," was at once laid over with a goodly number of mats, leaving two or three openings in the roof which answered very well for windows and also for letting out the smoke of the fire, which was built inside in cold weather. The door, too, consisted of an opening two feet wide by four high, left in one side of the building, over which hung a small mat or covering, which served as a good door. The rich marbles of Italy were not needed for a pavement; that was perfectly supplied by the green grass in summer and by the hard frozen ground in winter. At one end of the Church, four timbers were firmly planted in the ground, whose upper ends were at the height of an altar; on these were laid two or even four other beams, the whole forming the sides of the altar. Upon this were fitted two or three layers of hard and tough bark from trees; all made a table six feet long and two wide; the bark was covered with one of the best mats, and lastly, a strip of linen or cotton which served as an altar-cloth. When candles were to be had, candle-sticks were quickly made,—a piece of bark cut in a circle about half a foot in diameter, forms the foot; another piece rolled into a cylinder to hold the candle makes the shaft, this fitted into the first and the candlestick is finished. The priestly vestments and everything else necessary for the holy Sacrifice were always carried with him by the Missionary, who in turn was always mechanic, workman and cleric.

In this church, with its frail walls of bark, the Indians of the Menominee tribe often united in assisting at the mysteries of Holy Faith. There was the holy Sacrament of Baptism received, there the humble Confession made, the Holy Communions administered with the greatest devotion, and the praises of God sung by his poor children in their own tongue. The complete absence of that sacred magnificence of God's House which rouses in one's heart sentiments of adoration towards God was compensated for by that lively faith and holy fervor which was the happiness of these poor Christians in the poor lodge of bark where their Saviour received their fervent prayers. The Missionary cannot recall the slightest instances of irreverence in these gatherings;

on the contrary, the most profound recollection which made one remember the holy cells of the faithful of the Catacombs in the early centuries.

When Divine Service was over for that time and place, the lodge Church of mats, as it was only a temporary arrangement, was dismantled and taken apart at once, and each worshipper carried away to his own dwelling the materials which he had employed in building it. This circumstance is a real and beautiful image of that blessed life to which the followers of our Blessed Lord will bring the rich gain earned by those Christian virtues which have built up the glorious spiritual structure of the Church militant. Let us also hasten each according to his vocation to help on the erection of that holy Temple of Christ on earth; assured of becoming one day a portion of that heavenly Jerusalem symbolized by the earthly city of God, His temple, in this vale of tears.

Chapter XXVI.

THE ANGLICAN MISSION AT GREEN BAY RECEIVES THE SUM OF TWO THOUSAND ONE HUNDRED DOLLARS, IN JUSTICE DUE TO THE CATHOLIC MISSION.

During the spring of 1834 the number of Christian Indians in the Green Bay Mission exceeded one thousand; this fact led our Missionary to believe that he could easily obtain from the Government the sum usually appropriated to the education of the Menominees. These had lately sold their right over a portion of that territory in which they were living near Green Bay, and for that were receiving from the United States Government a stipulated sum of money, besides two thousand one hundred dollars for the education of their children. Animated with the hope inspired by the chiefs of the tribe, the Priest somewhat imprudently began the building of a frame house large enough to serve exclusively for the instruction of the Indians. The resident agent of the Government, contrary to the expressed wish of the Indians, chose to give the sum above-mentioned to the Protestant Missions of the Anglican sect, who already possessed not far from the Catholic Church, a large and commodious building, erected by the contributions of the followers of their sect throughout the United States. The agent himself, the Anglican minister, and all the Protestants of the vicinity were witnesses, that the Menominees had not become Protestants, but Catholics; on Sunday everyone saw them making their way to the Catholic Church and not to the sectarian meetings. The chiefs of the tribe when holding councils with the agent had clearly expressed their predilection for the Catholic Mission; moreover, public opinion was to the effect that this Religion alone had the power by its influence to improve the intellectual and moral condition of the savages; facts abundantly proved this truth. Notwithstanding all this, the Catholic Mission was defrauded of that means which would have facilitated the conversion of the entire tribe.

It would be entirely wrong to attribute so great an injustice to the laws or to the spirit of the Government, for this is absolutely disconnected with any religious belief, and it protects the rights of individuals of any religion whatsoever. The wrong always lies at the door of the officials to whom is entrusted the impartial administration of business affairs. In our case it was contended that the Protestant Mission had been appointed for educating the savages with their consent, and that the yearly sum of two thousand one hundred dollars ought to be paid to them. But the distances, the one-sided influence of officials, according to the opinion of the more prudent, rendered any effort useless for remedying so unjust a distribution of that money. Notwithstanding their pecuniary assistance, the Anglican Mission could not boast of having wrought any conversions among the Menominee tribe; some children of Canadian fathers, a half dozen of really native Indians at times were supported at their Mission, usually for the sake of a living, and on some occasions an adult of that tribe pitched his temporary dwelling in their neighborhood, urged to this step as the public well knew, either by hunger or by an objection to earn his living through his own industry. And yet in the reports submitted to print, the sectarians failed not to boast of having made a number of proselytes among the natives, while that was exclusively the work of Catholicity.

Chapter XXVII.

FALSE METHODS OF THE PROTESTANTS IN CONVERTING THE SAVAGES.

The system of modern sectarians being nought else but perversion of the true Religion of Christ, finds its way with difficulty into the spirit of a heathen; for this system of teaching Biblical truth presupposes a great Catholic truth, that is, the divine origin of the Bible itself, which can rest solidly upon no other foundation than that of the infallible testimony of the Catholic Church. The heathen in becoming Protestant, according to the fundamental doctrine of the sectarians, ought not to believe in the inspirations of the Holy Scriptures upon the simple assertion of a Church or of a minister, but he must, rejecting all human authority, be convinced by means of his own private examination and study that the Bible is truly the Word of God. To pretend to convert the savages to Protestantism by obliging them to a private examination of the truth of Scripture and of the doctrine contained therein would be a veritable chimera. The Catholic Missionary never had the good luck of encountering an individual of the Menominee tribe, who, after reading the Holy Scripture, had become a Protestant. Take the case of the adults among the Indians, especially the aged, unaccustomed to abstract reasoning, with ideas so narrow in the extreme, so material, so simple, how could they learn to read the Gospel or comprehend its expressions, even if it were read to them in their own language? I do not doubt that religious fanatics, wise in the privacy of their closets, with the help of their imagination, have discovered the possibility of such intelligence in these people. But he who, not satisfied with suppositious cases, tried the experiment, was convinced that such plans were the aeriest air-castles. It is probable that the children of the savages with the help of some education may be able to become Protestants in the broadest sense; that is, to believe in the little or nothing that is suggested to them by the study of the Holy Scriptures.

It is only too true that Biblical fanaticism deprives man of his intelligence and throws him into a certain degree of dementia for which medical science has not yet found a remedy. All the world knows that the Bible is full of difficulties both in letter and sense; that the learned in every country have spent every power of their mind upon the study of the Bible; that the many Protestant sects for three hundred years have disputed over the true sense of the words of the Gospel, without thus far deciding anything with certainty; for all that, our Missionary has conversed with Protestants who believed that they could convert the tribes by the distribution of copies of the Bible—these, by the way, usually incomplete and poorly translated. Such a supposition a thousand times disproved by facts could only enter the head of a man deprived of common sense.

The Catholic Priest preaches the truths of the holy Religion of Jesus Christ to the Indians as he would preach them to the most learned persons of the world; without reference to their ignorance of their knowledge he only announces the spotless, unalterable Faith in which he himself has been instructed and which all the Catholics of the world have believed from Apostolic times. And in truth, such is the command of Jesus Christ: "Go ye into the whole world and preach the Gospel to every creature. He that believeth and is baptized shall be saved; but he that believeth not shall be condemned." (Mark XVI, 15.) By this means the most simple minds receive all Christian truth, without the aid of books, and Biblical studies, for which the greater part of humanity is unfitted either from natural incapacity or the laborious circumstances of their lives.

The Protestant method employed in the conversion of the savage to Christianity supposes a degree of intellectual power which in general they do not possess; that is, the ability to read the Scriptures and to discover therein through reasoning, those truths called fundamental truths—yet learned Protestants themselves are still divided in opinion upon these very points. In the second place, the savage, wandering, struggling for subsistence, could find neither the time nor opportunity for making such a study of the Holy Books as in truth few Protestants have made. It is absurd, then, to expect these unlettered minds to search out through Bible study these verities eternal, indispensable to salvation which their preceptors themselves have not yet discovered.

The Catholic method requires of the savage only the giving up of vices and the will to believe in those doctrines which independently of mere reason, are learned without arguments or disputations, and even without books, but simply by hearing, as says Saint Paul, in his Epistle to the Romans, X, 17, "the Faith cometh by hearing." If the Christian Religion is a body of truths revealed, it follows that these truths are learned not through reason, but through preaching, that is "by hearing." The experience of three centuries has proved that Christ's priest can make more converts from Paganism to the great truths of the Christian Religion by the simple preaching than a thousand Protestant ministers with their millions of Bibles aided by their numberless commentaries and studies; their mission appears properly not calling the idolater to the Light of the Gospel, but rather perverting him whom the Catholic has converted, teaching him to protest against any and every doctrine that he has learned and leading him by degrees to a state of negation or at most to one of mere opinions and doubts.

Chapter XXVIII.

PROTESTANT MISSIONS AMONG SEVERAL TRIBES OF INDIANS IN WISCONSIN TERRITORY AND VICINITY IN 1834.

It may not be useless to give a short account of some Protestant missions existing just at this time in Wisconsin Territory and its vicinity. The subject of the conversion of the Indian Tribes to Christianity had engaged every Religious sect of the United States and of Europe, and in point of pecuniary contributions they rival the generous piety of Catholics. The Protestant Missions possess very many institutions scattered throughout that vast region then peopled with Indians much more than at present.

The Island of Mackinac boasted of a very large establishment belonging to the Presbyterian sect. A minister with his wife, several assistants, naturally some of whom were women, had the direction of the household, consisting of about one hundred persons. The pupils for the most part were children of traders of European descent, but

PART ONE

married to Indian wives or those of mixed race. In the schools they were taught the English language, reading, writing, arithmetic, geography and smattering of history. The principal subject, however, was the reading of the Bible, according to the translation approved by King James I of England. This they committed to memory so that not a few after some years were able to repeat a considerable portion of the text. The Calvinistic teachings from their nature permeated with hatred towards Catholicity, formed the subject of the prayers, the sermons and of the religious instructions in which the youth of that Mission was trained. It is not to be wondered at, that several of the daughters of Catholic parents, though baptized Catholics, should become Protestants at this school, after several years' residence in the Presbyterian Mission School; for they had been educated far from a Church or a Priest, without any knowledge of their Religion. Yet many of these young girls who had left the institution returned to the bosom of the Holy Church. At the Mission, so great was the hatred to the Catholic Religion that the practice prevailed of praying for the conversion of the idolaters, as they designated the Catholics, and whom in prayers and in various ways they accused of worshipping the images of Christ and the Saints. The rather heavy expense of maintaining so many individuals was met chiefly by the Protestant Societies of the United States, and by the liberal contributions of many others who in their zeal forward money, clothing and provisions in abundance for the support of the Mission.

At Sault Sainte Marie, ninety miles from Mackinac, near Lake Superior, there was a Mission under the direction of the Baptist sect. A minister with his wife was director of the establishment, which for hatred towards the Church was in no wise behind that just mentioned; the number of its pupils was small, and contributions were in proportion. To say that this Mission had wrought any spiritual good to the poor people of the country would be idle words; as an elementary school it had its merits.

Green Bay, as is shown in Chapter XXVI, had a quite extensive institution for the Anglican Mission, whose erection, according to report, cost the goodly sum of ten thousand dollars; the support of the teachers, men and women, was therefore no slight amount. The number of pupils often ranged from sixty to one hundred; a few of these made some compensation, the rest were kept at the expense of the Institution, which was furnished with everything necessary through the wealth and generosity of the Anglicans in the large cities of the Eastern States, and probably by their zealous coreligionists of England. Many children of marriages between Europeans and natives were educated at this school. This rather unusual circumstance must not be passed over in silence, the fact that the minister at the head was a man greatly beloved, gentle and courteous, yet without a wife, although he had reached the age of thirty-five; assuredly, he would not find fault with the celibacy of the Catholic Clergy.

Ascending the Fox River about twenty miles from the Anglican Mission stood another building for the propagation of the Presbyterian belief among the remnants of several tribes who had come to the West from the State of New York. These were called the Six Nations, the Abenakis, and also the New York Indians. They spoke the English language as well as their own, as these tribes had been trained among the English settlers in New York. They had sold to the Government their rights over the land of their forefathers, and had received as price, a stipulated sum of money and an extensive tract in Wisconsin Territory near Lake Winnebago. Two Calvinistic ministers, with a yearly salary, superintended the Religious instruction and schools of these half-civilized natives; but the habits of many of them were a scandal to the place. These tribes had a more intelligent knowledge of agriculture than the others.

The Iroquois Indians who had emigrated from the Eastern States, also their ministers in this part of the country. The Christian Religion, however, seemed to them a subject undefined, a name rather than a doctrine.

Different Protestant ministers had striven vainly to convert the Chippewa Indians who occupied the western shores of Lake Superior. After many years, long voyages, and lavish outlays by the Bible societies, the Scriptures had been preached from a central point called Fond du Lac, but the preachers had not seen the natives embrace their belief.

Along the Mississippi River from Prairie du Chien to the Falls of Saint Anthony, a distance of about three hundred miles, the various sects, but chiefly the Presbyterian, sent out their Bible Readers or Exhorters, for the most part accompanied by their families. Both time and money were spent profusely and vainly, for the Indians of the Menominee, Chippewa and Sioux tribes had not yet learned to read either in English or in their own native tongue. This state of affairs usually led the ministers to seek their own support and provide for the future needs of their large families; some among them had the merit of having a sure means of support secured, by cultivating with their own hands a tract of land in some pleasant and picturesque site along the river bank.

Two French Preachers, sent by a Protestant Society in Europe, according to report, commenced a mission among the Sioux Indians; one seems to have failed in perseverance and abandoned the undertaking; the other, marrying a young girl of the region, continued there his fruitless preaching on the letter of the Bible.

More notable was the establishment begun in 1834 at the expense of the Winnebago Indians and put under the direction of a Presbyterian minister; it was a few miles from Prairie du Chien near the western bank of the Mississippi. In 1832 this tribe, the Winnebagos, had sold to the United States a rather extensive stretch of land which their forefathers had inhabited; in addition to the annual payment of many thousand francs, which the Indians received for the sale, the Government was to build a school and support it for thirty years at a yearly cost of three thousand one hundred and fifty dollars. In the summer of 1834, the chiefs of that tribe had demanded through their agent, Captain Robert A. McCabe, that the Catholic Priest be appointed director of their school; in spite of this, a Calvinistic minister was assigned to the place. So he with his wife and sons came into possession of a fine dwelling, as much land as he desired, and the aforesaid annual sum with other sources of revenue which it would take too long to enumerate. In this school a few Indian children of Canadian or English fathers received the first rudiments of education, but the chief benefit fell to the minister, who then became the Indian Agent with a good salary from the Government. If it were asked how many adult Indians were converted to the Presbyterian creed, I believe that no one could answer to the very difficult question.

Now let the reader imagine the immense sum expended for the various establishments here mentioned, that is, for the building so many houses, the amounts paid out for so many ministers with their families and assistants, traveling expenses, food and clothing of the pupils, books, managements, and so many other things inseparable from the carrying on of such institutions. The Protestant Societies, as has been said, contributed the greater part of the funds necessary for these foundations; another portion came from the grants made by the Government for civilizing the Indian tribes; while a small sum was received from the parents of some of the pupils. The periodical Reports published by the different sects teemed with most marvelous accounts of the unheard-of-progress of the Gospel among the natives, of the great usefulness and great need of Bibles and of evangelical laborers in the matter of the conversion of the people of the West. One minister of New York City, in 1832, did not hesitate to use the accounts of the progress made by the Catholic Religion among the Indians, and the zeal of the Priest, for the purpose of rousing his own coreligionists to devote themselves to the missions. Similar statements were printed by them. Through these means were won the hearts of their readers in the great cities, as also those goodly sums without which the Bible Readers could make no progress.

In 1834, the Missionary who writes these Memoirs, seeing himself surrounded by so many sectarian establishments, and anxious to prevent, if possible, the Indian youth from imbibing false principles, undertook to build a House of Education. But not having received from the Government Agent the yearly appropriation of $2,100 assigned for the education of the Menominee children, to which, as is stated in Chapter XXVI, he had every right, he found himself without the means of paying for the expenses already incurred, and with a sense of self-blame for thus incurring expense through too great trust in justice. The Bishop of Detroit contributed the sum of $1,000 with funds furnished by the Propaganda; this did not suffice to pay half of the indebtedness, but it was liquidated afterwards when the Redemptorist Fathers in 1835 took charge of the Church and house of Green Bay.

Before closing this Chapter, it will be of use to make this observation, that Protestantism, unable to convert the adult savage, limits itself to training the tender youth, in whom it may hope to infuse the faith in the divinity of the Scriptures, which they must afterwards examine by private judgement. Thus, only the sects flatter themselves with the idea of collecting in time an assembly of followers. On the other hand the Catholic Priest found the conversion of the tribes more ready, by directing his instructions to the mature, capable of receiving the truths of the Gospel; their children become Christians because they are attracted by good example or by the wisdom of their parents. This unfailing result could well be brought forward as a new and irresistible argument for the Apostolic Mission of the Catholic Clergy, for they, like the Apostles, call to the light of the Gospel, first those of ripe years after whom follow their children. The Protestant minister, in his powerless must needs leaves the Pagan of mature years in his blindness and puts all his hope in the little children. The Catholic Priest finds his power over the Pagans in preaching, that is, in the words of Christ: "Go ye and teach all nations." The Protestant minister finds his power over the Pagans in educating their children. Had the Apostles followed the Protestant system of converting the nations, where would they have found the way to establish so many schools, and how many centuries would have elapsed before attaining the object desired?

Chapter XXIX.

MISSIONS AMONG THE WINNEBAGO INDIANS IN THE YEAR 1834 —CONVERSION, BAPTISM AND BURIAL OF AN INDIAN WOMAN —AN EXPERIENCE WITH RATTLESNAKES—HOW THE PROGRESS OF THE FAITH WAS IMPEDED.

In the spring of 1834, Monsignore Rèsè, Bishop of Detroit, sent to Green Bay a brother-Priest to assist our Missionary in the varied offices connected with that Church, on which devolved the spiritual care of more than two thousand Catholics, scattered far and wide over an immense space of wild country. Then, therefore, it became possible to visit again the Winnebagoes, many of whom had received Baptism the year before. After a journey of one hundred and ten miles on horseback through the wilderness, the Priest reaching the Wisconsin River was met by a party of Indians, all intoxicated with the whiskey just sold to them by the traders, and all boisterous and quarrelsome accordingly. One of the Christian Indians advised him not to attempt to reach the lodges which were about six miles distant, for as nearly all who were not Christians were drunk and would continue so until next morning, he was afraid that the Priest might be molested that night. In spite of this wise advice, the Priest, with a great deal of difficulty, crossed the river, and before night dismounted in the valley where three hundred of these Indians were living; most of these, poisoned with the liquor, were yelling and quarreling over the last remains of the whiskey barrel. The lodge of one of the Christian Indians gave shelter to the Priest with his interpreter, and there they ate the scanty meal that Providence had provided them.

Next morning before sunrise, the first sound heard was the voice of an aged Indian convert, who passing up and down among the huts gave notice of the Missionary's arrival and reproved the bad conduct of the young men who had given themselves up to vicious behavior the day before; he concluded his self-imposed office by admonishing them to be converted to the Christian Religion. This mode of publishing the orders and warnings of the Chiefs is said to be an ancient practice still observed by the well-disciplined tribes.

To avoid repeating what has already been said of the manner in which these people were converted, it may be briefly stated that more than three weeks were spent in instructing, baptizing, hearing Confession and administering the Sacrament of Matrimony to the new Christians. Provisions were obtained from the traders, and we share the common table with the poor Indians; the bed consisted of a mat laid upon the bare ground or perhaps upon strips of bark, with a blanket. A kind Providence ever supplied their real needs and blessed their temperance by granting them perfect health. The holy Sacrifice of the Mass was usually celebrated in one of the lodges, all things necessary for this having been brought by the Priest on horseback, the bread and wine for the altar also forming part of his little burden. The Winnebagoes showed themselves more docile than usual; those who did not wish to become Christians, gave no annoyance to those whose were attending Catechism; indeed, they often came to the instruction themselves, but chose to stay outside, listening to what was spoken within, so the truth was making a little progress.

A noteworthy circumstance was the baptism and funeral rites of an Indian woman of this tribe. During her last prolonged illness the poor creature had put into operation every superstitious charm known to the savages, hoping to obtain a cure of her sufferings. Her husband, a noted warrior, was equally famous for his pretended gift of curing diseases in virtue of the secrets of what might be termed magic. In the sick woman's lodge, sacrifices were offered both to the good and to the bad spirit, who were both invoked with strange prayers a thousand times repeated, in noisy ejaculations. He tried the efficacy of a snakeskin, the skin of several other animals, but each failed him, while the poor woman was plainly drawing near her end. As the Indian doctors were unable to discover the cause of the severe pains that the patient was suffering, one of them professed to discover by means of a tortoise-shell; he thrust the head part of this into the mouth of the sufferer, declaring that the spirit formerly dwelling in that shell had entered into the woman's body to examine into the condition of the disease; withdrawing it after a few minutes and lifting that portion to his ear, he told the bystanders that he heard from the turtle the account of the true condition of the malady. With such superstitions are the poor creatures deluded, for they not only obtain no relief, but they even obliged to reward the pretended wisdom of these medicine men who will not move a finger without pay.

The Priest had heard of the desperate case of the invalid, and went to her lodge; there with his interpreter's help, he succeeded first in convincing her of the false and foolish doctrine of those who had promised to cure her; then explaining the consoling promises of the Christian Religion, he awakened her to the Unity of God in the Trinity, and in the Incarnation and Divinity of Jesus Christ. At the close of the second day, with the gift of grace, and with a limited but sufficiently clear knowledge of the Divine Truths, the sick woman received Holy Baptism and died that night. Happy the soul passing so speedily from the waters of Regeneration to the life of the Blessed!

This was the first Christian death in that tribe, and the Priest thought it might promote the cause of Religion to carry on the funeral rites with all ceremony, and thus teach the Indians the sanctity of the true Faith not only in her doctrine, but also in her care for the dead. The corpse was borne to the lodge which was called the church; everyone was invited to the religious services, pagans as well as Christian, those who could not find room within, stood outside. During the celebration of Mass, the Baptized Indians were repeating from memory the few prayers that they knew, the others looking on, assisted most respectfully and in profound silence. After Mass the Priest began to explain the saving grace of Baptism coming upon one who has died after receiving it with Faith and contrition, as he hoped the deceased had done. The doctrine of the Resurrection of the Dead formed the principal theme of his discourse, for this great truth has greater power than any other to touch the hearts of these people, and lead them to God; a natural consequence of this doctrine is the respect due to the body of the dead, who will rise again, vivified by the soul which inhabited this body.

After the funeral ceremonies in the Church, the procession was formed, composed of the whole tribe, men, women and children, Christians and pagans; then followed four boys, who filled the place of clerics; the body was carried by four Indians; the father of the dead woman, chief of the tribe, although not yet a Christian, walked before the bier carrying a cross in his right hand; the Priest with several assistants closed the procession. Proceeding thus about a mile, they reached the summit of a hill, the site of the cemetery where a grave was dug, and the mortal remains of the new Christian were solemnly deposited therein with all the ceremonies of the Church's Ritual. And here the Missionary took occasion to discourage the practice of burying the favourite possessions of the deceased in the same grave with the body, a practice common to nearly all the North American Indian tribes, according to their affectionate wish that these objects may be of some use of consolation to the dead hunter in the "happy hunting grounds." The immortality of a man's soul might well be called an article of faith among the tribes of North America.

This village where the Priest was staying was called Decari after its tribal chief; the place and its surroundings were infested with rattlesnakes, whose bite is most venomous, usually deadly. One morning just as he opened his eyes at daylight, he discovered one of these rattlesnakes called round a beam which crossed the lodge. Knowing that these creatures do not attack unless molested, he waited quietly until it crawled out through a hole in the side. Later while he was attending a sick man, the Missionary sat upon the ground near the patient for more than half an hour; on rising to leave the place there lay an enormous rattlesnake quietly sleeping, which had been all the while coiled up under the folds of his cassock. The Indians present cried out and instantly killed the reptile which this time at least had done no harm. There was a Winnebago there, who to display his daring and peculiar power, used to grasp a rattlesnake by the neck and let it coil its full length around his naked arm; then he would throw it from him and circling round it to escape its deadly thrust, would grasp it again by the neck. Wherever these venomous snakes are found, is also found a provision of loving Providence in a certain herb, which when chewed and quickly applied to the wound made by the poisonous fangs, neutralizes the effects of the venom.

Continuing the brief history of this Mission it may be noted that in September of 1834 the Priest paid another long visit to this tribe. On that occasion, a number of the Indians manifested a great opposition to the true Faith for the reason that they feared being influenced by the example and authority of the chiefs, in the matter of giving up the practice of polygamy, the use of ardent spirits, an important article of trade, as also of relinquishing the superstitious practices to which they were accustomed to resort for averting sickness or war. One proof of this was the means employed that very year in order to avert the cholera. The superstitious nation had heard the news that there had been some deaths from this plague at Prairie du Chien, a hundred miles to the westward. That same day when the sun was about setting in a clear sky, the braves set to work loading their guns and shooting them off towards the west in order to kill the cholera, as they said. This warlike fusillade against the setting sun was kept up for more than half an hour.

The eldest son of the venerable chief Decari discovering that his mother and several of his younger brothers and sisters had been baptized, threatened to kill his own father, if he would dare to follow their example. The good old man, intimidated by these threats, did not dare to join the Christians openly, although he often came to the services. His own exemplary life, free from those vices which are really the true cause of obstinate unbelief, merited that God's Mercy did not abandon him at the hour of death which occurred in the winter of 1836. Then remembering the holy truths which he had so often heard repeated by the Christians, he longed to die like a Christian; he could not have a Priest at his death-bed, so he sent for an old Canadian who like himself spoke the Chippewa dialect, and begged his friend to baptize him, received the saving Sacrament with the greatest devotion and rendered his soul to God a few days later. Who could doubt that the good life of the aged chief Decari won for him the Sacrament of Regeneration in this life and the fruit of our Lord's Redemption in Paradise?

It was not only the wickedness of some of the people of the village where the Missions were given that hindered the progress of Religion among the Winnebagoes; various other causes contributed to the same result. In 1834 the tribe numbered more than five thousand persons, two thousand of these having sold to the Government their lands on the east of the Wisconsin River—had imposed themselves and their vicious practices upon the few Christian Indians; the money which the newcomers received every year, only swelled the tide of immorality among them; the traders, greedy of gain, fostered their craving for brandy and in the train of drunkenness all vices followed. Just at this time there was under discussion a plan to remove the whole tribe to the west of the Mississippi, and in fact the plan was carried into effect the following year. This naturally threw the Indians into a state of apathetic indifference towards their present abiding-place and towards that Religion whose duty was to restrain them within the bounds of social and community obligations. The Protestant Mission to the west of the great river, with its abundant means and influence, both pecuniary and sectarian, put many obstacles in the progress of Catholicity. The Missionary found himself entirely destitute of means, even the most necessary—for instance, to pay for the services of an interpreter, expenses of travel and even of food; on one occasion he lived for a week on bread and butter only, which he had brought himself in his scanty luggage, for the bad weather and absence of the hunters made it impossible to procure other provisions. Once pressed by hunger he made a meal off the flesh of a prairie rat, which turned out to be eatable in an emergency, though rank and ill-smelling.

For effecting the conversion of these people, known as one of the most immoral, intractable and least amenable to virtue of all the tribes, more powerful means would have to be employed than those at the disposal of one solitary Priest. A permanent abode with these people, a thorough command of their language, with the necessary time for its acquisition — none of these was possible for one laborer, compelled to give his time also to the service of those Catholics of many different nations, scattered far and wide over a vast country. Money was sorely needed for building some structure to serve as a Church, for a cabin as dwelling, for paying an interpreter, for even supplying the daily wants of the Indians themselves, especially in winter, for establishing a school, and lastly for introducing agriculture among these poor people. In the total lack of all these things the propagation of the Faith would be a miracle in truth.

God has ransomed through His own Precious Blood His elect of every tribe and every tongue as is written in the Apocalypse, and He has called to the knowledge of the Gospel, to the participation in the merits of His Precious Blood, and to the glory of His Kingdom, a few souls among these Winnebago people, notwithstanding the great, almost incredible difficulties in the way of their conversion. The heavenly seed of the Divine Word will yet in the decrees of God's Mercy be able to produce greater fruit of eternal life, and give new consolation to the heart of him to whose lot it fell to first sow the seed in the midst of these poor people. The few faithful Christians among them having learned the saving doctrine of Holy Baptism bestowed on their children, in danger of death, are continuing this holy practice.

Chapter XXX.

MISSION TO PRAIRIE DU CHIEN IN 1835.

The Catholics of Prairie du Chien on the Mississippi, about five hundred in number, had not seen a Priest who could announce God's Word or administer the consolations of Religion to them since October 1832, so in 1835 our Missionary determined to set out for that station, which belonged to his Mission. On the first of February he left Fort Winnebago in company with one f the traders, and traveled by sleigh down the frozen Wisconsin River for one hundred and fifty miles; thence crossing a tongue of land he found himself at his destination, a village by the Father of Waters.

On the journey the travelers saw in the distance a fine buck attacked by nine greedy wolves, who cunningly contrived to force the fleet-footed creature flying for its life, to cross the river; here on account of the ice, it could not keep up its swift flight, slipped, and fell into the ravenous jaws of its famished pursuers. They were tearing it to pieces and devouring it alive, when the whip was laid to our horse and the two travelers came up to the poor victim. The wolves with mouths full of the yet warm flesh, taking fright at the sudden rush of the horse, fled off the ice to the bank nearby, leaving behind them more than two-thirds of their prey. In this unforeseen manner did Providence supply needy travelers, who this time shared the game caught by the cunning and skill of the very wolves. The night was spent in the woods on an island in the Wisconsin, and as a company of traders reached the same place of encampment at evening, most of the night was devoted to roasting and feasting on the venison.

The faithful of the village were better disposed this year to frequent the Church and the Sacraments than had been the case in 1832, and therefore the occasion was more favorable for preaching the truths of Faith; every Sunday of February, and part of March, was spent in that house where Mass was celebrated for the time being. Many of the people received the holy Sacraments for the first time, many savages of the Menominee and Chippewa tribes were regenerated in the saving waters of Baptism. Yet notwithstanding all that could by any possibility be said and done in those few weeks, ignorance and scandalous lives prevailed for some years among many who could hardly be called Catholics, until, as will be recorded in the Second Part of these Memoirs, a Priest was permanently appointed there, and a fine large Church was built in the village.

Here must be related an edifying circumstance which took place in March 1835 — the return of an aged blind man to the Religion from which he had strayed. Born in Montreal, Canada, of parents in easy circumstances, he had enjoyed the advantages of a good education, but in early youth had come in the capacity of a trader to live among the Mississippi tribes, and in the course of time had entirely forgotten, at least in practice, the teachings of his holy Faith. Now he had been blind for three years, and near the end of life; but was striving towards a reconciliation with God so fervently, that often as he sat weeping over years gone-by, he trembled in every limb like a leaf shaken by the wind; tears gushed in torrents from the eyes which, as he said, could not tell night from day. On the Sunday when the Priest bore the Blessed Sacrament to the bedside, the people thronged thither praying on bended knee, in the room and on the ground outside the house, offering petitions for the poor blind Christian whose words and edifying demeanor moved the throng to tears of tender compassion and joy. All without distinction gave thanks to God Who in His Mercy had granted to that soul so great a spiritual delight and so prepared the dying Christian to open his eyes to the light of Heaven.

Chapter XXXI.

STATE OF THE MISSIONS AMONG THE TRIBES WHEN THE MISSIONARY LEFT THEM TO THE CARE OF HIS SUCCESSORS.

The mission of the Island of Mackinac which comprised Point Saint Ignace and the surrounding islands at the time when it was placed under the spiritual charge of another Priest, counted more than one hundred and twenty-five savages of the Chippewa, Ottawa and Menominee tribes. In addition to these, and much greater in number, were many baptized Christians, children of Indian mothers and of Canadian, English or American fathers; a few of these possessed some education, but the others were hardly distinguishable from the native Indians. These new Christians for the most part persevered in the Faith and in the practice of good works; almost all the adults were practical Catholics. Since 1833 the cause of Christianity in that Island had never been deprived of the services of a good pastor.

At the time when the Bishop of Detroit had stationed a Missionary at Sault Sainte Marie in 1833, the number of natives, chiefly Chippewas, who had been baptized, was not less than sixty. Here as in other trading-posts there was found a population of mixed Indian and white descent, who were baptized and could claim many zealous Christians.

Green Bay in Wisconsin had more converts to the Faith than the other Missions in that section. At one time the Menominees numbered a thousand at least, with more than two hundred and fifty practical Catholics among them, well instructed in the truths of Faith; about five hundred had enjoyed the privilege of receiving Confirmation from Bishop Edward Fenwick, O.P., and also in 1834 from the Bishop of Detroit. The adults were faithful to the Sacrament of Penance, which as Confession required the services of an interpreter, was more exacting on the time of both Pastor and parishioner. After the year 1834, the Redemptorist Fathers and other Priests attended to the Religious wants of these Christians; many of these good people died the deaths of true Christians, many still serve God in the devout practice of their Religious duties, while a few among them, by force of evil environments and bad example, allowed themselves to be led away perhaps not from the Faith, but at least from exemplary lives. At Green Bay there were probably about five hundred Catholics, who either on the father's or the mother's side were akin to the Menominee and Chippewa Indians; these although Catholics were not numbered among the real converts, who are natives.

In January 1835, the Register of Baptisms administered among the Winnebagoes showed three hundred and ten names, including children, who constituted the greatest number, and here and there thirty or more Baptisms of natives which had not been registered. Up to this time only four of the natives had been considered sufficiently prepared for the reception of the Most Holy Communion, and seven others, children of Winnebago mothers and Canadian fathers, had the same privilege. The Sacrament of Matrimony was conferred upon about twenty-five couples. Many of the Christian Indians passed to the next life confirmed in grace, we have reason to hope; while many have persevered until this day in Faith and in the practice of the obligations of a good Christian, others have strayed from the right path because they were too far from the Priest, and exposed to temptations in the midst of heathens and deprived of those instructions necessary in their case to perseverance.

Such was the state of the Mission among the savages when our Missionary left them to the zeal and good example of his successors in the toilsome service. The lack of a school building for the children of the different tribes was felt to the quick by one who knew too well the importance of such a building, at a time when its erection would have given wonderful results. Neither the means nor the men for such an establishment could be found among the Catholics, while the Protestants were building and supporting among the Indians in many places, not a few schools for the purpose of converting the people. Although this fact serves to bring out more resplendently the superiority of the Catholic preaching, which yields its own fruits even without the aid of educational establishments, nevertheless, humanly speaking, the Catholic Missions in Wisconsin, assisted by a good school, would have preserved the Faith much more effectually among the converted Indians and in all probability have brought about the conversion of all the tribes.

The Priest who up till 1830 had made the first advance into a region situated upon the confines of civilization and inhabited by tribes of Indians with their many white traders, could do nought but scatter a few seeds of the Faith here and there, while planting the Cross of Christ and introducing solemn observances and teaching the beauty of Catholic worship. Other missionaries came afterwards to foster and encourage by example and words the growth of those truths announced by their predecessor, which were in time to bring forth fruit worthy of eternal life. If the Lord permitted that, in its first establishment in these regions, Religion should be deprived of the means which human wisdom considered necessary to its maintenance, we ought to adore His inscrutable decrees and those wondrous mysterious ways of God, by means of which He calls unto Himself His own elect, and for reasons to us unknown, punishes the soul that renders itself unworthy of the grace of holy Baptism.

It may be well for the reader of these Memoirs to know that the Catholic Missions among the Indians of Wisconsin and Northern Michigan have now almost ceased to exist, for within the last few years, the Government of the Republic has bought up those tracts. The Ottawa and Chippewa tribes sold a great part of their lands in the vicinity of the Island of Mackinac and migrated elsewhere. The Menominees ceded the lands along the Fox River, the Bay and Lake Winnebago and have withdrawn more to the northern section of the Territory. Since the year 1836, the poor Winnebagoes have possessed nothing of that immense tract of country which they had occupied to the east of the Mississippi and have been provisionally settled upon the opposite shore of the great River only to be ordered to move yet farther away, in a brief time. The tribes of Sacs and Foxes who made war against the United States in 1832 had been occupying the lands in the vicinity of the Mississippi, but after their outbreak evacuated all those regions and are now found not far from the Missouri River. A similar case is that of the Pottawatomies who have been living in Wisconsin Territory along the shore of Lake Michigan where they used to have a Missionary. And thus are the savages slowly moving towards the setting sun. But change of place alone would be an affair of no importance as regards Religion, were it not accompanied by many and varied fatal circumstances opposed to the propagation of the Faith. The money received in payment of their lands ceded to the Government is a source of many disorders, and setting in a new country in the midst of heathen tribes, contributes not a little to shake their Faith and demoralize the Christians. Besides all this, it is exceedingly difficult and costly to send Priests and to build new Churches in places which are almost wildernesses and destitute of all things necessary.

PART ONE

Chapter XXXII.

RELIGION IS THE ONLY MEANS OF CIVILIZATION FOR THE INDIAN TRIBES — THE GREAT OBSTACLES IN ITS WAY.

Before closing the Memoirs on the subject of the "Missions Among the Indians of Wisconsin Territory," it may be satisfactory to many readers to give some general idea regarding the civilization of the tribes who live within these United States; this may also assist in correcting some erroneous impressions made by different writers, who either through lack of sufficient knowledge of the facts, or carried away by a certain spirit of enthusiasm or else by views of self-interest, have declared very easy of accomplishment a work which under existing circumstances has shown itself to be a difficult and an almost impossible one.

The Catholic Religion has the power to call the Indian from his wild, roving, barbarous mode of life to a participation in the spiritual gifts of Redemption and to advantages of Christian society. In order to become a follower of the Teaching of Jesus Christ, the savage, without changing his mode of life, has only to abandon his superstitious practices, to believe the truths of Faith, to perfect in himself those ideas of morality already imprinted upon his soul by Almighty God Himself, to do what is good and avoid what is evil. When circumstances are favorable, such a transformation of the tribes is not so difficult as some imagine; for, as creatures endowed with reason and destined for the glory of the children of God, they were redeemed by God the Saviour, as were the other nations of the world and thus made able to receive the gift of Faith in all its plenitude. Then Religion with the Heavenly power of her virtues, but especially with the spirit of fraternal love and of true charity, brings mutually individual to individual, family to family, village to village, tribe to tribe, and thus lays the foundation of society, unites its varied parts, and little by little builds thereon the entire superstructure of the arts and sciences, in a manner lasting and beneficial to humanity.

If these salutary effects of Religion among the uncivilized Indian tribes are not always manifest, it is not because Christianity itself by its very nature does not produce them, but because of the immense obstacles in its path. These great obstacles to the propagation of the Faith are found in man himself, in his passions and in society generally when this does not cooperate with example and influence.

A Christian who comprehends the sublimity of revelation and sees how perfectly it is adapted to rescue men from the misfortunes of his present state, does not make civilization consist in the form of government, in civil laws, in the regulations of society, in human sciences or arts, in the courtesies of life, in riches, in social elegances, but he believes it lives in the knowledge of God and in the practice of the moral virtues. The savage, become Christian, may in truth be called civilized in an eminent degree, for the reason that his knowledge of God and purity of morals illumine his intellect and fill it with religious science, infinitely beyond the entire array of human discoveries. And besides, to what does it all really aim — this world of books, of studies, of gold, of grandeur, of elegances of life, of progress, whether civil, literary or social? Their one object is to attain to a certain degree of happiness. But the Catholic Indian is put in possession by his religion of that moral and social felicity, which not Solomon himself with all his wisdom and royal magnificence could enjoy.

In order to better develop this great truth, let us put before us the case of an American savage, instructed in the Law of God, faithful to the promises made in Baptism, who goes to Europe for the purpose of beholding the grandeur of the nations, the magnificence of cities, of palaces and assemblies, the luxury, fashion, wealth, all that civilization has found of beauty or utility. After this review, he is then taken to the courts of justice where he is informed of the numberless civil and criminal processes against the citizens; he is given an idea of the codes, the laws, of their severity towards delinquents; he visits the prisons and there to his intense surprise sees numerous malefactors, among whom are many condemned to death. Everywhere he notes iron-barred doors, not only in the prisons but even in the houses; here and there along the streets he meets groups of armed men, and others who stand guard with their guns day and night. It is a mysterious spectacle to him, from which he has reason to consider the country at war. This is not

PART ONE

enough; the good savage is led to the arsenals where he beholds a prodigious quantity of ammunition and gun-powder; the sight of the cannon strikes him with dismay. From their size and number he forms an estimate of the slaughter they can cause; a few steps further and he enters a fortress where are seen all the engines of war for devastating the country by fire and sword. Lastly, before him in a broad plain are drawn up in battle array the thousands of soldiers on foot and on horseback, armed with guns and swords, all well skilled in the art of exterminating their own kind; then follows the dreadful artillery with its vast convoy of horses and men. Yet more; if by chance this man is present a one of those moments when the troops, drawn up simultaneously, discharge their guns, the cavalry in its sudden and tumultuous onslaught, threatens destruction and death, while the artillery shakes the very earth, makes the air resound with thundering explosions, darkens the sun with clouds of blinding smoke, so that the sky seems convulsed with the tempest and thunder and everything breathes terror, fire and death — the poor Indian at such an unexpected and terrible spectacle may well cry out, "My God, where am I! What civilization is this!"

A friendly citizen draws near to comfort the terrified spectator, makes him take note that he is no longer among the barbarians in American forests, but in Europe among a cultivated people, where there exists so many beautiful things that not even an idea of them can be formed. And this friend adds: "The tribunals, the laws, the prisons are for the good order of society; the guards whom you noted in our country serve for the protection of the person and the property of our citizens; the weapons, the soldiers and the military exercises which so deeply impressed you are indispensable in a civilized people. Woe to our societies if they were not here! No, the perfection to which the art of war has been brought up to this day is a proof of our progress in culture."

Now our good Savage, impressed by the novel and immense wonders that have passed before his eyes would say to the European, with all his native candor and sincerity: "You have shown me many, many beautiful things, which are unknown to my tribe; yet notwithstanding all these, the civilization brought to us poor Indians by the Priest, is far superior to that of Europe, for from the moment that we became Christians, disputes, feuds, acts of revenge, drunkenness, theft, immorality, and murder were entirely banished; the people of our village live in peace, day and night with no guards, tribunals and prisons. When we were heathen we loved war and we desired the death of our enemy; yet now, we live in harmony with the neighboring tribes; but you, to judge by what I have seen, are still studying the art of murdering your kind. Moreover, it seems to me that the manners or the morals of Europe must be very imperfect since it needs so many laws and so many formidable fleets and armies to make the people honest and obedient. I would advise you to become good Christians like us, then you would be just and would be happy in each other's society and would enjoy in this life the consoling hope of a blessed eternity."

Thus would one speak who should judge of the intellectual progress of society, not by the material aspects, but rather by the peaceful and happy condition of the individuals who compose it. From this may be inferred what the Missionaries found to be a truth, that is, that the first means for civilizing the savage is Religion; this alone surpasses in influence every art of human knowledge, and carries with it a principle of industry which is able to ameliorate his condition, both physical and social.

Many persons in Europe suppose that the American Indian tribes can be raised to the same grade of civilization as the other nations of the earth. Such progress does not seem possible under the circumstances existing among those tribes within the limits of the United States, and this for several reasons. First, the present generation of Indians is incapable of taking such a step, by reason of their extreme poverty and of the necessity of changing their abode in order to give place to the European settlers who take possession of their lands; the vices introduced into the tribe by the traders offer an insurmountable obstacle to any education and to morality, without which there can be no civilizing process. The missions and schools of the ministers of the various sects serve more to confuse than to teach the aborigines; moreover, self-interest seems to be the ruling principle in these establishments.

But granting that a tribe had taken a step towards progress, when the Government buys their land, the tribe is removed to the midst or to the neighborhood of other tribes in regions entirely uncultivated, and there it is subjected anew to the influences of the savage life as at first. There is another very convincing reason for supposing civilization morally impossible in these people; it lies in the fact that the United States Government pays to almost every tribe on the borders of the States, an annual sum stipulated in the sale which they made of the lands that they were occupying. The money, instead of being a means of self-improvement, is the moral and physical ruin of the Indian, who spends it unwisely or abandons himself to indolence. It also attracts around him many individuals who have no aim outside their own interests, and are on many accounts the least capable of propagating the social virtues.

It must not be inferred from all this that in the United States are not found tribes among whom there is practice in the mechanical arts and intellectual culture. But these are rather remnants of tribes and, for the greater part of mixed race with one parent of European descent, who have lived for many years in the midst of a civilized population from whom also they have learned the English language. This was the work of at least half a century, and the attentive observer will find in addition, that the progress is not general throughout the tribe, but is limited to individuals. The accounts of this subject given to the press and circulated throughout America and Europe are usually so exaggerated that the reader is led to draw from false suppositions, inferences which through a number of contrary facts are entirely unwarranted.

But someone may say: Then will it no be possible to bring the tribe to the state of civilization? In theory, there seems to be every possibility, yet experience teaches the contrary. In fact, in South America where the aborigines who inhabited it at the time of the discovery of that continent were formerly much more skilled in the arts and lived in community, they have advanced in civilization exactly in proportion as their race became amalgamated with Europeans. Three hundred years of intercourse with uncivilized nations, left in these countries a great number of Indians in an uncivilized state. But to treat of the causes of their present condition, would be beyond the limits of these Memoirs.

In North America up to the time of the discovery of the country, the tribes were less advanced in civilization than those who were living in a milder climate, and in spite of the great efforts made at different times both by governments and by Religious Associations they are still with very few exceptions almost in their primitive state. Wherever the European has built cities and cultivated the soil, the Indian has entirely disappeared. This is the case especially in the United States, where from the Atlantic Ocean to the Mississippi River are to be found only a few wretched remnants of tribes, and already throughout the Territory of Iowa, the States of Missouri, Arkansas and Louisiana, the Indians have been gradually scattered towards the vast regions at the headwaters of the great rivers Missouri, Platte, Kansas and Arkansas.

The reason why in Canada the original tribes still live near the Atlantic coast, lies in the fact that the first settlers of that province now under the English government, were French, who instead of driving out the Indians, were satisfied to occupy the country with them; their villages were adjacent, and each respected the rights of the other. Catholicity consolidated this peaceable mode of living side by side. Then emigration to Canada was never on so large a scale as to the Republic whose Government was compelled to harbor the Europeans for the increase of its own population while the English government had no the same anxiety on that head.

From this we may gather that morally speaking, the training of the tribes even to a moderate degree is almost impracticable under the present circumstances, and these appear so permanent as to foretell their future destiny, that is, their continuance in their wild, roving and uncivilized state until the day when the civilized population of Europe shall have filled the entire continent, and then the poor Indian will have left in the land hardly a trace of his existence.

The true friend of the Indian must be satisfied to bring him to the knowledge of the truths of the Gospel, for these, as experience teaches, are within the grasp of his intelligence and are practicable in the physical and social conditions wherein Divine Wisdom has placed him. Religion will find in her treasures of heavenly knowledge gifts that will gladden and assist these people; agriculture, the mechanical arts, writing, reading and a fixed social order shall be the inseparable accompaniments of holy Faith. It is this substance which can be done for the benefit of this poor race, and in truth, nought else is necessary for their present or future felicity. To begin this without the Faith would be to build a house without a foundation.

If the Catholic Religion in accord with the United States Government could exercise absolute influence, both religious and political, over the tribes who live beyond the borders, in such manner as to exclude traders, sectarians and any person whose presence would be injurious to them, and if the Indians could be entirely isolated under the sole direction of the Missionaries, a few years would suffice to make them all followers of Jesus Christ, and to form them into well-regulated communities attended by the advantages of industry and the knowledge of the principles of the arts and sciences of our civilization. This is impossible, however, because of the great majority of Protestants in the Republic and from the spirit of Religious and political liberty which influences many citizens to force themselves in among the tribes. The Government by Acts of General Congress has many times made generous grants of money for the instruction of Indian children, but differences of Religion and conflicting interest make each attempt of every little utility; even if a few pupils have learned to read the Bible, to read and write in English, these usually have lost much of their innocent simplicity and when grown, have not proved themselves examples of morality to their own people.

Lastly it may be noted that Catholic Missions among the Indians have ever been most flourishing in proportion to their distance from trading-posts and from the white men in general; a proof of this is the mission of Arbre-Croche, and that Mission in Oregon Territory amid the Rocky Mountains, which was begun a few years ago by the Jesuit Fathers.

Part II

Chapter I

HOW THE MISSIONARY, AFTER HAVING SERVED IN THE PROPAGATION OF THE FAITH AMONG THE INDIANS IS APPOINTED TO THE MISSIONS ABOUT THE HEADWATERS OF THE MISSISSIPPI.

In Part I of these Memoirs mention is made that the Missionary in question was appointed in 1830 by Bishop Edward Fenwick of Cincinnati, afterwards by Monsignore Frederic Rèsè, Bishop of Detroit, until other Priests were able to settle there. Early in 1835 not only the Indians recently converted to the Faith, but also the white settlers received through the unwearied and charitable zeal of several Priests, the sweetest consolations of our most holy Religion. Then our Missionary cherished the thought of visiting his own Brethren of the Order of Saint Dominic in Ohio, and of consulting with them as to the place where it would be most suitable that he should fulfill the duties of his ministry. At it had come to his knowledge that in that part of Wisconsin on the Mississippi, where it borders on the State of Illinois, there were living many Catholics with no guidance or assistance from pastoral care, he planned to take that direction; and for this reason leaving Prairie du Chien early in April where he had spent part of the winter, he traveled on horseback first to a village called Mineral Point. At this place it pleased Divine Providence to grant him means most timely and necessary for continuing his long journey. A gentleman of the place desired him to baptize his three children and invited him also to preach in one of the houses. He willingly consented and this having been done, as he was remounting his horse next morning, the father of the newly baptized children put into his hand the sum of twenty dollars. "May God be thanked!" was the only word the recipient could utter, for without this assistance he would not have been able to accomplish a tenth part of the distance yet to be traversed. The keeper of the hotel, too, although a Protestant, declined to take his just due for the traveler's entertainment. A ride of forty miles from Mineral Point brought him to Galena, a little city, but important as the centre of the rich lead mining interests of that region.

In this northern section of the State of Illinois there were at that time about three hundred Catholics who had neither Priest nor Church; in like deplorable case was also the city of Dubuque, then a tiny village on the western bank of the Mississippi River. The Missionary interrupted his journey to minister to the spiritual needs of the faithful of these two places and their surroundings. Many Baptisms, Confessions and a few Communions were the slender but salutary effect of his words during the brief stay of two weeks. The people would fain have kept the Priest near them, but he desired first to obtain the permission from the Bishop of Saint Louis, who then held the jurisdiction over that part of the country.

Reaching Saint Louis after a journey of five hundred miles, crossing the river in a steamboat, he had the happiness of becoming acquainted with the venerable prelate Monsignore Guiseppe Rosati. (This holy Bishop laden down with merits and virtues rendered his soul to his God, in Rome, September 22nd, 1843.) From Saint Louis he pursued his course along the Mississippi and thence passing up the Ohio River, he landed at Cincinnati, where the zealous Bishop John Purcell was occupying the episcopal chair. Finally he reached Somerset in Ohio, one hundred and fifty miles from Cincinnati, and there took counsel with his brethren of the Order Saint Dominic who have the charge of many parishes in that town and in the surrounding country. It was judged necessary for the greater honor of Religion that he should retrace his steps in order to use every effort possible in those Missions to which he appeared to be imperatively summoned by the circumstances. This plan compelled our Missionary to undertake a fresh journey of one thousand and three hundred miles in order to return to the Upper Mississippi region where he arrived July 4, 1835.

The Catholic inhabitants of the rising cities of Galena and Dubuque, with the hope of securing the Priest's permanent residence among them, early in the next month, August, wrote to the Superior General of the Order of Preachers residing in Rome, to the effect that they begged him to be pleased to consent that the Priest in question might exercise his holy ministry exclusively in that part of the Republic of the United States. The Most Reverend Hyacinthe Cipolletti, the zealous Master-General happily governing, who illustrates the Dominican Order by his wisdom and his true devotion to its interests, animated by the same spirit which inspired our holy Founder Saint Dominic in the thirteenth century to send forth his brethren in every direction to extirpate vice and preach virtue, with full consent and expressions of his satisfaction acceded to the great desire of these people who with great reason asked for a pastor.

Thus did the Lord manifest His Will to His humble servant who ardently desired the spiritual advantage of the faithful and went to them, glad of being permitted to make his principal abode with them, and with whom he remained until the spring of 1843.

Chapter II.

THREE CLASSES OF MISSIONS IN AMERICA.

The Catholic Missions in the United States may be divided into three classes; the first is that of the Priests in the civilized sections of the Republic, especially in cities already provided with Clergy and with Churches, although these are rarely sufficient in number for the needs of their people. In this first case, there are required on the part of the Priest a store of general knowledge and a mode of expression clear and concise, in order to agree with the genius of the people, his hearers, who fairly hang upon his words. The Faith often vilified and insulted in works sent to the press by sectarians, imperatively demands that the Catholic Priest be found ready to defend it fittingly by employing the same means for defense. The general corruption, wealth and luxury with the manifold attractions of the age in a country where in his exterior appearance God's minister differs little from the laic, and where his duty often calls him into the very midst of worldly vanities, these and many other like circumstances put all his virtues to the test. In the larger cities, Protestantism being more divided, more indifferent and for that reason less influential, leaves to the Catholic Priest a broader field for making conversions through his preaching the Word of God. Placed in these circumstances, his duties differ little from those of the zealous Parish Priest in Catholic countries. Generally he can derive from the liberal contributions of the faithful that fitting support which is by right due to him for the sacrifice which he makes of life and talents. The extent of his mission is seldom one that calls him from his residence for a longer time than one day.

The Priests who are alone in places thinly populated, far from cities, form another class of Missionaries. Their condition is for the most part that of those who live in the Territories of the Republic, in newly settled States and near the unbroken wilderness, and differs in many particulars from that of the clergy exercising their ministry in cities, for both naturally share in the circumstances common to their own sections of the country. In the second case, everything has to be done, the land must be cultivated, cities have to be built, and society must be constituted. The citizens constantly migrating from one place to another with hope of improving their conditions by the cultivation of the land and by the elegant arts, find themselves for years deprived of what forms the wealth and common conveniences of life. The land is only here and there barely touched with the plough; a state of rude nature without streets or bridges and containing very few settlers, and consequently poorly provided with dwelling houses, and these only frame structures, small and poorly constructed. In the great number of those who seek their support by emigrating to new lands, there are many Catholics, principally from Ireland and Germany; therefore preserving the Faith in this scattered population, organizing new parishes, and building churches constitute the most important duties of a Missionary. To his zeal is often contrasted and opposed that of the Protestant ministers, who almost always precede him in great numbers under the protection of various associations, and well supplied with means. The vast extent of these Missions bordering upon regions already civilized, obliges the Priest to long and frequent journeys for the purposes of spreading the Faith, comforting true believers and giving help to the dying, and the varied difficulties encountered on these journeys are often such as could not easily be overcome except by one ready to give up everything for his duty, and who has the true spirit of sacrifice. Contributions for the bare necessities of life are more slender and more uncertain in this second class of Missions than in the cities, but Divine Providence never fails in desperate need.

The third and most distinct class of Missions in the United States is that among the Indians; it may itself be again divided into two classes;

one among the tribes in contact with civilization which imparts to them more vices than virtues; the other among the tribes, distant, and beyond the confines of civilization. As to the character of this class of Missions enough has been said in Part I of these Memoirs. The object of this classification is to put in clear light the relative position of the Clergy, and thus enable the render to understand well not only these narrations but also the Ecclesiastical history of North America.

The Missions to which our Priest was appointed by the Divine Will were from 1830 to 1835 among the Indians who lived intermingled with a half-civilized people, of whom we have already treated. From 1835 to 1843 he then had his own Missions in a country newly settled, wild, wherein a fresh beginning was necessary for each and every venture, and be it noted that until 1839, the year in which other Priests came to that part of the country, he found himself alone and distant from a Brother-Priest by more than a hundred miles. From this it may be shown that his labors are connected with the beginning of Catholic worship in various parts of that country, and if it seems to anyone that these brief records may seem just now of but little importance, it must not be forgotten that one day it may be a great assistance in the Ecclesiastical History of some Dioceses of America.

Chapter III.

ORIGIN OF THE EPISCOPAL CITY OF DUBUQUE IN THE TERRITORY OF IOWA—ITS FIRST CATHOLICS AND PRIESTS—BUILDING OF A CHURCH BEGUN IN 1835.

The little Episcopal City of Dubuque dates its origin from the year 1833; before that all the country west of the Mississippi which forms the great Territory of Iowa was still inhabited by different Indian tribes. The Government having bought from these tribes the lands adjoining the river, after various treaties, or to speak more correctly, after the expenditure of generous sums of money, many thousands of the citizens of the Republic settled there within a few months, but especially in the vicinity of Dubuque, on account of the lead mines. The traffic in this valuable metal created the city of Dubuque, named for the last French trader who after spending many years of his life in that place with the Indians, died in 1811. The lead mines to the west of the Mississippi as far as latitude 42 1/2° N had been worked at first by Mr. Long, then by his successor in the Indian trade, M. Cardinal, followed then by Mr. Dubuque. This account was given in 1835 by an aged Canadian, an octogenarian, who during the course of about twenty years had been in the service of the last mentioned gentleman.

In July 1835, the rising city of Dubuque numbered about two hundred and fifty persons, perhaps a thousand with the people in the environs of the town, where the mining was carried on in search of lead veins. The Catholics might have numbered two hundred, the rest were in the matter of Religion a mixture of different sects and of persons indifferent to any Religion. Although removal from the ordinary sources of sanctification and evil occasions may draw the souls to what is wrong, nevertheless one who has imbibed sound principles and has once tasted the sanctity of true Religion, always finds a sentiment deep in his heart which inclines towards the good. Such in brief may be considered the state of the episcopal city question. Nearly all Irish by birth, on their first emigration thither, on the discovery of mines, not a few had acquired a considerable fortunate, but the wealth acquired more by chance than by industry served more to their harm than to their well-being. Nevertheless, the Faith which seemed as if dulled, was not extinguished in these souls who had once imbibed Catholic principles.

In 1834, a Reverend John McMahon, sent into these parts by the Bishop of Saint Louis, visited the few Catholics of Dubuque, but that same year he died in the city of Galena, State of Illinois, where he had been living for nine months. The Reverend P. FitzMorice who succeeded in the same place, ended his days that same year, three months after his arrival. When our Missionary set foot in Dubuque in the July of 1835, he firmly believed that as this place was destined to become an important city by reason of its situation, that he could by nothing give more honor and advantage of Religion than to devote all his efforts, with every obligation, to the building of a Church and the formation of a parish. With this object the people assembled in the house of Mr.

P. Quigley, who, notwithstanding his large household, kindly welcomed the Priest, and provided a room wherein to celebrate the Holy Sacrifice. As the site whereon he hoped to build the House of God had already been selected, the Priest roused the faithful to contribute towards it with all their might, and visiting them personally in their own homes, he persuaded them with kindly words to promise the largest sum that their means would permit. Money was plentiful at that time in Dubuque on account of the discovery of new lead mines and the high price of the metal. Not only Catholics but many Protestants gave the impulse to this noble enterprise, contributing from five to even twenty dollars; several of the faithful, more favored by fortunate in their mines, offered forty and one hundred dollars. The Missionary having himself drawn the plan of the Church, in order to save the expense of an architect, speedily engaged the workmen, who at that time were neither many in number nor highly skilled, but Almighty God so prospered it, that on the fifteenth day of August everything was ready for laying the first stone.

Almost all the inhabitants of the village, Protestants as well as Catholics, assisted at this ceremony, for as it was the first Church in that great Territory, all the people without distinction were satisfied and happy to see in a country just springing into existence, a monument raised for the propagation of the Christian Faith.

A manuscript inscribed with the name of the reigning Pontiff, of the Bishop of the Diocese, of the President of the American Republic, and of the Governor of the Territory, with current year and day, was deposited in the hollow of the corner-stone. And in such wise was celebrated publicly the feast of the Assumption of the Blessed Virgin at Dubuque, in the year 1835.

The building was carried on with such uninterrupted and zealous application that at the end of October, when the work had to be interrupted on account of the cold, besides the foundation, there were five feet of the wall built round the whole circuit of the building. This Church was dedicated to the Archangel Raphael. It measures seventy-eight feet in length by forty-one in breadth. The walls are of stone brought with extreme difficulty from the hills nearby; to the small number of Catholics, although endowed with generous piety and inspired with zeal as they were, success seemed impossible, and that labor too costly; but eventually, it surpassed all expectation whatever, because it was a cathedral that was being erected which the faithful make use of today in order to cherish their own devotion.

Chapter IV.

THE CITY OF GALENA: ITS ORIGIN — THE FIRST PRIESTS WHO VISITED — IN 1835 THE FIRST STONE OF A CHURCH IS LAID.

The Mission received by our Priest had, within its confines, not one rising city alone or one Province alone, but finding himself in a vast region and by himself, he was obliged to succor the spiritual needs of the faithful who inhabited Iowa Territory, the western part of Wisconsin Territory, and the northern portion of the State of Illinois. In the latter state and about fifteen miles from Dubuque, the city of Galena is situated, which in 1835 numbered about eight hundred souls; the Catholics were almost two hundred in number but others lived in the vicinity.

Galena is situated upon a little stream called the Fevre River, distant six miles from the great Mississippi; the business connected with the rich lead mines in Wisconsin and Illinois gave rise to this town in 1820, and at present it controls this traffic and is distinctively connected with it. It is the principal site whence this precious metal is forwarded on steamboats to every quarter of this prosperous Republic, and here, too, for the same reason, are the traders who purchase the lead with money or merchandise. In 1843 it contained more than three thousand inhabitants, and the lands in its vicinity are quite cultivated for a new country notwithstanding its somewhat cold climate; there is no doubt that in a few years, with such riches of its own producing, it will be able to become a populous city.

The Irish, emigrating from their own persecuted country, were the first to penetrate these regions, for the purpose of benefiting their condition by industry, but deprived as they were of the efficacious helps to the practice of Religion, with few exceptions they possessed

PART TWO

the Faith without the works which give it life. In 1828, the Reverend Vincent Badin and a few years later the Reverend Father Van Quickenberg, a Jesuit, and the Reverend G. Lutz from Saint Louis, visited the Catholics of Galena and the surrounding country; but the Missions were only of a few day's duration, and left not the slightest trace of the formation of a parish. Monsignore Rosati, distinguished for his charity and wisdom, in 1833 sent there as Missionary the Reverend J. McMahon, an Irishman, who, as the preceding chapter recounts, died nine months after his arrival and was buried in the public cemetery at Galena. The Reverend P. FitzMorice, of the same nationality, succeeded him in the ministry the next year, only to follow him to the tomb at the expiration of the third months of his Mission. The bodies of these two Priests, the first who passed to a better life in this western part of the Republic, without the last Offices of Religion, will be exhumed during this present year, God willing, and will be reverently laid in the new Catholic cemetery of the parish.

In July 1835, when our Missionary arrived at this place, for the purpose of exercising the holy ministry, he found not a vestige of the sacred things necessary for the celebration of the Holy Sacrifice. A good Catholic offered his house and on the second floor of this, the Priest erected a substitute for an Altar which transformed the room into a Church, poor and narrow indeed, but of precious remembrance as it was the cradle of the good, model congregation of the faithful which was afterwards gathered there. In that same room at the right of the Altar, upon a miserable bed, he tranquilly passed his nights planning the best means for carrying out his intent of raising in that young, promising city a House to the service of Almighty God. The short distance from Dubuque allowed him to divide his time so as to do in the one place what he was not neglecting in the other. In short, there were such efforts, such visiting and such stirring words among the people, that the necessary funds were finally obtained, wherewith to make a beginning on the building. The greatest difficulty was in finding a site suitable and central for the Church; Galena, closely surrounded by high hills, has very little space for a city; land suitable for building sites costs considerable here in comparison with other places; it was necessary to incur a debt of seven hundred and fifty dollars in order to secure sufficient land. In this place, the Protestants supported a Calvinistic minister, and a building which served as a temple, but in a spite of the secret opposition which was made, a number of them who were not dominated by prejudices of who were influenced by the worldly policy common in the United States, contributed generously to our religious enterprise.

For greater economy, the Priest acted here also as architect and superintendent, and with Heaven's help found himself able to lay the first stone on the twelfth day of September. There was a great concourse at the place of the ceremony; there were more Protestants than Catholics, called thither more by curiosity than by Religious feeling. He who presided at the function deemed it well to render a service to truth and an act of justice to Catholics by explaining the nature of the civil obligations of a Christian who from the sanctity and perfection of his religion is literally led to be a good subject to that form of government, whether republican monarchical, which is permitted him by Divine Providence for its own inscrutable designs. He proved besides that Religion has always impressed a sacred and inviolable character upon all political and civil institutions and has set the seal of consecration upon that obedience to law without which they lose their worth and are reduced to simple material forces. The grand truth of an All-Seeing God, supreme Judge and Rewarder of good and of evil, obliges man as member of a civil society, to keep the law both in private as in public, that he may thus receive an eternal recompense from the Divine Lawgiver. Thus does the Religion of Christ serve as a solid foundation to human societies, by sanctifying the laws upon which they rest.

The discourse upon this subject in the presence of a large gathering was delivered in answer to a calumny spread by certain malicious or ignorant persons to the effect that Catholicity cannot put itself in harmony with a Republican Government. This was once an error widespread throughout the United States, yet always confuted by the fact that the Catholics of that country give thanks to the supreme Moderator of events, that through the civil independence of that form of government, He has also rendered their Religion independent of those who were persecuting it.

The names of the Supreme Pontiff, of the Bishop, of the President, and of the Governor of the State, with the day and date of the ceremony formed a simple inscription placed in the foundation stone, which when settled in its proper place, served as a receptacle for the sum of more than two hundred dollars given on that occasion by several zealous persons for the church building. The church was dedicated to the Archangel Michael, Prince of the people of God. The dimensions are seventy-four feet in length by forty in width; and in that year it was too spacious for the number of Catholics, but now it is able to hold only half the Congregation. The principal utility of this House of the Lord was made manifest after a few years in the faith and zeal of the many who hitherto relaxed and lukewarm in the Faith returned to the strict observance of the holy duties of Religion; and it was made manifest too in the conversions of some who were living far from the Truth, who are now giving beautiful examples of loyalty and of all evangelical virtues.

Chapter V.

SPIRIT OF THE CIVIL LAWS OF THE UNITED STATES IN THEIR RELATIONS TO THE CATHOLIC RELIGION AND TO ALL THE RELIGIOUS SECTS EXISTING AND TO EXIST.

The erection of two Catholic Churches simultaneously in a country where Protestants are four times as numerous as Catholics, where the Priest stands alone, isolated from his brethren in the Priesthood and where there are many ready to spread prejudices against the Faith, may seem to some a circumstance difficult of explanation. Yet to one who understands the political spirit which dominates human happenings in a society made up of peoples of every nationality, of every imaginable religious belief, it ought not to appear an incredible thing to see one Catholic, alone, unlettered, in one of the large cities of the American Union, protected in his form of Religious worship, even though that form is believed to be a false one by all his other fellow citizens. Any form of worship under its most striking manifestations and surrounded, if its devotees so desire, by the most extravagant accompaniments, is considered by the public as the personal, private property of the individual, is protected by law, not, to be sure, as a religious belief or rite, but as his house or the right of eating and drinking what seems best to him, would be protected.

Whoever wishes to thoroughly understand the status of Catholicity in the United States should study its relations to the nature of the existing civil laws. Then will he discover the line within which every Religious association, true or false, may enjoy rights, and outside which they would become amenable to secular authority. It is not the writer's intention to refer in this article to any politico-religious principle, still less to ensure, to offer blame, or vituperation to existing forms of government upon their relations with the Church; his is simply stating facts which deserve attention of one who desires to know the causes of the progress of the Faith in North America.

The world has ever and always been divided in its politics in relation to Religion; some governments have given their protection exclusively to one particular creed or form of belief, and have declared the public and private profession of all others an offense against the laws; this policy unable to maintain itself long has been reduced to the prohibition of proselytism or exterior practice of proscribed forms. Some governments have by force protected a chosen religious system, and with generous bestowals of privileges, while tacitly tolerating those who profess different ones. There are also governments who have supported a veritable Pantheon of all creeds, however diametrically opposed, and have lavished upon each a special and direct interest. The imagination or the ignorance of some misguided persons has actually conceived the idea of a government without religion. Lastly, there exists one government which while completely without any religious system whatever, is content to protect its subjects in the free practice of their own particular belief, without either adopting or repudiating any one of them by law.

Now, coming to our subject, it must be noted that at the epoch of the war between the United Colonies of America and England, the people who were fighting for independence were an intermixture of almost every European nation and of every religious belief. After independence was secured, the question of Religion seemed to settle itself by each individual's belief in his own right to profess whatever he liked, with fullest liberty; a republican government in its infancy was not in a position either to protect or proscribed any particular form, since it owed the freedom of its existence to the blood shed by its defenders of every creed, and was not empowered to extend any right of inspection over them, otherwise, the administration of public worship would have proved a wider, more complicated, more difficult department than the entire political administration.

The Constitution of this great Republic was framed by representatives of the people, who all on one plane of equality, were not willing to yield to the laws the very least right over their particular and multiform religious creeds; on the other hand, the design of the Constitution was simply to provide for the well-being of each individual, giving him a guarantee for everything pertaining to him as personal property. The legislators of the United States had in view the establishment in their laws of that straight line which separates the civil power from conscience, leaving to this last, all doctrines true or false, with all their present and future consequences, good or bad. In such wise did the various Christian sects, Judaism, indifferentism, unbelief and all the systems which divide the world in religious matters, become neither recognized nor repudiated by law, but simply disjoined from it as heterogenous, as a thing with which the civil power had nought in common. From that moment the whole enormous mass of so many systems with all their inseparable woes and paradoxes were laid on the shoulders of the people who were considered under the law as one simple citizen, and never under a religious aspect.

The immediate consequence of the separation of the civil authority from any connection whatsoever with religion was the obligation on the part of the Government of the Republic to protect not to religion, but the citizen in the practice of the religion. For the same reason and in the same sense that every government in the world does not interfere with its subjects in indifferent matters, but merely protects them, as for instance in the cultivation of their own farms, the form of their dwellings, the color of their garments, etc., just so in the United States are the citizens protected in whatever is mere matter of conscience. Even when religious practices conflict with the laws in a way, if these practices are not in themselves immoral, unjust or detrimental to one's neighbor, they are respected by the laws; for as they concern the conscience alone of the individual, they are held as entirely free of the governing authority. But should the religious practices of any citizen turn to the prejudice of good order, of administration of the law, or of the rights of a third party, then the secular power can and must interfere to correct the delinquent, not as guilty of following a false doctrine, but of an act which violates the law or the rights of other parties.

Such in brief, are the relations of all forms of religion with the governmental authority in the United States, so separated, that they might be considered equally independent and free of each other, although in a certain manner they lend each other mutual assistance. The laws are obliged to respect and protect the citizen in the exercise of his religious belief, and the religious bodies in order to preserve that very liberty of worship must observe and respect the laws of the state, upon which that liberty is founded. So in this government the independence of the civil from the religious official is due to the independence of worship from the civil power, or to express it more concisely, the liberty of one is the liberty of the other. It might also be called a mutual contract of independence and protection between the Government and all Religious bodies present and to come.

There are many who ascribe this state of things to the high standard of the political spirit compared to that of the old world,—of those legislators who framed the Constitution of the United States; and nearly all the citizens of this country pride themselves on being wiser than other nations in their policy regarding Religion. One who has acquired a clear understanding of the singular circumstances attending the Declaration of American Independence will readily see that to these circumstances more than to any others is due the independence of religious from civil affairs. The many religious sects that were existing in America and were united in the struggle for freeing themselves from the yoke of England, the example of so many bloody wars and persecutions under nearly every government of Europe resulting in these new sects during the past three hundred years; the universal longing for the same liberty in worship as that prized so dearly in civil matters; the impossibility of adopting one sole religion or of forbidding any of them, —these were the moving causes of the total dissociation of legislative authority from the religious doctrines and modes of worship of the citizens of the great Republic of America. To the same causes is due this day, the continuation of freedom in religious matters. It is to the irresistible force of the circumstances just noted, and not to mere human wisdom, that the thoughtful observer will attribute this remarkable state of affairs, probably the only example in the world.

In a country where the people constitutes itself the supreme legislator through its representatives, the Government must at times recognize religious authority and the latter not seldom depends upon the former, according to the ideas of the ruling majority. This may happen in particular State legislatures, where some laws might concede too much to a religious sect or sects or on the other hand curtail their liberty. Such deviations from the true spirit of the Constitution would be only the imperfections inseparable from human affairs.

Some have thought that the Government of the United States, because of not recognizing any particular religion must naturally be itself skeptical or atheistic—a most false conclusion in our case, for in one State where the republican system is carried out in full, there can be no laws for direction of worship there, while the citizens are divided on the matter of religion. The very fact that the civil authority is obliged to protect the citizen in the practice of his devotions, is the very strongest proof that the majority is religiously inclined, even though by reason of ignorance and error of the people they may be led away to varied and false doctrines. Woe to that country if the mass of its people shall ever become unbelievers! Then will religion lose that protection which makes it now so free to act, and enslaved by general corruption, its ruin and disintegration, humanly speaking, will be irreparable.

A Republic demoralized is worse than any form of Government whatever, for in such an event the demoralization of the will and the general manner of living will take upon themselves the force of laws. In a real Republic, the loss of Religion and the general corruption of morals keep pace with anarchy, with dissolution of civil society and at last with absolute despotism. This might not be the case in a Monarchical Government, which not being wholly in the hands of the people might if guided by wise policy and helped by force of arms preserve some degree of order even if the masses were entirely corrupted.

Notwithstanding the freedom of worship guaranteed by the Laws of the Government the people of the United States, when under the influence of blind bigotry, of false notions and sometimes of mischievous religious sectarians or crafty politicians, are at times guilty of violating the sanctity of Religious tolerance. We have a humiliating example of this in the burning of the Ursuline Convent near Boston in 1835. These and other riotous demonstrations are not enough to destroy freedom of worship, because they are acts of individuals in opposition to the laws and severely condemned by these laws. Abuses of liberty might even insinuate themselves into State legislatures, and even into the National Congress, but ever contrary to the spirit of the Constitution, and this of itself would deprive them of the force of a law.

From this brief explanation of the spirit of the civil authority in its relation to all the forms of Religion now existing or to exist, the reader can easily comprehend that the building of churches is no more a matter pertaining to the laws, than would be the building of an ordinary house; and that the assembly of a congregation of the faithful, the organization of a parish or the ecclesiastical authority of a Priest has no more to do with laws than would the meeting of a few friends around a festal banquet presided over by the head of the family. In the great Republic of North America one may build a hundred Catholic churches without asking for permission and may convert them to other uses if it so please him, with the same case. For the same reason, the greatest of fanatics is free to preach a new religious creed and organize a new sect and when it suits him may change it for another absurdity.

Chapter VI.

THE MISSIONARY RARELY HAS THE OPPORTUNITY OF APPROACHING THE SACRAMENT OF PENANCE—ACCOUNT OF HIS MINISTRY UNTIL THE SUMMER OF 1836.

Among the privations which a Priest must bear when isolated in far countries, that most keenly felt always was the deprivation of the opportunity for frequent Confession. In fact while our Missionary was occupied in the building of two Churches, from the month of June until the following December he had not once the happiness of seeing a brother-Priest to whom he might humbly confess his faults. There was one Priest at the distance of two hundred miles away, but the roads and all the circumstances of the journey were so dangerous, so beset with difficulties, that the journey to the city of Saint Louis proved easier and took less time, although it was distant from Galena five hundred miles by way of the river and about four hundred miles overland. The cold season having arrived, the river was frozen over, and at the expense of many days' travelling and a considerable sum of money, he was obliged to follow the latter route in order to receive the spiritual refreshment of the Sacrament of Penance.

In the case of him who is under obligation to remain constantly in a state of grace for the celebration of the Holy Sacrifice, it would be neither prudent nor permissible for him to remove himself far from the opportunity of frequent Confession; but when the fulfilling of those words of our Lord "Go ye and teach all nations" separates us long from this holy tribunal, it is not unreasonable to believe and hope, first, in the existence of a special grace preserving the preacher of the Gospel from grave faults, when he is faithful to the high duties of his calling; and secondly, in that sorrow that in his case may suffice to take the place of the Sacrament of Confession. Without such confidence in this special grace and in this abiding sorrow, there would be no God-fearing soul able to acquire that Apostolic zeal which has moved so many from all ages to forsake all things, that he might proclaim the truths of the Gospel to the very ends of the earth.

Now he is sure that on the borders of the American Republic as well as in many remote corners of the different States, there are many Priests of the Altar, who for the sake of preserving and propagating the Faith, are toiling at such a distance from each other that they are unable to frequent the Sacrament of Penance oftener than three or four times a year. These taught by experience to comprehend the supreme advantage of that sacred Tribunal, which in Catholic countries is often neglected or even abused by those who have access thereto at their own pleasure.

On his return to his scattered little flock, the Missionary devoted himself to preaching continence, justice and the desire of the gifts of Heaven with the view of correcting the erring ways of those, who, deprived of means of grace, had been living with souls all relaxed and enervated in neglect of their eternal salvation. To satisfy the good desires and spiritual needs of all, it was found necessary to distribute his time according to the different seasons between the two little cities of Dubuque and Galena and their environs, but for the most part in those two cities where the Catholics were most numerous. The entire month of February was spent at Prairie du Chien continuing in that parish of more than five hundred souls, the little work for good that had been accomplished the previous year; during this visit a gift was received from a generous citizen of the place, who presented a tract of four acres in the very centre of the town for the erection of a Church; this project, however, could not be begun before the year 1839.

Thus occupied in his Priestly duties he passed the long winter, and at the solemnization of the Feast of the Resurrection, saw but a few at the Holy Table. The cause of this was the life that those faithful lead, their continual association with non-Catholics, when they gradually grow lukewarm in spiritual matters and unfortunately lose those leading virtues in which they used to abound, and lead worse lives,—above all when they are destitute of Churches wherein the sacred offices and the preaching of God's Word contribute to preserve the Faith and vivify it with good works. The labors and fatigues borne by the Priests of the Gospel for long years, the gain among souls, these all stand in constant risk of being lost. The lack of zealous Priests, of Churches, of catechetical teaching, of good example, the never-ceasing attacks by the Protestant ministers upon Catholic truths, the assumed piety of many who merely pretend to be true followers of the Gospel, the influence of numbers, of wealth and the general prevalence of sectarian influence and of many other circumstances of the same nature form a huge stumbling-block in the way of the poor faithful, making them totter and sometimes casting them into the mire of skepticism.

To all this must be added the sorrowful effect of the scandalous conduct of some among the Catholics in the very midst of the sectarians who, in spite of their many dogmatic errors, believe themselves the true disciples of the Divine Master; and as facts speak a language far more convincing than that of arguments, the sanctity and Truth of the Church are disfigured in the eyes of men and the shade of Protestantism wrapped in the mantle of virtue is taken for a reality. Now it must not be believed that reviving the Faith and inflaming anew the devotion of cold and indifferent Catholics, inviting them to different devotional exercises,—that all this is the work of a few days or is more easily accomplished than the conversion of pagans to the Unity of the Church. Experience has taught our Missionary that the reestablishment of Religion in the regions appointed him by Divine Providence has required more sacrifices, more time, more patience, more burning words than were required for the conversion of the Indians.

In April 1836, the Priest traveled a second time to the city of Saint Louis by the way of the Mississippi River, and the purpose of his journey as before was to seek the grace of the Sacrament of Penance. On the return voyage about a hundred miles from Galena, he left the steamboat in order to land on the famous island called Rock Island, where at that time stood a Fort to keep the tribes in check. Here he celebrated the Divine Mysteries, after which he crossed over to the western shore of the River to administer the consolations of our holy Religion to the only Catholic family dwelling there, a charming spot, formed by nature herself as a site on that gently sloping and verdant hill of that young city, now with more than a thousand inhabitants. A certain Mr. Antoine Le Claire, a man of most amiable temperament and exemplary character had his home there in the midst of a square mile of an estate; this had been presented to him in his character of a lifelong benefactor and faithful interpreter of the united tribes of the Sacs and Foxes, when these latter, a few years before had ceded to the United States Government the lands whereon hitherto they had dwelt, on the borders of the Great River.

Chapter VII.

THE CHURCHES OF DUBUQUE AND GALENA.

In a country where commerce, the arts, the cities and society itself, are yet in their infancy, the erection of Churches becomes a work not only of grave importance to the cause of the Propagation of the Faith, it is besides an undertaking not easy of accomplishment. The scarcity of necessary means, the inability to procure on the spot materials that are absolutely indispensable, the exorbitant charges of workmen, with various other circumstances, put to the last test of the perseverance and application of one who strives to build a House of God, however small. This was the state of the things when in the summer of 1836, the walls of the Church of Saint Raphael, now Cathedral of Dubuque Diocese, were in process of erection. The contributions of the preceding year were then entirely exhausted, yet the Missionary took heart with all the more earnestness and never-ending anxiety; by dint of which, little by little, doing the office of collector, of superintendent, of architect, of watchful inspector or accountant, of treasurer, and sacrificing unreservedly every trifle that the faithful gave to the Priest in the name of charity, he had the inexpressible satisfaction of seeing the building under cover toward the last of September, and in such condition that divine service could be suitably conducted therein.

In order not to refer to this subject again in these Memoirs it may be stated here that before 1839 the Church of Dubuque had already cost $5,000,000, without counting the labor gratuitously bestowed by many of the faithful or any expense of conducting the work. Of this sum, not the very smallest portion was received outside the limits of territory over which the Church was to serve, so that it owed its existence to the great unity and disinterestedness which prevailed.

As the Missionary was occupied during the summer of 1836 on the western bank of the Mississippi, he was able only with much difficulty to devote part of his time to urging on the building of the Church of Saint Michael in the little city of Galena; yet of that also several feet of the wall were raised, all around. The Holy Mysteries were celebrated in different houses of the village wherever it was most convenient, but to provide a more suitable and permanent place, a little frame house was built upon the Church land which until 1839 served as a Chapel and dwelling for the Priest. The expense of this most useful frame building was $800.00.

It would be of no advantage to make mention of the various stations, visits and missions throughout that part of the country which was beginning to be settled by emigrants, for from the idea already given of the circumstances surrounding the first settlers situated on the borders of a perfectly wild region, the reader may be able to judge also of the nature of the duties incumbent upon the Priest. On the occasion of one of his customary journeys to Saint Louis in the autumn to meet a brother-Priest and go to Confession, he delayed several days near Rock Island for the consolation of a few Catholics, who as will be seen later, were themselves to construct a little Church within the next year. On the fifth of December, the steamboat that was struggling against the current of the Mississippi, completely blocked by the masses of ice coming down the river, and, by their dangerous momentum, in danger of total wreck, was forced to put into a bay on the shore of a little island, and stay there for the rest of the season. The Priest with many other travelers finally reached Galena after a journey of three days on foot across a country then uninhabited. This little circumstances must be told as an example of the supreme respect that the Irish race holds for the Catholic Priests. The first night of this last journey, one of the Irishmen courteously observant, seeing the Priest lying on the bare ground, instantly divested himself of the single covering in his possession and brought it to the Missionary. This voluntary privation in such extreme need, may surely be called an act of heroism worthy of a spiritual and everlasting reward, for did not Savior say "Come, ye blessed of my Father, take possession of the kingdom, for I was naked and ye clothed Me." (Matt. XXV.)

Chapter VIII.

THE TERRITORIAL GOVERNMENT OF WISCONSIN IS FORMED — THE PRIEST ATTENDS THE FIRST ASSEMBLY OF LEGISLATURE — HOW CHURCH PROPERTY IS SECURED BY CIVIL LAW.

By an Act of Congress of the United States, held in the city of Washington, capital of the great Republic, during the winter of 1835-36, the Territory of Michigan, then extending to the west as far as the Mississippi, was divided to form the Territory of Wisconsin. This Territory formed from Michigan is bounded on the east by Lake Michigan, on the west by the great river; on the north it borders on Canada, on the south, the State of Illinois. Until 1838 the Wisconsin Territory comprised within its limits the vast Territory of Iowa. The first Assembly of Legislature was held in the early part of November in a very small and obscure village called Belmont. The Legislative body of a Territory is composed of thirteen members forming the Council, and of twenty-six other members who compose the House of Representatives; all of these are elected by the people for whom they are to make the Territorial Laws. The Governor of a State is elected by the people of that State; in a Territory the Governors is appointed by the President of the United States.

It has been seen in Chapter V that the spirit of the Constitution of the United States takes no cognizance of religious convictions but grants all religions perfect freedom; therefore Catholics are sometimes chosen by the majority of the people to occupy the first official positions in the Republic. In Dubuque County two Catholics obtained the majority of votes for the first Legislature of Wisconsin; the Missionary himself had a small share in this diplomatic gathering, having been elected to make a speech to the houses before the reading of the Governor's message. He opened the daily sessions of this Legislature with prayer, but his more important obligations as Priest did not permit him to perform this office longer than one week. Facts like these prove that to the spirit of the great Confederation is entirely due that superior liberty enjoyed by the Catholic Church under its protection. It would be difficult to find in the history of any country whatsoever, a diplomatic body wherein Protestants outnumbering the Catholics eighteen to one have conferred upon the Minister of the Altar the office of Chaplain. In this case, even if one chooses to take much Religious indifference for granted, yet he must perforce recognize that spirit of impartiality in the organic laws of the Government which severs them completely from religious functions.

In the legislation of the Territories, of the States and of the general Government, Catholicity, as well as all the religious sects, can obtain civil privileges which may prove useful and even necessary to the security and prosperity of all her institutions, whether colleges, seminaries, regular corporations, church buildings and such like, always however, so far as in the face of society they are the rights of one or more individuals. Since the governmental authority does not recognize ecclesiastical dignity or authority in the holding of property, but simply the person to whom the property belongs in the face of the law, so whenever a religious association deems it wise to secure this property under the immediate care and control of that association, it petitions the proper authorities for the legalization of certain rules or constitutions proposed by that association. Thus, each of the various institutions, religious and literary, although subject to the authority and superintendence of many individuals, in presence of the law, becomes as it were one sole individual, in the very same sense as do the mercantile firms recognized by the laws of all the governments. In this way Catholic possessions and institutions in the United States, while independent of the Government as far as pertains to spiritual affairs, are able as to civil properties and associations to take deep root and lay solid foundations as immovable as the constitution which holds firm the Republic itself. One who feels the full force of this can readily see how the goods of the Church can share before the law in that stability and security which can never give way unless by the fall of the government itself.

The wisdom of the first Council of the Bishops of the Province of the United States which was held in the month of October, 1829, in order to prevent any inconvenience which might arise in the future, from permitting secular persons to become owners of Church buildings, ordained in Decree No. 5 of this Council that no Church should be built or consecrated in future, without being first given over in writing, to the Bishop of the Diocese, for the purpose of Divine Worship and the advantage of the faithful. But as there may exist circumstances wherein this Decree might not easily harmonize with Religious interest, the Council has added "when this can be done."

This Decree however, does not bind the Church property of the Religious Orders, which enjoy in America all the privileges granted by Canon Law and by the constitutions of the Roman Pontiffs. So that said Orders may hold their Churches and other ecclesiastical property in the name of their respective Superiors dwelling in any part of the world, or in the name of several members of the Community, provided these obtain, from the legislative power of the State in which they are, an act of incorporation as a moral or literary association.

The title or the holding of Church property put into the hands of one individual, whether Bishop or Superior of a Religious Order, carries with it this grave inconvenience; for instance, supposing the case of heavy personal debts, of bad management or even of lack of strict honesty, the Church building, Seminaries, might be in danger of passing out of the control of the Church, for the reason that they might be considered as personal property of an individual who could, legally, sell them or give them away,—or be deprived of them by his creditors. It is to be hoped that the paternal solicitude of the Supreme Pontiff will soon provide for the greater security of Church property in America.

Chapter IX.

LONG JOURNEY THROUGH WISCONSIN TERRITORY IN A SLEDGE.

The beautiful broad natural prairies of Wisconsin Territory usually offer the traveler in the cold season an easy and commodious passage over the snow which covers them with its white mantle for the space of many months. In February, 1837, the Missionary took advantages of this curious phase of nature of make a journey to Green Bay, two hundred and ten miles from Galena, his object being to recover some articles needed for the Church, stored there two years before. It is not easy to give an idea of a course of four hundred and twenty miles, all alone, across a country still unbroken and unsettled, in the very depth of winter severity, in a sledge drawn by a single horse, crossing prairies, woods, rivers, frozen lakes, over a road at times smooth and easily followed because marked by the tracks of many other vehicles, at other times hardly discernible because little used and hidden under the snow drifted there by the wind. It may be observed that in this part of the country the snow is seldom so deep as to render the road too hard or entirely impassable; so in winter the highways from one little village to another are generally well traced through the snow by the sledges of the wayfarers, while in the vast prairies the tracks do not remain plain and well-defined as in the woods, on account of the wind which blows there as it does over the sea, and carries with it the frozen snow like dust, obliterating in an instant the tracks just made. Many are the difficulties to be encountered by the inexperienced traveler; there are streams with high banks and of course with no bridge, whose waters fed by springs near, do not freeze over; the ice is not always solid upon the lakes and is very treacherous and dangerous certain rivers; in the hollows of the undulating prairie the snow is often drifted by the wind in a mass to the depth of six or seven feet. The greatest, most dreaded peril on these vast prairies is caused by the falling snow, so as to completely cover the track, and shutting out the slightest view of the surroundings, even of east and west; desperate is the condition then of one who finds himself in such a strait when the fury of the freezing wind, with the dense, powdery snow, so confuses him that he loses his way and is forced in spite of himself to stop his horse under the stormy sky, and wait until thee fury of the storm passes by. In these desperate straits many are found frozen to death. The prudent forethought which counts its steps before taking them, and prepares for possible dangers will ordinarily prevent misfortunes of this nature.

 On the occasion if the journey, the Priest visited his Menominee Indians who were engaged in fishing at Lake Winnebago; great was the consolation and spiritual gladness he experienced seeing again those good Christian whom he had won but a few years before from the superstitions of the savage to the truths of the Gospel and on their part his presence gave them the greatest delight. To sanctify such a meeting, forty-two of them received from his hands that Heavenly Bread which divinely unites hearts in the love of Jesus Christ. As he made his away towards his destination, he stopped at various stations to provide for the spiritual needs of the Catholics dispersed throughout the western part of the Territory. He who bears the word of Truth should imitate his Divine Master, who went about doing good, lightening the burdens of the heavy-laden and sore oppressed.

Chapter X.

DESCRIPTION OF THE BEGINNING OF THE CITY OF DAVENPORT ON THE MISSISSIPPI — HOW CULTURE AND THE ELEGANCIES OF LIFE ARE INTRODUCED INTO THE NEWLY FOUNDED CITY.

One who has lived long enough in the Western States and particularly in those just settled has been eyewitness of the sowing of those first seeds which later grow into the great city. Where he now paces streets regular and filled with noise of traffic, a few years before he was gazing at nature in all her simplicity and silence. This growth, budding and blossoming as it were, of cities, carries one's imagination back to the living complete picture of what were once the sites of the proud old world centers, before man decreed to build his dwelling there.

Among the most beautiful and charming sites on the western bank of the Mississippi is that one opposite the famous Rock Island, more than a hundred miles from Dubuque down the river; nature herself seems to have shaped this regular verdant slope girdled and shielded by hills that man might raise a city there. A certain M. Antoine Leclaire, an devout Catholic, noted no less for his integrity, than for his wealth, for many years had his happy home there, alone with this wife, and held his estate of the a square mile along the river; this had been presented him as a free gift by the tribes of the Sacs and Foxes in their gratitude towards their faithful friend and beneficent adviser on the occasion of the ceding of that section to the United States Government.

PART TWO

It was in 1836 that Mr. Leclaire began to convert his estate into a city, which he named Davenport, which was first designed upon a map with streets straight and of noble breadth, leaving at regular intervals spaces for squares and public buildings, with a broad spacious expanse on the river front for commercial purposes. His faith did not let him forget the cause of Religion, for in the city he was planning he devoted a square in an advantageous position, for the erection of a Church. Many speculators and others desiring to enjoy the advantages offered to the first settlers in a new country, in 1836 bought an immense tract of land near the new city of Davenport, and many and various were the frame houses raised there before the spring of the next year. The emigrants who for two or three years before, like colonists with their families, had been dispersed throughout the vast extent of Iowa and near the river had given a great impulse to the trade which in that section all centered in Davenport. Thus the farmers gave the young city its importance, and this in turn served to make their condition more convenient and agreeable, and their farms more profitable, because brought into the neighborhood of trade. This mutual advantage made the welfare, prosperity and material riches of both.

It is a circumstance worthy of note, that in the young cities of America, where the Indian has abandoned the country, culture enters with the very first settlers; this happens from the fact that these settlers with their families come from other large cities and are expert merchants, lawyers, physicians, mechanics of all trades, in a word, they are members of a little society who change their place of abode in the hope of bettering their conditions. The first who make up the city are usually men who having suffered losses elsewhere, seek to retrieve them by retrenching in business and practising economy; young physicians and lawyers more easily find practice there where they are alone in their particular sphere; the building of many houses employs more workmen and at better wages; this is the reason of their emigration. There is another numerous class, often well educated and in good circumstances who bring their families to the new city, and these are the aspirants to political offices. In America with its peculiar system of legislation, everything is organized quickly and easily; the country is at once divided into counties, and the cities, no matter how small, have the same privileges as the largest of them; the people of the State or Territory elect the members of their legislative bodies, the counties elect the officials needed for establishing good order and keeping the peace among the citizens; those who live within the limits of the city appoint their own authorities. Nevertheless, to occupy these various offices whence is derived some gain and honor, many enter the western country with the first settlers in order to secure their esteem and good will.

The newspaper is not last with its editors and printing presses in the new villages; it is a common thing even where only four or five hundred citizens can be counted; for politics in which everybody takes part, is the daily bread which feeds or supports those newspapers that in America find their way into the houses of the poorest and most illiterate, as well as of the men of letters.

There are two causes besides those already mentioned, which contribute to facilitate the founding of new cities; one is the Postal System which in the United State penetrates, as best it can, into wilds where only a dozen of families can be found; in this way even in new and sparsely settled countries a man is put several times a week into touch with all affairs, political, literary or business, that take place in the great Republic. The other element that promotes the establishment of towns is the absence of walls, of gates, of tolls which are always burdensome to the traveler, the trader or the citizen. Taxes are entirely national here. The States, accordingly, the country and the cities are in free communication with one another, without the least hindrance. In this way the prosperity of trade is not dependent upon personal rights or legal privileges, but simply upon local advantages and industry. Almost all the American cities owe their origin to the industry of their citizens, and to their taking advantage of the beautiful or suitable sites presented by nature herself in every form adapted to that phase of trade that serves the wants of the people.

But coming back to our story; the Missionary with the assistance of Mr. Leclaire, principal proprietor of the new city of Davenport, in the month of April 1837, laid the first stone of the church which was called Saint Anthony's. The first bricks manufactured in the place were used in the construction of this building, which was only forty feet by twenty-five, and built with two stories, so as to accommodate on the lower floor, a Priest, who later made his home there.

In 1837 Davenport numbered one hundred inhabitants, one-fourth of whom were Catholics; in 1843 it numbered more than twelve hundred, with about three hundred Catholics, and possessed five Churches of different denominations, a fine hotel, a courthouse (for it is at present the county seat), several school-buildings, — people devoted to trades and to luxury, professions of every kind, a flourishing trade with smaller towns in the interior, two weekly newspapers and literary associations. One who saw in 1835 the tepees of the poor Indian dotting the verdant plain, and sees it now covered with new buildings of brick, presenting to the traveller's view a gay symmetrical city where many elegant steamers land, is tempted to wonder if what passes before his eyes is not an illusion rather than a reality. The plain whereon Davenport is built is not the only one to undergo so great a transformation, but the hills which surround it and the sweep of country for many miles around, which only a few years ago was feeding ground for wild beasts, are now studded with dwellings, are reduced by industry to rich cultivated fields, providing sustenance for every species of domestic animal. If seven years has wrought such changes, what will Davenport be in half a century? The beautiful city of Cincinnati on the Ohio River furnishes an answer to this question; it has enjoyed but sixty years of existence and at this present time will number more than fifty thousand inhabitants within its circuit.

Although not every American city can boast of so prosperous a beginning or possess the same possibilities of speedy growth, yet it is a historical truth that all of these new towns owe their existence to the immense, unrestrained immigration of the people, bringing with them those gifts, both intellectual and mechanical, that go to the formation of a culture society. How great is the need then that our holy Religion should closely attend the giant growth of this new world we shall treat of later.

Just now it will suffice to remark that the little Catholic Church of Davenport was finished during the spring of 1838 and a worthy Priest officiated there since 1839, but at this present time it does not accommodate half of the parishioners; so some measures have already been taken for the erection of a large new Church that will hold fifteen hundred. That church built in 1837, at the cost of more than two thousand dollars, will serve as a habitation for the Priest and for school purposes. And thus in a few years do matters grow and change in the New World.

Chapter XI.

THE PROTESTANT MINISTERS IN THE WESTERN STATES AND THEIR PREACHING—EFFECTS OF A RELIGIOUS EXCITEMENT—ADVANTAGES OF THE CATHOLIC PRIEST OVER THE MINISTER IN MISSION WORK.

The arrival of a number of Protestant ministers in 1837 in the regions that the Priest had been visiting, affords to the compiler of these Memoirs a favorable opportunity to give some account of their mission, character, preaching and way of making a livelihood, which may serve to give an idea of the people by whom he was surrounded.

There is no corner, however remote, that a settler has reached, where a minister of some sect has not made his voice heard, extolled the Bible as the sole rule of Faith, directed his enthusiastic prayers to Heaven and of course in one way or another, vilified the Catholic Church. The axe that hews down the first trees and clears the road for the emigrant cannot always boast of first breaking the profound silence of wild nature, for not seldom has it been preceded by the loud and boisterous voice of the religious fanatic. Among the first to settle country places in the West are many ministers of different sects but principally Methodists and Baptists, who with their families while seeking in the possession of the land and in the trade for a little of the kingdom of this world, on Sundays, preach that of the older. In this way while losing nought of the advantages of secular life, over and above this, they draw from the Gospel that moderate gain and that influence in society which may serve to the well-being of their usually numerous offspring. We must not be astonished then, if everywhere in the New World, we meet so many ministers and so few Priests. This results from different causes; for instance, the greater number of Protestants, and the assistance supplied by their various societies, to those who leave the populous cities for the purpose of exercising the ministry of preaching in the most remote districts of the Republic.

Generally speaking, those ministers who live in those districts on the borders of civilization, are well-versed in the letter of the English translation of the Bible and possess great facility in speaking acquired by constant practice; but apart from this they possess very little erudition, they do not study theology at all, the history of the Christian Religion, the origin and dogmas of the Protestant Reformation. The Methodist and Baptist sects which predominates over the most illiterate class, naturally have a greater number of preachers whose eloquence consists in much noisy speaking, in quoting the Bible in every sense that may suit them, in uttering the name of Jesus constantly, in inveighing furiously against sinners without explaining morality, in inviting everyone to conversion through simple Faith in the Saviour, in extolling the word of the Gospel, and readily promising Paradise to their hearers. In vain might one seek throughout their discourses for one word on the unity of the Faith, the doctrine of penance, the obligation of restitution, obedience to the Church, the necessity of an Sacrament of which they know only "The Lord's Supper" and Baptism as mere symbols. To make up for this lack, they do not fail to render their speaking more agreeable and impressive to their hearers by mingling therein all ridicule, calumny, insult and hatred against the Catholic Church, by persuading the ignorant that the Church is Antichrist, and providing it by the prophecy of the Apocalypse.

The ministers also posses a peculiar art, or rather trick, which enables them at their meetings to weep whenever they please and to pass from grave to gay with the utmost facility and quickness. This peculiar mode of eloquence, which is decidedly their own, is accompanied by loud cries, prayers, exclamations, sobs, frenzies, trembling, sweats, contortions and all that the violent commotions of a strangely troubled soul can produce in the body which is its victim. The influence that some of the ministers obtained by this means over religious fanatics, over the youth, the hypocrite, in a special manner over the weaker sex, could not be easily described by one who was not an eyewitness; suffice it to say that the audience often broke out into violent weeping, cries and ejaculations, so as to drown the preacher's voice. This is called by them the work of the Spirit of the Lord, which enters into and takes possession of the souls of the elect, justifies them, washes away all their sins, putting into their hearts that true love of our Savior, manifested by certain and visible signs of the operation of the same Spirit.

The Priest had occasion of seeing the disastrous effects of the rousing of this religious frenzy in the city of Burlington, Iowa;—it was at a "Reviving of the Spirit," as it is called by the Methodist sect, during which for the space of eight days or more, several ministers preach many times a day, principally however at evening until nearly midnight. Preaching, praying and singing are carried on at any or every hour, according as the spirit moves the preacher or the audience; this exercise becomes so animated that it excites many persons, women especially, to leave their places, to rush from place to place here and there and finally to leap into the air, to shriek and weep, attributing it all to the work of the Divine Spirit. Among the victims of this diabolical illusion, a spectacle to excite as much compassion as horror, he saw a woman who fainted and after vain attempts had been made to restore her, the bystanders had to carry her to her own home. Another in the course of the night fell into a swoon and remained till morning lying on a bench like one dead, entirely destitute of sensation; when they finally carried her home, it was found impossible to put her in a carriage on account of the rigidity of her figure. The more easily impressed and the most powerful in the matter of praying, weeping, sighing and being moved and convulsed by the "spirit" are not always the more moral among them, — for it often happened that they had to be expelled from the meeting, as happened to one who seemed always more inspired than the others, and could lengthen out her enthusiastic prayers and hymns for entire days without any intermission. Behold how God's Justice punishes those who, forsaking the Church of Christ, become the prey of Religious fanaticism and the impostors of so many sects of our day!

Since 1837 the Presbyterians or Calvinists sent out many ministers into the villages along the Mississippi and they failed not from the press and from the pulpit to falsify the Catholic Church unceasingly. Few are the Anglicans and ministers of the other denominations, for the reason that the teachings of the Methodists and Baptists are more fanatical and more tumultuous in their expression, and so appeal more strongly to the simple people in the country places and generally speaking, to the most ignorant who are more readily influenced by loud words and cries than by good sense.

A religion which has no exterior form of worship as Protestantism, can be fully established in all its requirements without altar, sacred appurtenances or church; preaching with the accompaniment of prayer, and the singing of hymns only, can be carried on with utmost facility either within walls, or in the open air; beyond this, since in their Churches there is no authority which can bind the conscience and speak to it in the Name of God, so the followers of these sects are not obliged under sin to assist at the public assemblies. From these facts it follows that Protestants have a far greater facility in exercising their ministry than has the Catholic Priest, to whom there is absolute need of sacred accompaniments to worship, and of altars for the celebration of the holy Sacrifice of the New Law, and above all, he must be armed with Charity, with Zeal, with Apostolic spirit and daring, which will sacrifice itself to the preaching of the Gospel, to the conquest of souls with no recompense except the merit of the labor, and which for conscience's sake will strive to extend the boundaries of the true Church and the Kingdom of God.

Yet despite of the difficulties as to Altar, Chalice, Altar Stone, Missal, which attend the lot of the Missionary, his condition in this regard is infinitely superior to that of maintaining a wife and family in new countries. Only the minister can describe his own anxieties and miseries, when he is forced to depend upon a poor and wide-scattered flock to whom he preaches the Gospel, for the support of his household. Outside the cities he rarely finds means for a livelihood without following some other occupation in addition to that of preaching the Word of God; necessity and his love for his children force him to put his hand to the plough, entangle him in the labyrinths of business matters, often to the occupation of carpenter, bricklayer, smith and other trades. This combination of the clerical with the matrimonial state results in making the former serve the interests and advantages of a family which imperiously demand from him a subsistence; so the ministry becomes a mere accessory to the great cares and anxieties inseparable from married life.

How much more advantageous to the people and how much less costly is the celibate life of the Catholic Priest in these remote and unsettled districts, is evident from the fact that the Missionary to whom these Memoirs refer, although alone and without any outside assistance, found wherever he was, the food and clothing that were needed. In the families of the faithful it was considered the greatest delight and held as a great honor to receive and entertain the Priest whose wants are so few; then too, on a journey it rarely happened that he incurred expense; most of the captains of the steamboats running on the Mississippi refused to accept fare from him whom they knew to be employing all his time and labor for religious motives only; at least two-thirds of his many enforced journeys were made without any expense, trusting in Divine Providence. In the same way, clothing was presented to him by the pious benevolence of the Catholics, a thing which could not be done for the numerous family of a Protestant minister. The Catholic Missionary, being unencumbered with those anxieties which extend beyond one's own person and into the future, after the necessities have been provided, if there should accrue to him anything in the matter of gifts, can and must devote them to the good of Religion; while the minister who is a father in the missions of the Western States must devote any superfluity to the future needs of his children. From all this it follows that a zealous Priest will find means to support life when a Protestant minister with a far greater number of followers, is forced to wrest a subsistence from some missionary society or from the labor of his own hands. Our Lord Jesus Christ has said that a good Shepherd sacrifices for the good of his flock his own affections, his own peace, his own life and with glad heart. With anxious care to lead them to rich pastures he ever walks at the head of his flock, often raising his voice to keep them from straying and that the wolf may not take them unawares; he spares no toil, and is ever on the watch prepared for meeting an attack upon his flock. But in these words of the Divine Master who does not recognize the picture of the Catholic Missionary elected to increase the spiritual riches of the Faith?

Chapter XII.

CREATION OF THE BISHOPRIC OF DUBUQUE IN 1837.

The emigration of thousands of families from the Eastern States of the American Union and from Europe, settling on the western border of Illinois, Wisconsin and in the Territory of Iowa, in the years 1835, 1836 and 1837, had so augmented the numbers of the Catholics in the Priest's Mission, that he found it difficult and almost impossible to provide even insufficiently for the spiritual comforts of them all. He was unable to remain longer than ten or fifteen days consecutively in any one station; the care of the sick in many and widely-separated localities, and his anxiety over temporal matters connected with the building of the Churches, made the disposition of his time a point of grave anxiety wherever he happened to go. The Bishop of Saint Louis, Monsignore Joseph Rosati, had it in mind to send him an assistant Priest, but was unable to carry out his intention.

On the occasion of the Triennial Council of the Bishops of the United States held in Baltimore, in May 1837, Monsignore Rosati proposed to his brethren in the Episcopacy to raise the small but rapidly growing city of Dubuque into an Episcopal See of one new Diocese formed out of the vast Territory of Iowa, which was then part of Wisconsin. The assembled Fathers of the venerable Council gave their approbation, and in the following August, it was recognized and confirmed with other Acts of that Council by the Apostolic See; and the Very Reverend Mathias Loras, already Vicar General of the Diocese of Mobile in Alabama for many years, was appointed with solemn decree by the same Apostolic Authority, first Bishop of the new See.

It was only on the tenth day of December, 1837, that the Reverend Mathias Loras was consecrated Bishop of Dubuque in the City of Mobile by Monsignore Michael Portier. The new Prelate then set out for Europe for the purpose of finding laborers for his Vineyard and the necessary means indispensable in a country where everything was to be established in order and harmony. During the long absence of this

Prelate, the Missionary who had been appointed by him as his Vicar General, exercised in the Diocese that ecclesiastical authority necessary in the case of the absence of its proper Pastor. Monsignore Loras, when he was in Rome, in the month of May, 1838, petitioned the Most Reverend P. Angelo Ancarani, at that time Master General of the Order of Preachers, that he would permit the said Vicar to remain in his Diocese and in those Missions wherein he had last exercised the ministry. This request was with all good will complied with by the pious and learned Master, ever zealous for the fulfillment of the Divine Will and the Propagation of the Faith.

This circumstance, a Diocese just created in a country only a few years before the abode of many savage tribes, may serve to give a just idea of the progress both ecclesiastical and civil of the American Republic. It was in June 1833, that the first cabin was raised on the site where now is built the City of Dubuque. On the fifteenth day of August 1835, was laid the corner stone of a Church, and just two years after, in August 1837, the place was raised to the dignity of a Bishopric by the Apostolic See; to in the brief space of four years, the spot which had first been the haunt of beasts and the solitary feeding-ground of roving herds, became a city of more than a thousand souls and an Apostolic Chair, by whose authority the saving bread of Gospel Truth was distributed to the faithful. This fact would have little significance if it were the work of a legislative act or some powerful individual, but as the combination of the temporal interests of the people and the interests of Religion, it deserves to be considered under this two-fold aspect.

To the free emigration of people from every nation in the world to any point in the United States where they believe they can better their condition, may be attributed the speedy formation of so many small cities on the borders of civilization. Trade, their very life, is concentrated in those places, and these cities by reason of their situation on rivers navigable for steamboats, offer the most direct and speedy communication with the rest of the Republic. The city of Dubuque owes its beginning not alone to these causes, but in an especial manner also to the lead mines which abound there, and which give it almost all its material importance.

PART TWO

Chapter XIII.

CAUSES WHICH CHIEFLY CONTRIBUTED TO THE FORMATION OF NEW DIOCESES IN THE UNITED STATES.

The reasons which induced the Church to create an Episcopal See at Dubuque, are the same regarding many other new Dioceses in the United States, therefore, it may be well to mention some of these, the better to make known the state of Catholicity in that nation. And first it must be remembered that the Bishoprics in this great Republic often extend over an area of more than hundreds of miles in length and breadth, and for this reason in the face of the expensive and most difficult journeys it becomes almost impossible for a Bishop to visit his diocese as often as the spiritual needs of the faithful would require, especially in the Western States. The communication of the Missionary Clergy with their own Ecclesiastical Superior, so greatly to be desired and sometimes so indispensable, is too often prevented by the great distance, to the disadvantage of the Priests and their flocks as well. In 1836 out of twelve Dioceses, there was but one, that of Cincinnati, which did not extend outside the boundaries of its own State. Now, however, over twenty-six States and three Territories, twenty-one Bishops rule, fifteen of whose dioceses are limited by the boundaries of the states wherein they are situated. Hitherto, it has not been the number of Catholics or of inhabitants in a province that caused the creation of the greater number of these dioceses; the real cause comprises two: the very great difficulty of exercising jurisdiction and beneficent Episcopal influence over two or three States, and the desire to propagate the Faith.

That motive, however, which more than any other contributed to increase the number of dioceses was the progress that the Faith has always made by means of such distribution of the labor of the Apostolate. In truth, since the Ecclesiastical Hierarchy is a Divine Institution, we must believe that it is needed for the spreading of the Gospel; therefore where by reason of great distance, this Hierarchy becomes like something unreal, almost unfelt by members far from its centre, then, indeed, is there need to multiply bishoprics, for thus are evangelical laborers multiplied, then is piety reanimated, then is raised up a new opponent to error, and the Faith, living and luminous, makes new conquests with yet greater ardor, with swiftness, with unwearied effort. That such were the salutary effects in the United States has been openly demonstrated by the fact that in several States piety was almost extinct; and the few Catholics scattered here and there without pastors seldom gave witness to the Faith which they professed, while the sectarians, availing themselves of such a situation with all the more readiness, disseminated error, and calumny against the Church. Moreover, there was not one to teach Christian Doctrine to the tender youth, with that sincere affection inspired by Faith and assisted by human learning. In certain places where even the probability of establishing the Faith was threatened with destruction, a remedy for this misfortune was sought by having recourse to the Order of the Episcopacy. This, spite of poverty and the obstacles inseparable from a new foundation, wrought a notable change as to the diffusion of the true Faith. Missionaries appeared in an instant, so to speak; churches arose and overflowed with worshippers; the Sacraments were frequented, preaching, schools and the example of the good, gave spur and impulse to the propagation and consolidation of the Faith. Of all this, the dioceses of Dubuque, of Nashville, and various others bear witness. Moved by these happy results, the Fathers of the Council of Baltimore, celebrated in 1845, petitioned the Holy Father to create five new bishoprics and one vicariate apostolic, and there is not the slightest doubt that their number will continue to increase by the subdivision of the present dioceses, according to the extent of their territory or number of their population; and the original design will not have failed, but will ever more inspire and increase the number of the devout.

The geographical extent of the country and the spiritual good resulting, are not the only reasons in favor of foundations of bishoprics in the United States; the facility with which church property is acquired is also an object of the greatest importance in connection with the temporal welfare of the Church, and depends in great measure upon the Episcopate. Now the reader must bear in mind that land is always secured more or less readily in proportion to the number of inhabitants in a country, so in the vicinity of newly settled towns, property necessary for the building and supporting all kinds of Religious institutions can readily be secured. On the other hand, the endeavor to secure land in States already settled and in large cities, finds everything very costly, and in general absorbs not only all means at hand but may even put the clergy under most hazardous responsibilities. The cause of Religion has much to suffer by reason of its restrictions and the want of assistance in the labor of diffusing the light of Truth among the people, through the medium of its sacred and literary institutions, and whenever the undertaking is deferred too long, the increase great expense and anxieties often too heavily overburden it.

The clergy, scattered here and there is States that are sparsely settled, with no certain and permanent abiding-place, are seldom able to secure either in growing cities or in the country places, those funds which could one day become of the greatest utility in the Propagation of the Faith. Small sums judiciously invested in the acquisition of Church property, though of little or no use for a few years, in the course of time might become necessary and valuable. As the population spreads and increases in the places near civilization, in exactly the same ratio does the need of Churches, schools, colleges and seminaries, etc., in such cases delay to provide the funds needed is only exposing one's self to the inevitable result of paying a price too great number and means of the Catholics of the place. Experience of many years has taught the Missionary that in the West, this is the invariable condition of all the new cities of any importance, and also of various rich and desirable places in the country.

The Bishops in the United States, since they hold nearly all the Church properly, are naturally under a greater obligation to secure it for the service of Religion; and in order to avoid heavy expenses, are induced to provide for the future by acquiring the necessary lands, while they are being offered at low prices. When this zeal for the glory and honor of God's House animates that soul endowed with experience and supreme disinterestedness, which occupies the Episcopal chair, then imperceptibly but surely in the course of a few years, does the Catholic Church come into possession of the means wherewith to win yet further victories. If a Bishop of a new Diocese was able to do nothing more than to prepare the way for Religion by the acquisition of Church property, he would accomplish a great work, and would deserve the esteem and veneration of his successors. In this respect the Diocese of Dubuque is happily provided for; within a few years she has secured possession of valuable land in all the young cities.

But even aside from the subject of securing means of support for Church purposes, the formation of Bishoprics in the United States hinders the diffusion of error and of calumnies against the Faith, especially in places where the people are few in number and at a distance from the Catholic Clergy. The ministers and various denominations not seldom take advantage of these circumstances to publish everything that malice has invented, in order to keep simple souls in the false principles of a Protestant education. The impulse that Truth receives from a zealous Prelate enervates the enemy of the Church and as it were, lops off the yet weak roots of so many prejudices, which strengthening and growing with the nation's growth, threaten to produce the saddest results upon a nation in its infancy. Humanly speaking, it might be asserted that in the new Territories or Western States, the outcome of the great struggle between Truth and Error depends in great measure upon which of the two, first holds possession and influence; and it would not be far from the truth to say that the same good or evil consequences that result from good or bad training in the case of a child, follow in the case of the young nation. From this one may infer the supreme importance of laying in the new provinces, however thinly settled, a solid foundation for Religion, that is the Episcopate.

As, however, the majority of the people's votes in the Republic elect the legislators of each State, and those of the general Government, it follows that the political influence of the Catholics is not to be despised in the defense of their Religious rights, when these are in any way violated through the hatred of their adversaries. In any part of the country, but more especially in the West, an Episcopal See never fails to exercise a beneficent influence upon popular opinion in all that regards the rights of conscience and the obligation of submitting to the civil law, so long as it does not oppose the Law of God. In a Government truly Republican, the Catholic Clergy well organized within the limits of its own spiritual authority and in obedience to its Bishop, commands the respect, the reverence and the deference of the laws themselves, because these are made by the legislators chosen by the people. Gaining the good-will and esteem of the people is equivalent, generally speaking, to gaining that of the legislators and the laws; a good clergy scattered over vast regions, and united in accord with their Bishop, constitutes a body sufficiently efficacious in the face of the governing authorities of the State which contains the diocese. How far the esteem and good-will of the Chief Magistrate could assist in the propagation of the Faith, is a subject not easy to advert to in this article, nor would it always be prudent to treat of it deliberately; it suffices here to know that the good opinion of those outside the Church in all civil associations offers a broad path to the preaching of the Gospel in public as well as in private.

From this brief digression it is evident that the extent of the country, the progress of Religion, the acquisition of Church property, the opportune antidote to error, the advantage of useful political influence can be considered as very grave reasons for the creation of new Bishoprics in the great Republic of America.

But you will say, how to provide for the dignity of surroundings due to a prelate,—for the expenses of a cathedral, for a suitable residence for a bishop, for a seminary? In a country where the majority of the people are living in the blindness of many false systems of Religion, the Church may be considered in the same position as in the time of the Apostles, when the first Bishops were as zealous and active parish Priests; in such case what suffices for the Priest suffices for the Bishop. This is the actual condition of almost all the American Bishoprics. And happy are they who for the propagation of the Gospel, are by the force of circumstances, deprived of the exterior tokens of honor and respect due to their dignity, while they are themselves bearing all the toils of their position. If during the persecutions in the first centuries there were Bishops without cathedrals, habitations or seminaries, why not the same in our day, wherever these cannot be had? Piety, zeal, disinterestedness and perseverance in the Prelate have ever built the cathedrals, the seminaries, and everything that conduces to the salvation of souls. To him in particular was this word of our Redeemer addressed:

"I have chosen you and have appointed you, that you should go, and should bring forth fruit; and your fruit should remain." (John XV, 16.)

Chapter XIV.

HINTS ON A FEW HARDSHIPS ON THE MISSIONS.

The summer and the autumn of 1838 were spent by the Priest in visiting, preaching and administering the Sacraments throughout the various newly formed parishes in the territories of Iowa and Wisconsin and the State of Illinois. The Catholics found themselves surrounded by many Protestant ministers who while organizing their own congregations, never forgot to accuse the Church of error and superstition; a Calvinistic minister, a Methodist and an Anglican were all settled in Galena and preaching to their own sects there; a Methodist, a Calvinistic and a Baptist were doing the same in Dubuque; and in the neighborhood of both these principal places there was a yet greater number of preachers of different sects. The Missionary, alone as he was, found himself unable to satisfy the desires of all his congregations, who would have wished to receive the same attention from their Priest that the ministers bestowed upon their own followers. For this reason until April 1839, he was obliged to divide his time among his many missions, — passing from one point to another as circumstances permitted.

The mode of traveling is on horseback, carrying in a valise the article indispensable to the celebration of the Holy Sacrifice, which formed a quite heavy burden. At the time, the Mission extended than two hundred miles along the Mississippi River and from thirty to fifty miles to the east, as many to the west of the River, — and counted not less than three thousand five hundred Catholics, of whom the greater number were of Irish descent, with many French and a number of German and American nationality; the roads although only bridle or wagon paths made by the passing to and fro of the settlers were passable enough in summer for a traveller on horseback, but exceedingly bad in the spring when the frozen earth thawed and the little streams now swollen by rains or heavy snowfalls melting, often completely hindered travelling. Among the Indians one had to be satisfied with a lodging in a wigwam of mats and sleeping a best one could wrapped in a blanket without a bed, but in the section above mentioned near the Mississippi, some habitation could always be found wherein to pass the night. But a house here consists of one or perhaps two rooms roughly built of logs laid one upon another, the whole covered with bark of shingles; these habitations of the first settlers might rather be called huts, often without window or floor, yet they often served the Missionary as shelter and even as Church. The houses in this part of the country are much larger and more commodious; the increased number of settlers coming from many quarters of the world has so changed and improved conditions that it no longer seems the rude country of seven or eight years ago. Custom and hospitality, or rather necessity, makes one forget the restrictions and the extreme poverty of those dwellings in which they cooked their food, slept, ate their meals from the same table which had served as an Altar, where also the Priest had preached, had heard Confessions and had administered the other Sacraments. There is no doubt that the Christian Religion was propagated primarily in the midst of poverty, and was born, as it were, in the cabins of the poor, for rarely were the rich among the first who submitted to the doctrine of a God-made man for us, born in a lowly manger.

Our Saviour said to His Apostle: "Be not solicitous, therefore, saying: What shall we eat; or what shall we drink, or wherewith shall we be clothed?" (Matt. VI, 31). In fact, even in the most remote places the Missionary found the necessaries of life without trouble. Sometimes Almighty God puts to the proof the confidence of him who trust His Providence, — permitting him no other food than that of the poorest sufferer, even the crust too scanty to allay his hunger. But how sweet is that very Hand of the Lord's Justice when it chastises us for our faults! The assurance that everything happens because God Himself wills it for the sake of spreading His Faith, gives to the poorest food the most delicious taste, and its scantiness becomes the price of the penalty due to sin and the pledge of the magnificence of that celestial Banquet that awaits us made ready in Paradise.

At times during the many years of missionary life, the particular circumstances of a family, or the lack of money on the part of the Priest, constrained him to sit at table with persons not alone poor, but the coarsest, roughest, worst of men, and what was especially repugnant to pride of heart, to eat their food an alms given him in charity. One who is not of ignoble birth, and who knows that his training and ecclesiastical career deserve consideration, is strongly tempted on such occasions to consider it too great a humiliation. And then Faith recalls to mind Jesus in the company and at the table of sinners; the Vow of Poverty which the Religious has professed, extinguishes in the depths of his heart the secret rebellion of pride, and he is forced to reflect that eating the bread of charity is a fitting thing for him who professes to be poor like his Divine Master. The poverty of the table should never be held as reason for changing one abode in search for a better; for this would be setting at nought the counsel of Christ to His Apostles: "And in the same house remain, eating and drinking such things as they have. Remove not from house to house. Eat such things as are set before you." (Luke X, 7, 8).

Generally speaking, on the missions, there is much kindness shown not only by Catholics but by Protestant as well, who supply with abundance the corporal needs of a zealous and disinterested Priest. Whenever he has to suffer any inconveniences on this score, he should thank the Divine Bounty that renders him worthy to participate in the trials inseparable from the preaching of the Gospel. Hunger, thirst, cold, heat, all the weariness and perils of travel, poverty, contempt, obloquy, and many humiliations are in very deed the glory and true merit of a Missionary, for Saint Paul says: "We glory also in tribulations knowing that tribulation worketh patience." (Rom. V, 3).

Chapter XV.

MISSIONS IN WISCONSIN IN FEBRUARY 1838—THE PRIEST LODGING IN THE CHURCH.

In spite of illness lasting about three weeks of January, 1838, in the next February, the Priest visited for nearly a month the many Catholics dispersed throughout the Territory of Wisconsin, their spiritual need calling for assistance. Gratiot Grove, New Diggings, Mineral Point, Dodgeville and Diamond Grove were the principal Stations, where in the houses of certain persons, Mass was celebrated. Preaching was carried on and many of the faithful received the Sacrament of the Eucharist. The Protestants of the neighborhood, through curiosity or through a sincere desire to understand the Catholic Religion, were accustomed to assist at Divine Service. It would have been of immense assistance to the cause of Religion if in that year he could have been able to set about building some kind of a Church, to put an end to the vast inconveniences of celebrating the Holy Sacrifice and administering the Sacraments in the little houses of the people. But where were the means to be found for such an undertaking? Or how divide his time among places so far away from his own congregations? For besides, there was but one lone Priest, and Churches so far distant from one another could not have been often in use. Yet although then it appeared an impossibility, he never gave up the hope of carrying out such a plan.

In preceding chapters mention has been made that in the spring and autumn, the Missionary had been obliged to go down the River about five hundred miles to Saint Louis, in order to make his Confession; he made this penitential journey for the last time in the April of 1838, as in the next autumn he had a visit from a Priest, and a year afterward came Monsignore Loras, with two Missionaries. The new City of Davenport in the Territory of Iowa, had not been forgotten by the Missionary on the occasion of his return from this journey, and he preached there many times to a hundred or so of Catholics in the new Church not yet entirely finished.

To give some idea of how the Priest on the Missions must be content with little, wherever by reason of poverty, he has no house of his own, we will here say a word about his lodging. While traveling, as has been said, he may sometimes find a decent place and a bed; and sometimes God wills that he be contented with a hut and the bare ground. But whenever he finds himself in a village without a Church, or is occupied in building one, he makes his abode in a Catholic family, to whom if it exacted, a certain amount is paid. But lodging with seculars should always be avoided, if in any way possible, on account of the little annoyances to which it subjects the Missionary as well as the people, who may desire to have free access to him without the necessity of troubling or putting themselves under obligations to a third party. During the autumn of 1836, when the Church at Dubuque was under cover, the Priest immediately took possession of a little room under the Sanctuary and this served as a chapel in winter, although it hd the bare earth for a floor and the walls were unplastered, which gave it the appearance of a cellar rather than a habitable place, but it served as a dwelling for more than two years. At Galena for the same space of time before the Church was finished, the Missionary abode in the little wooden Chapel, where on one side of the Altar he had his little cot hidden away in a tiny closet whose dimensions were six feet by five, while on the opposite side of the Altar was a Confessional; the body of the little chapel was used as a study and reception room. One who has not had the opportunity of living in the Church and sleeping near the Altar cannot readily imagine all its advantages, the grandest of which is the honor and privilege of abiding in common, in the same room with that Lord and Redeemer Whose delight is to be with the children of men. His Presence alone infinitely surpasses the grandeur and glories of the palaces of kings of earth.

Chapter XVI.

THE PRIEST IN PERIL OF HIS LIFE ON THE MISSISSIPPI RIVER, IN MARCH 1838.

During the course of many years, various were the perils to which the Missionary's life was exposed, but that which happened to him in the month of March 1838, was worthy of special mention. By his office as a Priest, he was obliged to cross the great River Mississippi from the State of Illinois to Iowa Territory where a sick man awaited his ministrations. He found that the ice no longer formed a solid support but, broken up by the change of temperature and by the wind, was carried along with the current.

Often during the spring this river is found in such a condition on account of its great length and many tributaries, so that many persons cross in little skiffs in spite of the drifting ice. The Priest with four other travelers found no other means of transport than a sort of narrow canoe, hollowed out of a single trunk of a tree, which had been left lying on the bank all the last winter; when launched they all embarked without discovering that the old boat had several open cracks along the sides. After pushing out almost half a mile across the River, the water began to pour in, and such was the fear of one of the sailors that he was pale and trembling. The steersman, however, experienced as he was, courageously managed the frail vessel, ordering those who were seated to keep perfectly motionless, "or else," he said, "we are all lost." The Priest alone remained kneeling and paddling with a single oar while the steersman gave orders to hasten his strokes.

But how comforting is the true Faith when in imminent peril of life! The Priest of the Altar on that occasion bearing with him Jesus in the Blessed Sacrament, had no great cause for fear, and as he found himself in the same peril as that which tried the Faith of the Apostles, when the tempest surprised them on Lake Genesareth, he cried out from the depths of his heart in their own words: "Master, we perish!" (Luke, VIII, 24.) A fixed sense of security in the Presence of the Veiled Divinity lying hidden upon his breast, gave no room for fear or doubt of reaching the shore. Nevertheless, the drifting ice fully a foot and a half in thickness, and in masses of enormous size, increased the peril not a little, for it one of these had struck the old log, it would assuredly have sent it to the bottom; we were compelled to turn from the course often to avoid this. The four passengers were already sitting in the icy water; the Priest and the steersman were kneeling in the water, for the rim of the old canoe was only four fingers length out of water, when thanks to God, we reached an island, and landing, every countenance showed thankfulness and joy. Then the steersman declared that as often as he had crossed that river in the most dangerous weather, he had never been so near death; adding that they had come across safe because they had had Faith rowing the boat and Perseverance at the stern guiding it; that is, the Missionary and himself.

The passengers, not being Catholics, knew not that they owed their lives to the Presence of that Omnipotent God who crossed with them under the humble guise of the Sacrament of the Eucharist.

Chapter XVII.

THE BUILDING OF THE CHURCH AT GALENA IS RESUMED—SALUTARY EFFECTS OF DISINTERESTEDNESS IN A PRIEST WHO IS ON THE MISSIONS.

The most important duties of the Missionary during the summer of 1838 were raising the walls of Saint Michael's Church in Galena, and caring for a very great number of sick persons. For want of means and also of necessary time, this Church had been neglected during the last year, with the hope that the Bishop-Elect of Dubuque would have celebrated his installation during that time; but he had been detained in Europe, and the Priest thought it necessary to set about the work notwithstanding his isolated position and the fact of having no companion in the ministry. Let the reader imagine a work costing at the least one hundred dollars a week, paid for with voluntary contributions collected by the Priest during the course of that same week. He was obliged to be architect, superintendent, financier and what was worse than all, collector; God alone knows the anxieties, the bitterness, the toils necessitated by such an undertaking, one which would have been a deed of consummate imprudence not to say a sin, under any other circumstances. The pressing need of a place of worship for a great number of the faithful prevented from assisting at Mass on account of the narrow limits of the little frame building used as chapel, was the sole reason that could by any possibility excuse the culpable temerity which dominated and held itself responsible for the whole expense. Many times during the course of the same, the work was interrupted for want of means to pay the day laborers; finally, and not without a heavy debt, the walls were raised and the building under roof before winter, but not till the next year was the building in a state to be of service to the people.

The amount expended up to this time exceeded seven thousand

dollars, none of which was contributed outside of the parish. From this fact someone might conclude that the parish must be rich to furnish such a sum; but it was not the wealth of parishioners, it was the expenditure of time, joined to economy, to tireless perseverance, to disinterestedness, and above all, to good will, which brought about so happy a result. About one thousand dollars were contributed by the people in labor and in materials; the rest was the result of the remarkable generosity of the Irish people especially, for the space of three years. Few of these were in easy circumstances, but nearly all earned enough for the bare necessities of life, by indefatigable labor in the lead mines which abounded in the district. Even the Protestants, animated by praiseworthy religious sentiments, or perhaps by human motives, contributed to the building of the Catholic Church.

It may be well to remark that the generosity of the faithful in these parts depends in great measure upon the disinterestedness of the Priest. If he manifests any desire for money, then all is lost for the Church, for he is the sole agent, secretary and treasurer. If he does not divest himself completely of self, and consecrate himself without one reservation to the propagation of the Truth, that indispensable boundless confidence of his people loses itself in doubts and suspicions and at last, vanishes utterly. The building of Churches in the western parts of the United States is not the work of the Government, of a powerful family, of a bequest, or of a corporation, as is the case in Europe or some of the large cities of America but solely of the Missionary who with industry and zeal hopes to receive from the people alms sufficient to pay for its erection. From this it is plain that reproach of Saint Paul: "For all seek things that are their own, not the things of Jesus Christ" (Phil. II, 21), would be incurred by him who would resolve not to build unless circumstances were extraordinary and favorable, for that would deprive him of all merit. His vocation should lead him far from seeking the comforts of this life, much less the goods of earth, which would render him unworthy of the sublimity of his Ministry.

The great secret, therefore, for finding money where it does not seem to exist, and to give it so speak, a marvellous existence, lies in the sincere disinterestedness of the Priest. In our case this virtue exacts that he be miserly towards himself, that is, in the matter of raiment and dwelling-place, that his requirements be reduced to what is barely necessary to his state, and no more; if he can receive support under the name of charity, it is of the highest importance to humble himself to the spontaneous courtesy of him who offers it. On journeys, economy that a Missionary should scruple to expend the smallest sum on things that have nought to do with his calling; for instance, in little trips for amusement, in curiosities, in objects of luxury and the like.

Example contributes more than anything else here mentioned to excite the generosity of the faithful towards the Temple of God. It would be of the very greatest advantage to one occupied in spreading the Faith, if he were bound by the Vow of Poverty, for a life immersed in business matters insensibly leads one to the possession of some personal means and this is almost always an occasion of coldness in the sacred ministry and serves as a false excuse on the part of Catholics for not ministering to the needs of the Altar. Our Saviour has told us to give of our abundance to the poor; he Missionary more than any other man in the world should despoil himself of all thing, even of himself, and make it a grateful sacrifice to his vocation. Now in the United States the church is generally the poorest of the poor, for either one must be built, or it is in debt, or else it requires repairs or necessary furnishings for the altar; so if the Priest desires to see the people liberal and full of confidence in his personality, he must himself lead the way, keeping nothing for himself and putting everything that he possesses in the treasury of the Church. The same Providence that cared for him in the past will not fail him in the future; forever true are those words of our Divine Master: "When I sent you without purse and scrip and shoes, did you want anything?" (Luke XXII, 35.)

Certain it is that this generous detachment and his voluntary privation are of the same importance in every place, nor can they be said to exist always even among Missionaries; but it cannot be denied that it is the true virtue and true riches of many among them. The wondrous effects of this spoliation of self in order to adorn the Church are principally an unbounded confidence, love, veneration, generosity, and obedience on the part of the people, even the Protestants; on the part of the Priest, zeal, evangelical liberty, activity, personal usefulness towards society.

Religion, therefore, through disinterestedness shines forth more beautiful, more beneficent, more holy. Experience has given certain proof of these truths.

Chapter XVIII.

SERVING THE SICK, IN 1838.

In the year 1838, the State of Illinois employed many hundreds of laborers in the construction of a railroad from Galena to the junction of the Ohio River with the Mississippi, that is, crossing the entire State from its northern to its southern boundary line, measuring more than four hundred miles in length. This great work was barely commenced, discontinued for want of funds, and left the State in debt for millions of dollars, and with no railroad. The majority of the laborers in and near Galena were Irish and German Catholics, as these generally perform the most laborious works of the nation. Unfortunately this year an intermittent fever broke out by which many were stricken even unto death. It was maintained that the principal cause of this disease was the high water in the Mississippi, which during the summer flooded the numerous islands and a considerable extent of the low lands lying along the banks; when the waters subsided in the month of August, the vegetation had decayed and was causing a most offensive odor throughout the atmosphere. Whatever was the cause, there were persons down with the fever in almost every house, and within two or three months no fewer than one hundred and fifty people died.

The Missionary was called every hour of the day and night to visit the sick, often to a distance of ten, twenty or thirty miles from his dwelling. Remarkable were the circumstances of the death of one man, a Catholic, who was unfortunately addicted to drunkenness, and who died without receiving the last Sacraments. This man had heard a few weeks before a sermon upon the necessity of being converted to God and doing penance; impressed by the announcement of the terrible of God upon the impenitent, he promised the Priest that he would go to Confession the first time he went to the city. Instead of being faithful to his promise, on coming to the city he became intoxicated and gave public scandal; on his return to the place where he had been working, about fifteen miles distant, he fell sick, sent for the Priest, but although the latter rode at his utmost speed on a fleet horse, it was too late; he found the poor man dead. Behold how the words of the Gospel upon obstinate back-sliders are verified to the letter; of these did our Lord prophesy when He said: "I go, and you shall seek Me, and you shall die in your sin." (John VIII, 21.)

During this dangerous epidemic, in his visits to the sick, the Priest was obliged to be fortified at all times with the Blessed Sacrament for the dying, to whom he was often summoned while passing by the public works. The houses temporarily erected for reception of the poor laborers, consisted of one room of planks in which slept thirty or forty of them, so destitute of help that there is no doubt that many died of want. Great was the consolation to find in many of the poor dying upon the straw, abandoned by the whole world, and in direst misery, to find, I repeat, a singular piety, fruit of a Christian life. Who could express the spiritual unction that consoled those souls when unexpectedly they saw a Priest beside them to whom they might make their last Confession, from whom receive the Most Holy Viaticum and Extreme Unction? Truly doth God know His own, nor doth He forget them in the perilous moment of their passage to Eternity; when all else fails, He never fails one who hopes in His Infinite Goodness and Mercy. On one of these occasions the Missionary divided among four dying persons the last Consecrated Particle left to him.

In these countries, the Viaticum is carried in a small case of silver-gilt which is hung around the Priest's neck and hidden beneath the exterior garment; in this manner has the Missionary often borne with him for days and many nights the most Adorable Mystery of our Faith. Such a device becomes necessary here in order not to expose the Holy of Holies to the contempt of so many unbelievers,—the same motive which led the primitive Christians not to reveal in public to the Pagans the doctrine and knowledge of the Holy Eucharist of which they preserved a profound secrecy.

PART TWO

Chapter XIX.

THE TERRITORY OF IOWA WAS ORGANIZED IN 1838—ITS PEOPLE, PRODUCTS, CLIMATE AND CITIES.

In Chapter VIII it was seen that through an Act of Congress of the United States, the Territory of Wisconsin was separated from that of Michigan and organized in 1836; two years later, by the same Congress, that part of Wisconsin to the west of the Mississippi, was made a Territory by itself in the same way, and named Iowa from the name of the beautiful river on which its capital city is now built. These lands extend from latitude 40.5°E to 49°E, and comprise about six degrees of longitude; on the east the waters of the great Mississippi bathe the boundary of the new Territory for more than a thousand miles; the Missouri River washes the western boundary; the Province of Canada on the north, and the State of Missouri on the south border this great Territory of Iowa.

When it was erected into a Territorial Government in 1838, it contained only eighteen thousand inhabitants; it had about six million acres of land along the Mississippi, the right over which the Indians by various treaties had ceded to the Republic. So great was the emigration to that Territory, that according to the census taken by Government in July 1840, Iowa contained forty-three thousand inhabitants, having received twenty-five thousand from 1838 to the middle of 1840, while almost as many more entered the Territory before 1843, so that, at present, the population is about seventy thousand. In 1843 by a treaty with the savages, the United States purchased eleven million acres in Iowa, which, together with the six million already in possession, would make twenty-six thousands, five hundred and sixty-two square miles, counting six hundred and forty acres to the square mile, but the extent of the Territory has been calculated as containing nine hundred and fifty thousand square miles; so that the lands of this immense section thus far occupied do not count a thirtieth part of its extent.

It would be difficult to give a correct estimate of the number of

Indians who still hold possession here; the principal tribes live in the northern part, that is, the Chippewas and Sioux; there are also a number of Winnebagoes from Wisconsin, Sacs, Foxes, Iowas and other tribes. All together, they number about fifty thousand Indians.

The Government will deal with them as they have been dealt with in all the western States of the American Union; that is, it will gradually acquire the ownership of their lands and give them in exchange, money or merchandise. In less than ten years, the southern part of Iowa will find itself entirely without Indian occupants; in the northern portion, because of the more severe climate and vast prairies, they may probably continue to live there during the next half century.

The land of this Territory is very fertile, especially towards the south; every species of grain can be cultivated there, domestic animals find rich pasturage for seven months of the year in the vast prairie lands. But no fruit bearing trees are native there, and those transplanted from other countries rarely come to maturity; the apple is the only fruit that seems to suit the soil and climate of Iowa, especially in the upper part of the state.

Near the rivers are large forests from ten to twenty miles in breadth; the settlers set much value on the forests, because the prairies constitute the greater part of the Territory, while this timber is used not only for fuel, but for building houses also and making fences around their cultivated fields. The rivers navigable for steamboats, are chiefly the Mississippi, the Missouri, the Iowa, the Des Moines, the Saint Peter, and some others of lesser importance. The climate is much colder than in Europe under the same latitude; from the month of November to the end of March the thermometer generally keeps below the freezing point, and in the depth of winter falls often to twenty or even thirty degrees below in the more northern sections of the country. Snow covers the ground for about three months and the rivers are frozen over so completely as to serve during the winter as the most solid of pavements, not only for men but for draught animals also, so that journeys of hundreds of miles are made upon their frozen waters. The months of June, July and August are quite hot but upon the immensity of the great natural plains, ordinarily even in summer, one enjoys a refreshing breeze.

The principal cities of Iowa are situated upon the Mississippi River, as Burlington, Dubuque, Davenport, Bloomington, Fort Madison and Iowa City in the interior, which last is now the capital of the Territory; the number of inhabitants in each of these varies from one to two thousand. There are also very many other little cities rising along the principal rivers and in the interior also, which will be important in the course of a few years for the business activity and population. The principal products of Iowa are the lead from the Dubuque Mines, wheat, Indian corn, potatoes and principally pork, which salted in barrels is exported to other countries. In the spring of 1834 the merchants of the city of Burlington despatched in this manner by their steamboats more than thirty thousand hogs raised by the farmers.

Chapter XX.

HOW THE GOVERNMENT OF THE UNITED STATES CAME INTO POSSESSION OF THE IMMENSE COUNTRIES ONCE INHABITED BY INDIAN TRIBES.

The fact of seventy thousand settlers within the course of ten years, crossing the Mississippi in order to find homes in the region of the vast territory of Iowa bordering the River, where, before this, the Indian tribes had been dwelling, must of its nature, excite in the reader of these Memoirs the wish to know in what manner the Government of the Republic obtained possession of these regions to the exclusion of the Indians. A few words will suffice to throw light upon such an acquisition of new land, to which must be attributed the surprising and exceedingly great emigration of settlers towards the West.

While the United States were English colonies, they contained less than three million inhabitants and held possessions of the lands along the coast of the Atlantic Ocean; the rest of that part of North America was in peaceable possession of numerous tribes many of whom are now extinct. After the establishment of the Republic, the emigration from Europe increased to such an extent that it became necessary to seek new countries whereon to locate, and then was inaugurated that system of treaties between the Government and the savage bands, by means of which the former got possession of the lands occupied by the latter. In this manner were formed all the Central and Western States, which up to the present century had been in a state of nature, with a few villages inhabited by aborigines to be found here and there, at great distances from one another.

Although the colonists had desired the civilization of the natives, they were not willing to sacrifice their own interests on that account, so they kept moving forward to cultivate the most fertile lands and most beautiful sites or most healthful positions along the great River. The traders greedy for gain introduced that traffic by which the simple native could never have any advantage but was a victim of one more wary than he, and one whose bad example taught him evil ways. From all this it was plain that the European and the native American could not live together peaceably, both their interests and their characters are so widely different and so completely irreconcilable. This state of affairs compelled the Government to demand sometimes from one tribe, sometimes from another, possession of a tract usually contained between two rivers and embracing many millions of acres. The Indians then would withdraw to other sections farther away, over which either they or the Government held possession,—but whenever for different causes this was found impracticable, the whole of the tribe or perhaps a part of it was left on a portion of the land which they had occupied, although surrounded on all sides by European settlers.

The geographical position of many Indians tribes deserves special attention of the reader. The tract of land thus set apart, is called in the United States an "Indian Reservation," that is, "riserba indiana" because reserved for their special use and independent of the Government, like all the lands of the Indians. Those who have lived upon the Reservation many years, have learned a little English and some small knowledge of Religion; at the same time, from the vicinity of the civilized people and constant intercourse with them they have become amalgamated with them to a great extent, so that they are no longer of pure Indian race. This is evident from the color of the skin which has changed from dark red to sallow white. Many of these remnants of tribes have adopted in a measure the customs of the civilized people, but have never reached such a degree but that the most superficial observer can recognize how inferior in all things they are to the European, and how incapable of real civilization. Their small progress is ever and always accompanied by a moral descent and it is an ever present fact that they have invariably degenerated from that simplicity, innocence and good faith which distinguish those who inhabit districts farthest away from civilization.

But to return to our subject, it will be observed that the Republic recognizes the right of possession by these many tribes over the lands where they live, although the vast extent of these lands is out of all proportion to the number of individuals who compose these tribes. The precise limits of the territory belonging to each are often undetermined. An actual sale, however, seems sometimes to decide these geographical uncertainties. On the borders of the States, the tribes usually hold less extensive possessions than those of the more distant tribes, and on this account, the Government secures from these last the right over immense tracts or the privilege of placing other people there. There are many who believe that the aborigines have no real right to the soil beyond what is necessary to their support and adapted to their manner of living, but others consider the Indians as the first lawful possessors of the entire country.

Any sale whatever that might be made by the natives to a foreign Government or to an individual, even an American, is held as null and void by the Republic, for she alone is recognized by conquest as mistress of all the countries between the boundaries of Canada and Mexico.

Whenever it is found necessary to purchase the proprietorship of a tribe over a part of the country, the Government authorizes certain individuals to assemble the chiefs who gathered in Council, listen in grave silence to the proposal made by the Commissioners; they then consult among themselves, and if they consider it advisable to accept the proposal without conditions, the matter is speedily settled; but in case they offer objections regarding the place or the extent of land desired by the Government, or if any matter regarding the proffered price displeases them, then delays and hot disputes follow until the parties come to an amicable agreement. The contracts of sale are written in

English and translated by an interpreter to the chiefs, and these in the presence of several witnesses affix a mark, each after his own name which has already been written down by a notary. Such treaties are of no value, however, until the legislative body of the Government assembled in the City of Washington has given thereto its lawful and final sanction.

In price for the lands, the Indians usually receive an annual sum of many millions of dollars (American) for a given period according to the extent and quality of the land sold, the value of which varies from five cents to one dollar per acre. But there is seldom a certainty as to the precise number of acres estimated in a sale, for the reason that these are for the most part lands of which little is known, and nearly all lying between rivers whose course has not yet been exactly ascertained, so an approximate value is agreed upon. The payments are made once a year by Government officials at some post convenient for the Indians; the heads of families receive a certain number of dollars in proportion to the total annual amount and according to the number of individuals who compose the tribe and of the family so represented by their respective heads. But this is not the only arrangement for all treaties; there are material differences both as to the manner and the matter of payments; these consist often of part in money and part in goods and provisions distributed among the Indians as is most convenient, besides pecuniary allotments for the education of their children.

The removal of a tribe to a new abode does not take place immediately after the sale but is deferred for one or two and even for five years. It may here be remarked that the money, the leaving one's native soil, the traveling to another land, and the circumstances of new surroundings are always accompanied by dissipation, disease, and various calamities which before our very eyes lessen the numbers of the Indians, who are leaving the county to the numberless civilized nations coming from the States and from Europe, destined to overspread that vast continent and to behold the entire destruction of the tribes.

PART TWO

Chapter XXI.

FIRST FOUNDATION OF CATHOLICITY AT SNAKE HOLLOW NOW POTOSI — THE CHURCH OF SAINT THOMAS IS BUILT HERE.

As a portion of these Memoirs may be of use one day as assistance in the history of the Diocese of Milwaukee, which comprehends the Territory of Wisconsin, it will not be out of place here to make mention of the first establishment of the Catholic Church in the place called in English, Snake Hollow, that is in Italian, *Scavi del serpente*.

About fifteen miles from the southern boundary line of Wisconsin, there is a valley three miles in length, terminating at the Mississippi River. During the War with the Indians in 1832, a cave was discovered here containing a great number of rattlesnakes; on this account when they began to dig there in search of lead, the place was called Snake Hollow. The Lead Mines in this part of the Territory being very rich, many flocked there in search of the precious metal, and in this manner many settlements were made in the valley under various names; the principal one at present where trade is centered is called Potosi, situated about three miles from the River.

It was in July 1838, that the Missionary made his way to Snake Hollow, celebrated the Holy Sacrifice of the Altar there for the first time in a poor little house, and preached the word of Truth. Notwithstanding the small number of Catholics, not more than one hundred and fifty, he decided to build a little frame Church. During that year the ground and nearly all materials necessary were made ready; so the next year, though not without much difficulty, they succeeded in putting the House of God in such condition that Mass could be there celebrated. The little Church was dedicated to Saint Thomas, the Apostle. To administer the holy Sacraments, to give instructions to the people, to lay the foundations of a parish, and to obtain from the faithful the means needed for the building of the Church, many were the visits during 1838 and 1839 made by the Priest to Potosi, which was only twenty-four miles from Galena. The Right Reverend Bishop Loras, after arriving at

Dubuque, visited the faithful of this district many times and sent a Priest there regularly twice a month until 1841, at which time the Reverend James Causse, a Frenchman by birth, was appointed Pastor. The congregation then counted five hundred souls. The Chapel cannot hold them, and a larger one will be built as soon as possible. There were several conversions of Protestants to the Catholic Faith, notwithstanding the great zeal of the Methodists and other sectarians.

There are two happy results following the establishment of a little Chapel in the new towns of sections in the United States that are just settled; the first is, that many Catholics are prevented from losing the practice of their holy Religion, by offering them at least now and then an opportunity of assisting at the celebration of the holy Mysteries and of hearing the Word of God, all of which cannot well be done in the small dwellings of the poor people; the cannot is that the Catholics who settle in new countries usually prefer the vicinity of a Church in order to avoid the great risk of losing the Faith when they see themselves deprived of Religious succor. Thus the Church becomes an important central point for the immigration of people, and not seldom is it the seed of cities or the chief cause why the settlers in its vicinity are all or nearly all Catholics.

Chapter XXII.

THE MISSION: ITS CONDITION PREVIOUS TO THE ARRIVAL OF THE BISHOP OF DUBUQUE IN 1839.

The progress which holy Religion had made in the Missions up to this time did not consist in conversions of sectarians, but in the improvement in the lives of the Catholics. The conversion of Protestants to the Faith is a labor much more difficult than that of persuading obstinate sinners to repentance; the former deprived of Faith, are found less able to give up the evil and practice the good, while the latter have only to rekindle with good will that Faith that is dead within them. Some, ever ready to believe that every marvel takes place on the Missions, imagine the conversion of Protestants to be a matter of daily occurrence, and the principal occupation of Priest in the sparsely settled parts of the United States, to be instructing and receiving them into the bosom of the Church. Facts, however, prove that this is only a secondary labor, for the Priest's principal mission consists not in implanting the Faith but in enkindling it and preserving it among the Catholics born in that part of the world, or those who have emigrated thither from Europe. From this circumstance, then, it follows that many, many times the good example of the faithful and the zealous preaching of the Missionary are the means which Almighty God makes use of to call many sectarians to the Unity of Religion.

Without pausing to reflect upon the truth of this widespread belief of the Mission of the Catholic Clergy, we shall content ourselves with observing that the work to which the Missionary was consecrated from the year 1835 to 1839 consisted in establishing among Catholics religious worship and the observance of the laws, both Divine and Ecclesiastical. It must be borne in mind that there were three thousand five hundred Catholics scattered over a vast expanse of country, midst a far greater number of Protestants,—without Church, without Altar, without Sacraments, without the Gospel preached to them; moreover the tender souls of the youth were exposed to the peril of being brought up in indifference towards Religion. Now let one consider the great distances between places, the coldness of those who have for a long time been living in the neglect of all Religious duties, the ignorance of Christian truths, the labor of erecting temples to the Lord, the poverty of the settlers, the many perils and difficulties of the ministry, and let him judge whether all that was not enough to occupy the time, the zeal, and the whole soul of one lone Priest, isolated from his brethren and without any exterior help whatever.

Much more important was it to the holy cause of Religion to call back to a Christian life those who through Divine Mercy had already received the Faith, rather than to turn one's energies towards one who had never known that light. Experience teaches us that the conversion of Protestants depends more upon the good example of Catholics than upon the power of reasoning.

Before the arrival of Right Reverend Bishop Loras with a few Priests, there were already three temples to the Lord wherein the Holy Sacrifice was offered; many hundreds of the faithful frequented the Holy Table; the truths of Catholic Doctrine had been the subject of very many sermons and familiar instructions in many places of the vast mission field. The people in general observed the laws of the Church; the prejudices and mistaken ideas of Protestants against the dogmas and practices of the true Religion had been overcome in part. Besides all this there was the visible improvement in the daily lives of many who had once been careless Catholics.

It is certain that the reception of the Sacraments of Baptism and of Matrimony assisted greatly to organize the various parishes. In the number of the newly baptized were five adult Protestants and many children of non-Catholic parents. Yet with all this, as will be seen later, very much more remains to be done by the evangelical laborers of our Redeemer who are destined to toil in that portion of His Church.

Chapter XXIII.

MONSIGNORE MATTHIAS LORAS ARRIVES FROM EUROPE—TAKES POSSESSION OF HIS CATHEDRAL CHURCH OF DUBUQUE AND VISITS THE CITY OF GALENA.

The worthy Prelate, Matthias Loras, consecrated Bishop of Dubuque on the tenth of December, 1837, in the Cathedral Church of the city of Mobile, State of Alabama, had prolonged his stay in Europe in this interests of his diocese until late in the year 1838. When he arrived at the city of Saint Louis, State of Missouri, distant five hundred miles from his own See by the way of the River, he was there detained by the masses of ice which even then had already formed in the northern waters of the Mississippi and was coming down in great quantities drifting on its majestic current. The Bishop had brought with him four French seminarians, whom he had placed in a Seminary in the diocese of Baltimore, that they might learn the English language; the Reverend Joseph Cretin and the Reverend Anthony Pelamourgues had also accompanied him from France in order to devote themselves to the missions of Dubuque Diocese. Notwithstanding the extreme anxiety of the Prelate to reach the place destined for him by Divine Providence, and which he had not yet seen, necessity compelled him to remain the entire winter in the Diocese of the Reverend Bishop Joseph Rosati, because on account of the severity of the season, navigation by the River was blocked until the next spring. The zeal which burned within his heart found a way there also to employ his precious time, as he was incessantly busied in the duties of his holy ministry, assisted by his learned and devoted Priest, the Reverend Joseph Cretin.

If Monsignore Loras was awaiting with holy impatience for the soft breezes of spring to open to him the way to his See, not less was the ardent longing of the Missionary, for as the only Priest in the vast Territory of Iowa, he eagerly desired to become acquainted personally with him who had been chosen to be his Prelate. With the hope of accompanying him to Dubuque for the solemnity of Easter of that year, the Priest left Galena on the nineteenth of March by the first steamboat for the city of Saint Louis, where he arrived on the twenty-third of the month. The good Bishop Rosati accompanied the Missionary on horseback for many miles to a village, where Monsignore Loras with Reverend J. Cretin were occupied in giving a Mission to the People of French descent. I leave it to the reader to form some idea here of the mutual consolation afforded be this first meeting of two, who for nearly two years loving one another in the Lord and conversing by letter, at last had the consolation of embracing and of more closely sealing that Priestly and holy friendship which has for its one aim the propagation of the Faith.

The honored and venerable Bishop of Saint Louis, who with his never-failing zeal for the holy ceremonies of the Altar was in person celebrating the solemn rites of Holy Week, desired that our Priest would assist him therein, in his Cathedral and that he would preach on Good Friday. Monsignore Loras being occupied on his Mission here until after the octave of Easter, it was not possible for him to go to Dubuque before the middle of April. On the twenty-first day of April, with all due episcopal solemnity, the Prelate took possession of his own Cathedral Church; assisting were Reverend Joseph Cretin, Reverend Anthony Pelamourgues and the Missionary who preached an appropriate discourse to the large audience of Catholics and Protestants.

To the heart of him who, since the beginning of the year 1835 until the event of the coming of the Bishop, had stood alone with the care upon him of a numerous flock scattered over a vast extent of country, did not the presence of a Bishop and two other Priests prove the greatest possible consolation? The edifying piety and zeal impressed upon their countenances on that solemn occasion, gave to the orator of the day that spontaneous and powerful eloquence which from a heart all stirred and overflowing with true joy, sank into the souls of his Christian hearers, drawing from every eye tears of loving gratitude to Almighty God, Who, to pour forth His Mercies upon them yet more abundantly, had erected a Bishop's See in their Church.

And thus after four years of isolation and privations of soul, the Missionary found himself surrounded by the sweet and edifying presence of other evangelical laborers, not to be separated from them except for the space of several months while the duties of his ministry were calling him to the remote stations of the vast diocese.

On the twenty-eighth of April, the Bishop deigned to officiate solemnly in the Church at Galena, and to give his Vicar an opportune occasion of preaching to a numerous congregation upon the divinity and nobility of the Catholic Hierarchy. The imperfect ideas held by Protestants upon such an important point arise from the fact that among them, the episcopal character is only a name and a mere distinctive mark of ecclesiastic preeminence, but deprived of that Apostolical authority to which the Catholic owes the perfect and uninterrupted organization of his Church. The Methodists, the Baptists, the Presbyterians and various other sects, to conform themselves to evangelical discipline, as they believe, have given the title of Bishop to some individuals among their ministers, who, however, do not confer the Sacraments of Confirmation or of Holy Orders, since they believe in two Sacraments only, namely, Baptism and Communion. The highest authority held by their bishops consists in superintending the good order of their churches, in presiding over religious meetings, and enjoying for the rest an unlimited jurisdiction over the ministers; in their religious functions they wear no garb which distinguishes them from lay persons, and they despise the use of Priestly robes in the Catholics.

On the occasion when Monsignore Loras was vested in Episcopal robes, many Protestants gathered to the Church, drawn thither by curiosity to see a Catholic Bishop. The Missionary who was well acquainted with the character of this people, spoke then upon the Divine establishment of the Catholic Hierarchy, adducing convincing proofs from both the Old and the New Testament, of the Heaven-appointed decrees upon that important dogma of the Church. To dispel the frivolous objections of the sectarians against the use of episcopal insignia, he commented upon that portion of the forty-fifth chapter of Ecclesiasticus, where the holy scribe speaks of the "robes of glory" and "majestic attire," of the beauty of the "mitre lovely to the eyes for its beauty," all of which in the holy Church of Jesus Christ serve to manifest the glory, the beauty and the authority of its Priesthood. These Scriptural quotations accompanied by explanations of the signification of each part of the pontifical attire helped to dissipate the prejudices of the Protestant hearers, to make the sanctity of worship shine forth more resplendently, and to confirm indifferent Catholics in the truth of holy Faith.

It should here be observed that sectarians in the United States are rather opposed to that phase of worship which manifests itself by means of sacred ceremonies and sacred garb, so that the forms of Catholic services rarely agree with the ideas which have been imbibed concerning the Christian Religion. In general, they suppose Religion destitute of any symbolic practice whatever, and knowing little of the present condition of man, they prefer to consider Religion as speaking truth to the spirit without directing itself at all to the senses through means of external symbols. From this it may be gathered how useful it is to treat this subject in a manner most fitted to combat principles so false.

Chapter XXIV.

SPIRITUAL PROGRESS AT DUBUQUE—DEPARTURE AND RETURN OF THE BISHOP—ILLNESS OF THE MISSIONARY—CONDITION OF THE EPISCOPATE IN THAT CITY.

The increase in the number of the Clergy added various temporal cares to the ordinary duties of the Missionary, since he was entrusted by the Bishop with attending to the erection of a residence for the clergy, and also to the completion of the Church in Dubuque. For the latter he had already expended the sum of five thousand dollars, contributed by the Catholics and Protestants of the parish, during the four years when alone he had exercised the ministry in that Mission. Where everything has to be done, and where the facilities for such labor so ready to hand in more populous places are entirely lacking, one who wishes to build must himself be architect and superintendent; therefore, although obliged to celebrate Mass and preach every Sunday in the Church at Galena, the Priest repaired every Monday to Dubuque, in order to attend during the week to the erection of the Bishop's house. Besides this, during the month of May he gave the May Devotions in the Cathedral, to prepare the people for the devout celebration of the Day of Pentecost, which was to be solemnized that year for the first time by the administration of the Sacrament of Confirmation.

Almighty God, Who in His goodness employs the Servants of the Altar to call the erring back to that conversion that bringeth forth fruits of penance, showed forth the power of His grace by the return, almost without exception, of tepid and negligent Catholics to the reception of the Sacrament of Penance and the Eucharist. The Holy Spirit rendered Himself visible in the moral conduct of many, who had led unworthy lives for years and who now began a course of Christian life and persevered to the end in the practice of virtue and penance.

As the Bishop could not perform the sacred Mysteries in the Church, on account of the labor going on within the building, His Grace with Rev. Anthony Pelamourgues, journeyed up the Mississippi River as far

PART TWO

as Prairie du Chien, a village often mentioned in these Memoirs. Thence they proceeded to a place called Saint Peter, about three hundred and fifty miles from Dubuque, where the Saint Peter river flows into the Mississippi. This Mission proved of very great advantage to the poor Canadians who were engaged in the Indian trade in that far distant section. On their return the rowed down the Great Waters in a little canoe hollowed out of a log and made a stay of several days at Prairie du Chien; there the Bishop laid with solemn service the corner-stone of the Church dedicated to the Archangel Gabriel, and for the good of the people he left there as Missionary the Priest who had been his companion. In the beginning of August, 1839, Monsignore Loras returned from his long Visitation to Dubuque accompanied by an Indian half-breed, with whom as they sat in the narrow canoe, he had shared the painful task of rowing for more than three hundred miles.

The Feast of the Assumption, the day appointed for the consecration of the Cathedral, was drawing near, when our Missionary exhausted with constant journeys and many temporal anxieties, fell ill of a malignant bilious fever. It pleased the Lord to keep him thus humiliated and suffering during a month, depriving him of the consolation of assisting in person at the solemn consecration of that Cathedral, the object to which he had devoted such bitter toil for many years. But as consolation upon his bed of pain, there was granted that Faith, which taught him that Almighty God in His Justice chastises our faults in this life, so as to receive us to the bosom of His innumerable mercies in the next. How consoling is this truth!

As we must not in the course of these Memoirs make further mention of the Mission of Dubuque, a few remarks regarding it must be added here. The congregation of the Catholics of this Church reaches the number of one thousand five hundred, many of whom live in the outskirts of the city which at present contains three thousand inhabitants. The Bishop has a residence capable of lodging seven Priests by allotting one room to each; the Bishop lives with the greatest economy, and has no other revenues than the voluntary alms of the faithful and the contributions of the Propaganda. His Missionaries in various parts of the Diocese are often compelled to depend upon him for assistance, in order to pay their expenses for travelling, clothing and sometimes for daily subsistence. The contributions from Europe, however, are almost entirely consecrated to the building of the Churches so necessary in these newly settled countries of the West. A man who attends to all the household affairs is the only persons employed in the Bishop's House. At this frugal table whereon is neither wine nor any delicacy whatever, his Priests also gather.

The duties of the Prelate are those of the Missionaries,—preaching, hearing Confessions, administering the Sacraments, traveling on horseback to sick calls when he is called outside the city, and often celebrating the Mass for the parish in the absence of other Priests. This is not the practice, however, of all the Bishops in the United States, but only of those who prefer to do so, or are obliged to supply the need of Priests.

The Church of Dubuque can glory in receiving to its bosom more than sixty converts and in presenting an example of exemplary lives among nearly all the Catholics. There are also well regulated schools for both sexes. The Clergy who never number more than two or three, enjoy even among Protestants, that good report that is won only by a stainless life.

The charity of the faithful in Europe bestowed through the Propaganda of Lyons, and also that of Vienna, has supplied the Bishop with the necessary funds for the building of the Episcopal residence, the completion of the Cathedral and the purchase of some lands near the Church. If the Associates in that most important and useful work knew how indispensable were these charities to the establishment of the diocese of Dubuque, they would be glad in the Lord.

Chapter XXV.

DOGMATIC DISCUSSIONS IN THE CHURCH AT GALENA, DURING THE AUTUMN OF 1839.

In a country wherein the restless religious sects have unrestrained freedom of speech and of the printing-press, there must arise disputes and contentions all springing from the animosity and jealousy that

PART TWO

each bears towards all the others. The Catholic Church also appears in the eyes of Protestants a subject of attack and angry contempt whenever she seems to rise up from a state of humiliation to any marked degree of dignity and moral influence; this is the motive which urges the various ministers to direct their discourses against the principal Truths of the Faith, which they reject as mere human opinions. Consequently, in order to reply to what had been alleged in the meetings of the opponents of Catholicity, the Priest was obliged to notify the public that the arguments on which were based the dogmas contradicted by these men, would be presented in the Church at Galena.

These dogmatic discussions were held during the month of October, 1839, in the evening after sunset, the most convenient hour for the greater number of the people, unable to attend during the day. For ten days there was a great concourse of sectarians at the Church, drawn thither mostly by curiosity. The Unity and Infallibility of the Church, the Sacraments of Penance and the Eucharist, the use of holy Images, the Intercession of the Saints, Purgatory, the Supremacy of the Pope and Indulgences, offered the Missionary almost inexhaustible subjects for discourses which were an hour and a half or even two hours in length.

Thoroughly heretical is the intense and obstinate opposition of Protestants to the Religious devotion of Catholics to the Most Blessed Virgin, Mother of our Lord and God, Jesus Christ; while they recognize the Divinity of the Son they deny to the Mother any privilege whatever over other creatures, and they mock at the prayer, Ave Maria, and at the practice of praying before her image, calling it pure idolatry. Could the heart of a Priest help being fired with holy zeal to defend the honor of her, who was declared by the Angel Gabriel to be "full of Grace, blessed amongst all women, upon whom was to come the Holy Ghost" and "whom the power of the Most High was to overshadow"? (Luke I, 28, 35.) No! He Who truly loves Jesus, has his heart filled with sentiments of love, and has a tongue ever ready to tell of Mary, chosen our most tender Mother by our Savior when He Spoke from the cross: "Mother, behold thy Son," and to the disciple, "Behold thy mother?" (John XIX, 26, 27.)

For the fulfilling successfully the office of controversial sermons, a very important duty of the sacred ministry, it was not necessary to commit to memory the dissertations or to write them out; it was sufficient, while comprehending the full force of the arguments to be discussed, to arrange them in such order as to closely connect them, and make them clear and easily understood by the hearers. To the practice of expressing one's own thoughts in public, is due that spontaneous, easy and persuasive manner of speaking which, spite of its simplicity and imperfection, becomes eloquent and persuasive, when the speaker on Religious controversy is animated by the holy Truth which he preaches.

No one ever attempted to disturb the peace and order of these assemblies though they were often composed of persons thoroughly opposed to Catholicity and even of sectarian ministers; therefore the Preacher was at perfect liberty to employ all those arguments which he judged helpful to the subject under discussion. He judged it well, often to cite the texts from the Protestant Bible, the opinions and beliefs of learned non-Catholics when these bore witness to the truth, thus all the better defending the teachings of the Church. A mistaken zeal calculated to offend against the charity due to those who are in the darkness of error, would tend only to drive the wanderer farther from the right way.

Before the controversial discourse, prayers were recited to invoke that assistance which alone gives life to the words of the Servant of the Altar; at the close the people were dismissed with prayer. The Religious Conference on the various Missions of which we speak were very frequent, but hereafter mention will be made of only the most noteworthy.

Chapter XXVI.

CONVERSION OF A LAWYER TO CATHOLICITY—WHY CONVERTS ARE GIVEN CONDITIONAL BAPTISM.

The Baptism of a lawyer, of his wife and daughter, consoled many hearts that autumn. He was a man highly educated, deeply learned in the law, well versed in the Greek and Latin languages, and on that account well able to study and to comprehend the full force of arguments offered either for or against Catholicity. Trained in the sect of Calvinism, termed "The Covenanters," he had received from infancy the most erroneous ideas that could be inspired by the hatred and ignorance of the true Faith. But as he himself related, having entered a Presbyterian Church in Boston through curiosity, he heard a portion of a discourse, by a minister of that sect, who in a fury, carried away by his own vain learning and his blind hatred towards the Church, with envenomed accents hurled against her the vilest, most unheard of accusations, all the more fiercely, because excited by the large audience that filled the place of worship. Among other things the Preacher announced that the Beast of the Apocalypse had set its talons on the city of Boston and left its track there in the Church of the Holy Cross. He wished to signify by this that as the Catholic Church was the Society of Antichrist, this monster had his followers and his abode in that Church. This blasphemy revolted the soul of the young Calvinist, and filled him with the determination to study that doctrine which was so horribly vilified by a fanatic declaiming as might a demon from the pit. Thus did Divine Mercy, whose ways are mysterious to men, lead one who knew not the Truth to its perfect knowledge.

Having emigrated from Boston to Galena, the lawyer with his wife began to frequent the Catholic Church and often to converse with the Priest, with whom he held many conferences in his own family. Directed by divine grace to which they corresponded with sincere determination to believe and practice all the truths of holy Faith, both, with their daughter, came to the Missionary's house to be baptized. Bishop Loras honored the occasion by standing as sponsor.

It must be remarked that these converts had already received Baptism in the respective Churches of which they had formerly been members; yet the Priest did not hesitate to administer to them the Sacrament of Regeneration, for the reason that the Baptism conferred by Protestants may be held as null and void. In the United States, few of the Religious sects retain that Sacrament as absolutely necessary for securing eternal salvation; many of them take no care to confer it upon their members, and as the ministers in general have no registration of Baptisms it often happens that persons advanced in age have no positive proof of having been baptized. Moreover according to the Profession of Faith of some Protestant Churches, Baptism is only a ceremony, in itself of no importance, simply a visible sign, by means of which one declares that he is a follower of Christ and a member of the Church. Moreover, the Presbyterians, who are very numerous in America, declared in their Confession of Faith, printed in 1824, that it is wrong not to receive Baptism, but yet it is not of absolute necessity for the salvation of the soul. This is the opinion of almost all Protestant ministers, who for remission of sins, including those committed before Baptism, recognize no other means of absolute necessity except simple contrition and belief in God. Not only the want of Faith would render the Sacrament of no effort, but also grave omissions in the manner of conferring, tend to render it if no avail. Some use the water so that it is not a veritable "pouring on," but they merely bathe the forehead or another part of the body; others so alter the form of the words as to render them unsuited to the Sacrament; there are also ministers, who allow so long a time to elapse between the pouring of the water and the words of the formula of Baptism, that of one act they make two and these entirely disconnected.

Since, in these cases there is the possibility of a doubt as to the validity of so great a Sacrament, there has been introduced into the United States the invariable practice of administering the Sacrament of Baptism (under conditions, however) to all converts from Protestantism in order to remove any doubt that might afterwards trouble the conscience of the new Catholic or of the Priest; persuaded that it is better to expose Baptism to the risk, of nullity (in case that it had been validly conferred by their ministers) than to fail in the fulfillment of a precept so solemn and divine, and thus deprive those who desire to enter the bosom of the Church of the benefits of the Redemption. Whenever Baptism is administered conditionally, then the convert to the Faith is under obligation to make a general Confession of his whole life, in order to receive Sacramental Absolution, since it would have been indispensable had the convert been truly baptized.

Chapter XXVII.

FIRST VISIT TO THE CITY OF BURLINGTON, WHERE SOME PREPARATIONS FOR WAR DID NOT PERMIT A LONG STAY.

In the autumn of 1839, Monsignor Loras had conferred Holy Orders upon three of his seminaries whom he had brought from France; one of these, Reverend Remigio Petiot, a native of France, was sent to Galena as Assistant to our Missionary, who through this acquisition found himself at liberty to visit other sections of the vast diocese. In the month of November, he made a journey overland to the little new city of Davenport, where the Reverend A. Pelamourgues had been appointed pastor of the congregation there; thence continuing his journey he reached the city of Burlington, about one hundred and eighty miles from Dubuque by the usual road. This city as well as Dubuque was founded in 1833.

The Territorial Government of Iowa held its sessions that year in the Methodist Church at Burlington. Here, although the prosperous city contained about two thousand inhabitants, after much investigation the Missionary succeeded in finding only twenty-seven Catholics, some of whom were from the surrounding country. The first Mass in Burlington was celebrated on the seventeenth of December, 1839, in the poor dwelling of a German family. After the Divine Mysteries, as the Priest looked at so small a number of the faithful midst so many sectarians, he found in the loving words of our Redeemer, "Fear not, little flock, for it hath pleased your Father to give you a kingdom" (Luke XII, 32), a subject of great consolation to his hearers, and of wondrous solace to his own heart, which that hour, felt to its very core the sorrowful effects of Protestant surroundings. He who announces the Word of God in non-Catholic countries should look upon such circumstances as a spur to his own zeal; for where unbelief reigns, there assuredly he has a motive for striving to extend the Kingdom of God.

A fierce dispute between the people of the Territory and those of the State of Missouri, about the boundary line which separated those two independent sovereignties, had filled the town with soldiers from the northern counties of Iowa. Government business was suspended, and the preparations necessary for quartering so many persons upon the contested line, during a cold winter, produced general confusion. However, the whole matter was amicably settled, for the Missourians abandoned the undertaking, leaving the Territory to the possession of that part of the land which it believed to be its own. In the United States, civil wars usually originate in the Printing Office, where also peace is concluded; the newspapers are the battle-fields, whereon there is a sacrifice, at the most, of the honor of a few citizens. Would to God that all the horrors of war might be reduced to simple typographical wars like these!

But in the midst of so much disturbance, the Missionary did not consider it wise to make a long delay; so after visiting and administering the Sacraments to a number of Catholics within the range of twelve miles, he returned to Davenport. In order to draw some good, however, from so long a journey in the depths of a severe winter, he used to preach Catholic Doctrine wherever a favorable occasion presented itself, mingling therein those moral reflections that make it more persuasive. In a village called Rockingham, during two evenings, he had a large audience of Protestants, who, instead of taking offence at hearing their condemnation in the speaker's exposition of their own contradictory beliefs, took the greater liking to him on that very account. The same circumstance happened in Savanna, a little town in Illinois; in the next summer, too, he had occasion many times to preach to large assemblies of sectarians, in the open air, under the shade of grand old oaks.

Chapter XXVIII.

CHURCH OF SAINT PATRICK, AT MAQUOKETA, THE CENTER OF CATHOLIC EMIGRATION — HOW A CHURCH BECOMES THE SOURCE OF CHURCH PROPERTY.

The vast unbroken tracts of land in the vicinity of Dubuque City were beginning to change their aspect, thanks to the many colonist coming there from Europe and from the eastern States of the Republic. The woods were falling beneath the axes of the new settlers intent on drawing wealth from the natural prairies, which their plough-shares had changed into meadows covered with rich harvests. Among the most remarkable places whereon the tide of Catholic emigration had checked itself might be considered that section of country called Maquoketa, so called from the river that borders it. The place is situated about twenty miles from Dubuque.

Many Irish families had settled there to gain with the sweat of their brow, that bread which was denied them in their own oppressed native land. Therefore in the beginning in the year 1840, the Missionary considered it is duty to go to this settlement, and to do his utmost towards the building of a little Church, and this, on account of the poverty of the people and the abundance of timber, could be built only of this material. He distributed among the forty-two men of the settlement the labor of preparing a great number of beams, from twenty to forty feet long; in the spring each of these men carried to the site of the Church, his own handiwork. As they were not in a position to contribute money, they gave their assistance in many ways to lessen the expense of building. Bishop Loras gave the sum of six hundred dollars out of the contributions from the Propaganda, with which to procure some building materials and pay the workmen employed by the Missionary for the erection of the Church, which was dedicated to Saint Patrick, the Apostle of Ireland.

The wonderful results of this feeble beginning were a sudden increase in the number of settlers in the neighborhood of the Church, so much so that the action whereon it stood was very soon occupied entirely by Catholics. When Divine Service was first held there in the summer of 1840 there were no more than a hundred Catholics; three years later the parish of Saint Patrick where the zealous Reverend J.C. Perrodin regularly attended and officiated, contained six hundred souls and possessed a school. The reader should bear in mind, that a Church in the forest, where Divine Service is held even occasionally, in the Western States becomes a point of reunion for the Catholics especially for the Irish and the Germans, who form real colonies, so there are many places in America called "Irish Settlement" and "Dutch Settlement," that is "Stabilimento Irlandese," "Stabilimento Tedesco." And since the sectarians always cherish a secret aversion to the Catholic Religion, so they usually prefer to settle far away from the Church, and if they find themselves in possession of any land near it, they readily sell it. Throughout the area of thirty-six square miles, forming what the American surveyors call a "Township," wherein Saint Patrick's Parish is situated, there is not a present, one protestant proprietor.

From this may be understood the important influence that even a simple frame Church holds in a new country. Already, the increased number of parishioners requires a building double the size of the present one, and their annual increase in numbers makes it evident that one Priest alone will not be able to fulfill all the duties of his ministry.

The building of Churches in sparsely settled districts, where the land owned by the Republic is not yet for sale, is equivalent to sowing the seed of considerable Church property; this originates in the recognized right of the first settler upon the tract of at least one hundred and sixty acres, to buy it at the lowest price, that is, at one dollar and twenty-five cents an acre, wherever the Government shall put it up for public sale. Now the right of a Church as represented by a Priest or even by a layman, is respected by the people, as is that of any individual whatsoever. But usually, there is reserved to the Church the privilege of possession over three hundred and twenty acres, or more; nor is there a necessity to pay for this immediately, or even for several years, for the reason that the Government after buying the land from the Indian tribes is obliged to spend three or four years in having these surveyed, and in preparing copies of the geographical map of each tract of land six miles square. Without these preparatory measures, the public lands cannot be offered for sale. The people who settle in the neighborhood of a Church, therefore, serve to enhance the value of the land, and thus in the course of time, to secure good Church property. And in this manner does Divine Providence little by little prepare a means of subsistence of the numerous bands of clergy who will one day be needed for the service of the Catholicity of the United States.

Chapter XXIX.

HOW SETTLERS OBTAIN POSSESSION OF THE LAND FROM THE GOVERNMENT.

It will now be in order to describe the mode by which Government dispose of the lands purchased by contract from the Indian tribes, as related in Chapter XX of this Second Part of the Memoirs.

As soon as the savages leave the country which they have ceded to the Government, many citizens of the Republic hasten thither for the purpose of taking possession of the most fertile and attractive places. No permission is required for this, because Government land, so long as it is not sold, is considered the property of whoever is cultivating it, so far as the use of it is concerned. And since five, ten, even fifteen or twenty years may elapse from the time when the Indians evacuate the land until the date of public sale, it often happens that various sections throughout the country are populated by many thousand families, who do not own one foot of the soil they have cultivated. This may take place in almost every Western State, but especially in the Territories of the Republic. Here is one of the reason why there are no poor in America, and at the same time the cause of the immense emigration to the West of the nations from Europe and from the Eastern States. They go there to cultivate the Government lands, which are yet so vast and so thinly settled that they can satisfy in abundance the desire of every immigrant.

Before the Government can dispose of these land in its possession, it must employ a great number of surveyors in different quarters of the country. First they divide the land into tracts six miles square, setting a permanent sign at each corner of these squares, either by a mark upon the trunk of a tree, or by a mound of earth, raised for the purpose. Only the most skilful men are appointed for this stage of the work, the most important of any on account of the extreme exactitude required; this is carried on over many hundred of miles without interruption. All of these tracts, six miles square, are then subdivided into thirty-six

English square miles, each marked at the corners as above. Maps are prepared of each section of land, that is of each of these six-mile squares, in accordance with the results of the surveyor's work; on each map is represented the precise course of every river, great and small, of the lakes, swamps, hills, prairies, woods, and of any noticeable or peculiar feature of the surface. And also each square mile on these maps is again divided into four equal parts of one hundred and sixty acres. Everything is numbered so as to avoid the least confusion.

This land survey is often carried on in places entirely destitute of inhabitants, and it serves to give us reliable knowledge of the geography and nature of the country; geographies and maps made previous to this survey are entirely untrustworthy. Three copies of these authenticated maps are prepared: one is kept in the office of the Surveyor General of that particular district of the Republic to which the Government has appointed him; a second copy is forwarded to the General Land-Office in the capital city of Washington; and the third is intended for the use of the respective offices where the lands are sold to the settlers.

When the Government has ready to hand the results of the work described above, a notification is sent through the public press, by order of the President of the United States, that in such a State or Territory, in such a County, certain sections of land, numbered, etc., will be sold at auction at a specified hour and place, etc. Six months after the notification, the lands on sale are put up at auction by the employees in their respective offices; the lowest price is one dollar and a quarter, American money, corresponding to about six and one half francs. Those settlers who are actually occupying and cultivating the lands put up at auction are the first to present themselves and bid at the sale, and ordinarily they have no competitors, as there it would be considered robbery to outbid those settlers, so the latter can buy eighty or a hundred acres at minimum price. Those sections that have not been occupied sometimes yield at the auction more than the lowest price.

The lands that do not find sale at the auction, can be secured by anyone at private sale in the office and at the lowest price. The first proprietors receive from the Government the bill of sale, made out in thoroughly legal form and on parchment; this is called "The Patent."

Only in such a way can the citizens or any foreigner come into possession of the domains of the Republic.

Some years ago, in order to encourage emigration to regions entirely uninhabited, the Government used to grant to anyone at all who would settle upon and cultivate those lands, the privilege of buying one hundred and sixty acres of these at minimum price, and to the exclusion of any other person who should offer more, but on account of various abuses and disorders inseparable from such a privilege, it was withdrawn by Act of Congress.

Although the Public Treasury annually receives many millions of dollars through sale of its lands, yet the profit is very small, for first the Government must buy these lands from the Indians, then must survey them; maps and charts must be made, very many who are employed in the work must be paid, and besides all this, are the extraordinary expenses that attend the sale itself.

Chapter XXX.

CONVERSION AND BAPTISM OF A MOTHER AND HER EIGHT CHILDREN.

Those causes by means of which Divine Goodness calls to the bosom of Mother Church those souls who are astray from her, may often appear mysterious to human understanding, yet whenever it is permitted us to perceive them, we find them always the same; they are innocence, sincerity, an upright intention, a heart disposed to piety and a sincere sorrow for faults committed. Among the many proofs of this truth, we may justly note one, the conversion of a mother and her eight children. This was in April 1840.

This lady was living in Illinois, fifteen miles from the city of Galena, in a place where the Priest had preached several times; a dangerous illness that threatened her life, had long confined her to her bed. In the midst of her sufferings, notwithstanding her very limited knowledge of the Catholic Religion, she was fond of wearing round her neck a little cross, which was the gift of a Catholic friend. But the Evil One, who always trembles and flees before the adorable Sign of our Salvation, strove to tear it from her breast, through the instrumentality of a friend, a Protestant, who declared it to be only an object of superstition, that keeping a cross about her was entirely useless, and unbecoming to one who professed the doctrine of the Bible. The temptress did not fail to employ force as far as possible, in order to carry out her purpose. But the heart of the sick woman was too innocent and devout to be deceived by so false a friend. Who can tell what burning prayers had already kindled a flame of love for Jesus Crucified and who knows if the adorable Sign of the Son of Man had not been impressed upon that suffering soul? In truth, the temptation served only to confirm her in her tender love for the Cross, to condemn even more earnestly those beliefs which hated it, and to strengthen the idea already conceived, of entering the bosom of the Holy Church. Happy victory of the Cross of Christ!

But other difficulties were to be overcome by this pious woman before receiving the Sacrament of Regeneration. Her husband who had been a Baptist minister for many years, could not regard this decision of his wife with indifference; the children of his first wife, already grown, angered by their own mistaken ideas regarding the Church, which they had imbibed from infancy, vehemently opposed their stepmother, and bitterly reproached her for the simpleminded weakness in believing a doctrine so base and unreasonable. To this were added the threats of friends and neighbors loudly declaring their disapproval and determination in cast her off. But a soul that sincerely loves God is ready to lose everything to gain Christ, and so this brave woman hearkening to the voice of Him Who said, "If any man cometh to Me and hateth not his father and mother and wife and children and brothers and sister, ... he cannot be My disciple," was ready to give up husband, children and friends that she might follow the Crucified. She openly declared that she was ready to be hated by all the world and banished from home, rather than shrink from professing that Religion which she firmly believed divine and the only one established by our Lord Jesus Christ.

Faith and the spirit of devotion overcame all the obstacles which had opposed themselves to the conversion of Mrs. N. The lady, now somewhat restored in health, sent word to the Missionary that at last she wished to receive Holy Baptism with her large family. He hastened to the home where Faith had made so fair a conquest; of the children, the five who had already attained the use of reason, at the sight of the Priest, manifested that spiritual joy and holy reverence inspired within them by the same Religious sentiments that burned in the heart of their tender mother. Their lively desire to become members of Holy Church and the earnestness with which they declared their belief in all the truths revealed by the Divine Redeemer supplied for the little Religious instruction that they had received. To assist them in the worthy reception of the Sacrament of Regeneration, the Missionary held a discourse upon the necessity of a true sorrow for sins already committed and of a firm determination to live and die as true Christians. After this he proceeded to administer Baptism, in their own home, explaining all the ceremonies prescribed by the Roman Ritual, and all the wonderful effects of the Sacrament, and preparing them for the solemn obligation contracted by those who receive it.

It was a consolation to the heart of him who served as the happy instrument of Divine Mercy to behold the modesty, the spiritual peace and the reverent silence which accompanied the prayers and the holy rites of the Priest, while he was reconciling to Jesus Christ in the Baptismal Waters, this mother and her eight children, and they could not conceal their holy anxiety to receive it. The father of the many children seemed well content, and remained in the room, a witness of the Catholic Profession of Faith as made by that wife and those children whom he loved so tenderly; he desired to know, however, why they did not believe it necessary to the validity of the Sacrament that there should be Total Immersion of the neophytes in the regenerating waters, as he had taught and practised many years as minister in the sect of the Baptists. The sons of the first wife, who were already grown, left the house on the occasion, that they might not be spectators of what they called a useless and superstitious practice.

Some time after the Baptism, the mother and several of her children were prepared to receive Holy Communion, which Bread of the strong, confirmed them in the Faith. The daily prayers regularly practised by this young family in their home could not but draw the heart of the father towards a Religion that could sink into the very heart of little children and give them the semblance in their devout attitudes of the very angels themselves. Once as the Priest was relating to one of the daughters just converted how a young Christian savage once wept over the unbelief of his father, who refused to submit to faith, all at once the happy face of the child changed in grief that bathed her innocent countenance with tears at the thought of her own father. In the conversion of this family the prophecy of our Divine Lord seemed verified when He said in Saint John: "And other sheep I have that are not of this fold; them also I must bring, and they shall hear My Voice, and there shall be one fold and one Shepherd." (X, 16.)

Chapter XXXI.

THE CHURCH OF SAINT GABRIEL THE ARCHANGEL AT PRAIRIE DU CHIEN, AND THAT OF SAINT PAUL AT BURLINGTON.

It would weary our readers to even attempt a detailed account of the many journeyings of our Priest during the year 1840; for this would necessitate a description of many voyages, for many hundreds of miles by the Mississippi and by land, and this account would serve no useful purpose; so we will content ourselves with a description of the building of two Churches at the same time, and in situations far distant from each other.

We have already narrated that in 1839, Monsignor Loras laid the corner-stone of the Church of the Archangel Gabriel in Prairie du Chien, Territory of Wisconsin. The Missionary was the architect of this building of stone which measured one hundred feet in length by fifty in breadth; so when work was resumed upon the building he considered it necessary to go often not only to direct the work, but also to rouse the people to contribute the necessary material and so diminish expenses. With this object in view for a number of days in June, he worked in the stone quarries with the people, helping to get out the rock necessary. Yet in spite of most extreme economy possible, the pecuniary resources of the Catholics of that section were not sufficient to complete the enterprise, so laudable and necessary, nor would it have been carried to the promising condition in which it now stands, had not Bishop Loras supplied the generous amount of fourteen hundred dollars. The Bishop's zeal impelled him to expand a portion of the contributions from the Propaganda upon the spiritual welfare of a young but extensive parish, outside of his own diocese.

The charity, the zeal, the learning, the entire holy and blameless daily life of the Very Reverend Joseph Cretin, Missionary at Prairie du Chien from 1841, will be forever held in benediction by that people, for whom he labored so earnestly to fix deep into their souls an enlightened piety. To this venerated Priest is owing almost all the spiritual good wrought in the parish of Saint Gabriel, now containing more than a thousand souls, and also the present fine condition of the Church which combines an elegant simplicity with solidity and spaciousness.

In the same year another House of God was built in the city of Burlington on the Mississippi in the Territory of Iowa, three hundred miles from Prairie du Chien. The very small number of Catholics there in the midst of a very large Protestant population was a powerful motive for introducing Catholic Worship there as speedily as possible, for delay in such a matter would have caused greater and insuperable obstacles to the spread of Truth in this place, an important position in the Diocese, on account of its trade. Our Missionary had the entire charge of this undertaking and to justify the confidence placed in him he was obliged many times in the course of the year, to leave his other Missions at Mineral Point, Dodgeville and Shullsburg in Wisconsin and betake himself to Burlington. As there were no Catholics there in a position to supply a piece of ground, it was necessary to purchase it from a Protestant, and before winter, thanks to indefatigable application, he had the consolation of beholding a Catholic Church upon a beautiful eminence in the centre of the town. It must be noted now that the Methodists owned a large building in this place, and other sectarians held their worship there while the true disciple of Christ was almost unknown; on this account the Church at first roused the ill will and much-haranguing of those who had always hated it. But the preaching at which not a few Protestants assisted, the Irish and the Germans who emigrated thither and increased the number of

Catholics, and the fact of the people growing accustomed to seeing their worship practised there reduced the opposition to a concealed aversion, and very soon dissipated many prejudices.

The Church at Burlington dedicated to the Apostle, Saint Paul, is fifty-five English feet in length, built of brick, with a basement to be used as a dwelling for the Priest, and for a school. The highest portion of the site whereon it is built has been left free for a Church of greater dimensions, which before ten years will be needed for the number of the faithful. This is the case always in all the new cities of the American Republic, where experience has taught that these plans are according to the dictates of Christian prudence, always solicitous for the spiritual needs of the future.

Chapter XXXII.

SEVERAL CONGREGATIONS OF CATHOLICS, VISITED BY THE BISHOP, ACCOMPANIED BY HIS VICAR—THE SENATE OF IOWA IN THE CATHOLIC CHURCH OF BURLINGTON.

The zealous Bishop Monsignor Loras, in the interests of his Diocese, in the autumn of 1845, went to the city of Mobile in the State of Alabama, distant about eighteen hundred miles from Dubuque, and our Missionary accompanied him by land into the Territory of Iowa, visiting with him the different Congregations of the faithful. From Galena they passed on to the little village of Charleston, on the western bank of the Mississippi, administering the Sacraments to the few Catholics of the place; thence went on as far as the beautiful city of Davenport. In this place the people were desirous of attending an exposition of the principal points of controversy contested by Protestants, so for eight evenings the Priest devoted himself to satisfying their desires. And on this occasion to impress the conviction more thoroughly upon the minds of the many sectarians attending, the Bishop publicly presented to the Preacher at intervals during the course of the argument, the very strongest objections that non-Catholics bring against the subject under discussion, in such fashion that the objections themselves only served to give yet greater testimony to Catholic dogma. The results of these controversial discourses always were the visible reconciliation of public opinion with the Church, strengthening true believers in their faith in evangelical truths, and sometimes, too, deciding certain well-disposed souls to undertake those preparations that precede conversion.

Continuing our journey along the River bank and through the city of Bloomington, on the third day we reached Burlington, after some serious obstacles in the matter of bad roads and streams swollen by heavy rains. Here the Bishop had the consolation of seeing the new Church. For the completion of this building and for the purchase of the site and other expenses the Association of the Propaganda contributed finally the sum of four thousand dollars. Leaving this place, the Bishop gave his blessing to his Vicar, and began his journey by steamboat to the city of Mobile, whence he was not to return until the spring of 1841.

The members of the Legislature of Iowa were beginning to assemble in Burlington for their annual session of seventy-five days, which that year, commenced on the first Monday in November, and the Methodist Church had been used provisionally for the session of the Senate and Representatives. Through the kindly interest of a number of his friends among the Senators, the Missionary arranged that the sessions of the Senate should be held in his Church which was not then consecrated to Divine Worship. Such a circumstance proves what has already been affirmed in these Memoirs, that the Government of the United States it its action has no regard or predilection for one Religion in preference to another.

Aside from the more kindly feeling towards Catholicity as one result of the occupation of our Church by the Senate of Iowa, another was the contribution of five hundred dollars and other considerable profits given for the rent of sixty days. This contribution added to that from the people served to cancel completely the entire debt contracted for erecting the building. During the Session of the Legislature, on November twenty-second, 1840, the Priest preached for the first time in the new Church, his pulpit being the same desk that was used by the President of the Senate.

Chapter XXXIII.

PROGRESS OF THE TERRITORY OF IOWA — DIFFERENCES BETWEEN ITS GOVERNMENT AND THAT OF A STATE—ORIGIN OF IOWA CITY—THE COUNTIES, AND THE ORGANIZATION OF THE TERRITORY INTO A SOVEREIGN STATE.

As the first establishment of Catholicity in the Capital City of Iowa must at present be our subject, it will not be unacceptable to the reader to know something of the origin of the City itself; this will be of very great assistance, in showing clearly the surprising results of that emigration to which must be attributed not only the formation of the Western States, but, indeed, the very creation of Dioceses.

According to the census taken by order of the United States Government in 1830, the vast region now forming Iowa, contained not one inhabitant except the Indians and a few citizens carrying on trade with the tribes; in 1836 it contained eleven thousand; in 1838, when a Territorial Government was established, their number had increased to eighteen thousand; and in 1840, to forty-three thousand; at this date there are estimated about seventy thousand. This population, which within the short space of ten years, from 1833 to 1843, crossed the great River Mississippi to seek in that rich soil and in trade the means of improving their condition, is an intermixture of Americans of European descent, with emigrants from Ireland, from Germany and other countries of our hemisphere. And as the agriculturist has need of the merchant and both are aided by the mechanic, so throughout the country in every direction cities rose as if by magic; forests were cut down by the settler's axe, wild prairies changed into blossoming fields, the trader, the traveller, the mail carries from every quarter traversed the land.

In the Act of the Congress of 1838 containing the legal organization of this Territory, the location of the Capital City, the centre of the governing power, was left to the choice of the Legislative body. This met in Burlington, where it was holding its sessions provisionally in 1839, and decreed that the Capital of the Territory should be built in Johnson

County, nearly in the centre, seventy-five miles from Burlington and eighty-six from Dubuque, on the east bank of the Iowa River, and decreed also that it should be called Iowa City. The principal reason for such choice was the providing convenient access of the Members of Legislature and the people in general, to the seat of their own Territorial Government, where the sessions are held in the State House, where the Governor is to be found, and all the State Officials, and also the Supreme Court of the Territory. The State Capitals serve the same purpose.

The more notable differences between a Territorial Government and that of a State are, the first is only provisionary in its extent and in all its laws, because adapted to a new and sparsely settled section, under the guardianship of the Governor-General of the great Republic, which forms and is able to change its organic constitution; the second is permanent in its boundaries and in its Constitution, which being made by the representatives of the people cannot be altered by the people, except for very grave reasons. The people of a Territory send a Delegate to the General Congress, who however has no vote in the affairs of the Nation; a State sends to Congress two Senators and Representatives in number proportioned to the number of inhabitants; all these Members elected by a State have a voice in the Acts of the General Government. The laws made by a Territorial Council composed of persons elected by its people, are subject to the authority of Congress, while the Acts of a State when they are not in opposition to the Constitution or to the Laws of the General Government, are entirely independent of Congress, for which reason the States are called Sovereign. The civil Officials over a Territory, as Governor, Secretary, Marshal, are chosen by the President of the United States with consent of the Senate; therefore the Nation pays the expenses of a Territorial Government, whereas the people of a State elect their own Officials, and the expenses of its Legislative body and all its Officials are paid from the revenues of the State. Lastly, there is another privilege enjoyed by the people of a State, that of voting for the President and Vice President of the United States, a privilege which the people of a Territory do not possess.

To return now to our subject, it must be observed that the site whereon Iowa City is now built was in June of 1839 an uninhabited solitude covered with trees; but on this very spot, the following month a city was laid out with broad streets, squares, sites for the Capitol Building or State House, Churches, Public Gardens, etc. In December following it contained about a thousand inhabitants, with hotels, Post Office, a line of stage-coaches, dealers of every kind, workmen, houses of brick and of stone, Courts of Justice, also lawyers, doctors, Protestant ministers with their Churches, Schools, a weekly newspaper, etc. All the lots in the city had been sold at auction; the money thus received together with twenty thousand dollars granted by the United States Government served to build the State House, a structure whose dimensions are one hundred and twenty feet long by sixty wide, with three stories, the whole built of stone. This building situated upon a beautiful eminence, on one side looks down upon the Iowa River, and from the other commands a view of the Capital City; it rises from the centre of a great square, it towers above the ancient oaks surrounding it, under whose shade but a few months ago, the savage pitched his poor wigwam. Notwithstanding the goodly sum of nearly one hundred thousand dollars already expended, the building of this State House is not yet complete in every part.

The surrounding country especially from the Mississippi to the Iowa River, which was a lonely wilderness in 1835, is at present inhabited by many thousand settlers, whose dwellings and cultivated farms have notably altered the face of nature. The sites most advantageous for trade, or in the centre of the lands most sought after by agriculturists are selected to found villages, which in time grow into important towns, especially those which from their central position in the county are erected into County Seats by the Territorial Government.

The Legislature of Iowa in its annual sessions held at Burlington from 1838 to 1841 and afterwards at the Capital has divided nearly all the tract of country bought from the different savage tribes by the Government of the United States, into counties about twenty-four miles square. This subdivision of the lands will continue with emigration, for it is indispensable to the executive power, to good order, to civil progress and to the popular elections. In Chapter XIX of this Second Part of the Memoirs, it has been stated that the part of the Territory at present settled and possessed by the citizens of the Republic is only the thirtieth part of that occupied by the Indian Tribes within the limits of Iowa.

We shall add, finally, that in 1842 the majority of its inhabitants, for several grave reasons, refused to be erected into a State Government and enter with all a State's rights into the American Union, notwithstanding the fact that there were a sufficient number of inhabitants to justify such a measure. This important change of public affairs, which cannot be carried out without the express consent of the people of Iowa and of the General Government, will be effected before 1846; at that time, a new Territory will be formed out of the northern part, in order to erect the southern part into a State whose extent will be inferior to no other of the entire Union. For the accomplishment of this purpose, the people elect several delegates who frame a Constitution for the new State. This after being approved or amended by Congress is remanded to the general vote of the people, and if they by a two-thirds vote, accept the constitution drafted by their own Delegates and approved by Congress, the Territorial Government passes to that of a Sovereign State which becomes part of the Nation and shares in all its civil rights.

Chapter XXXIV.

BEGINNING OF CATHOLIC WORSHIP IN IOWA CITY, 1840—ERECTION OF A CHURCH—CAUSE OF A CONVERSION.

By an Act of the Iowa Legislature several lots in its Capital City were set aside for Church purposes, but on condition that those Religious bodies who desired to obtain them, should raise thereon a Church building of not less than one thousand dollars in value. In December, 1840, our Missionary hastened from Burlington to the new Capital and giving over to the proper civil authority the required security of two thousand dollars secured to the cause of Catholicity one of the finest of the lots reserved for building Churches. The Primitive Methodists, the Methodist Episcopalians, the Presbyterians, the Unitarians did the same for their own sects.

The first Mass in Iowa City was celebrated on December twentieth,

1840, in the house of a German mechanic, not far from the State House and the first dogmatic sermon was preached in the Hall of a small hotel; the following morning the Holy Sacrifice was celebrated in an unfinished log cabin of an Irish family ten miles from the City. See in how lowly a manner did the Faith manifest itself the time in that part of the vast Territory! But the Bishop's absence compelled the Priest to hasten to Dubuque for the solemnity of the holy Feast of the Nativity; thence to Galena in the State of Illinois, from which place he traveled again to Burlington, having thus traversed a distance of four hundred miles all alone, part of the way over the ice on the Mississippi.

It will serve no useful purpose to recount particulars of the different Missions given throughout the country concerning the establishment of Catholic Worship in Iowa City, therefore we will depart from the chronological order here, and anticipate the memoirs respecting them.

With the cordial approval of Monsignor Loras the Priest made the necessary preparations for building a church, under the auspices of the Assumption of the Blessed Virgin Mary, for as she is the Patroness of the Diocese it was fitting that to her should be dedicated the first church of Iowa's Capital. On July 12, 1841, the Bishop laid the first stone of the building and the Priest addressed the large gathering present on the subject of the Religious and even political advantages resulting from the practice of Divine worship and that the truths of the Gospel are the basis of true liberty and true patriotism. A pile of earth left by the workmen after digging the foundation served as pulpit for the orator.

In the autumn of that year the stone walls of the basement story had been built; in the summer of 1842 the brick walls of the Church were raised and the building was in a condition to be used for Divine service in the following spring. The dimensions are sixty feet in length by thirty-five in breadth. It is so constructed as to allow of two small rooms in the basement as a lodging for the Priest and another large one to be used as a school-room. So when the increase in the Catholic population will require a more spacious church, the present structure can then be divided into two stories and used as a school or as a house for a Religious Community. In the existing state of things poverty necessitates keeping everything under one roof, leaving to posterity the task of raising a more commodious and costly edifice. To this work of such vital importance to the cause of Religion, the Bishop of Dubuque contributed three thousand two hundred dollars out of the alms from the Propaganda Association. The Catholics of Iowa City and its vicinity, although poor and few in number, yet contributed about six hundred dollars, partly in money, partly in material, partly in labor. The site, whose value is one thousand six hundred dollars, was granted by the Territorial Government of Iowa, as before stated.

To these Religious Memoirs of Iowa City which may one day be of service in compiling the history of Dubuque Diocese, we will add that during the years 1841 and 1842, the Divine Mysteries were often celebrated in private houses, where also the Word of God was Preached and Confessions heard as well in the city as in the homes of the first settlers living near the lands then in possession of the savages of the tribes of Sacs and Foxes. In a hall temporarily used as a Court of Justice, many times in the year 1842, the Missionary held controversial discourses in the presence of large audiences consisting of sectarians, in order to dispel as far as possible, the prejudices arising from a false Religious education.

Several converts to the Faith comforted the heart of him who was striving to establish Catholic worship. Among these was the mother of a family, who had been baptized by total immersion ten years before, according to the practice of the Baptists. As she had read in her Bible that the Priests of the Old Testament made use of sacred symbols in their worship in the Temple, she argued with simplicity and with justice that the Catholic Religion conforms more closely with Holy Scripture than do the sects. For they reject every sign of Religion and devotion ordained by the Lord in the Law of Moses, and practised by the Saviour Himself, while the Church animated by a spirit of holy fervor still manifests her living adoration of the Divinity by means of those holy venerable rites that have accompanied the sacrifices and prayers of the Patriarchs, of the Prophets and of all the just, from the beginning of the world.

It is much to be desired that our brethren of the Protestant sects would take pattern by this good woman and take heed of the form of exterior worship recorded in their Bibles, remembering that the

Messias came not to destroy but to fulfill, to make perfect the adoration of the Divinity, to Whom we ought to consecrate our soul's affections which are inseparable from exterior worship, remembering the words of Saint Paul: "I beseech you, therefore, brethren, by the mercy of God, that you present your bodies a living sacrifice, holy, pleasing unto God, your reasonable service," (Romans, XII, 1).

In 1842, Reverend Antony Pelamourgues, often visited the Catholics of Iowa City, about sixty miles from his station at Davenport. In the Mission of this Capital City of Iowa may be counted five hundred Catholics, principally Germans, who continue to immigrate to this part of the country. Within a few years, these settlers together with the Irish settlers and the converts will form a large parish, and one of some importance also, in the matter of the influence exerted by any city wherein reside the members of the Legislature, the Governor and State Officials.

At the public sale of lands lying near Iowa City, held at Dubuque in March 1843, at the suggestion of his Vicar, the Bishop purchased eighty acres in the suburbs, paying to the Government one dollar and a quarter an acre. This tract is to be used as a Catholic cemetery, as also to furnish fuel for the Church and the Pastor.

Chapter XXXV.

CHURCH OF SAINT MATTHEW AT SHULLSBURG IN WISCONSIN—
NOTES ON THE LEAD MINES.

From what has been started, the reader may see that the Missionary was often absent from Galena in Illinois, which was his principal station; but this large and important parish was not only attended by the Assistant Priest, Rev. Remigius Petiot, resident there, but was also visited very often by the Missionary, since it was situated on his road from Iowa to Wisconsin Territory. From 1835 to 1841, in that part of Wisconsin just above the northern boundary line off Illinois, the Priest was accustomed to officiate in the houses of the settlers, who worked in the Lead Mines; therefore it was decided to build a frame Church that year in a place called Shullsburg and Gratiot Survey, eighteen miles from Galena.

As the structure was to be of wood throughout, according to that described in Chapter X of Part I of these Memoirs, all the parts composing the building were prepared and wrought out by skillful carpenters in Galena. As soon as these materials had been transported to Shullsburg, the workmen put the whole together in six days and formed a beautiful little church, thirty-five by twenty-five feet in dimensions, serving very well the needs of Catholic worship, and presenting a certain symmetry in appearance that makes it an ornament mid the poor dwellings of the miners. The chapel is consecrated to the Apostle Saint Matthew, and at present costs one thousand dollars, almost entirely the voluntary offering of the incomparable generosity of the Irish. A Priest celebrates Mass there and administers the Sacraments once a month, for the spiritual welfare of three hundred or more Catholics scattered throughout the vicinity, within a range of eight or ten miles.

This part of Wisconsin Territory is extremely rich in Lead Mines; thousands of men in every direction are carrying on extensive excavations under ground in search of the precious mineral. It often happens that after many months of hard labor, boring through the limestone strata, they find their time and money entirely thrown away. But horizontal fissures are often discovered between the strata wherein Nature, as in a vast store-house, holds the lead in large masses interspersed with clay. Many of these veins are found at a great depth under ground, under water, and while these are usually rich in mineral, the labor becomes so difficult and expensive that the miner is often forced to abandon them. The lands containing these mines are for the most part of still in possession of the Government, but this fact does not prevent all the lead extracted becoming the property of the discoverer.

Chapter XXXVI.

FIRST ESTABLISHMENT OF CATHOLIC WORSHIP AT BLOOMINGTON IN IOWA TERRITORY.

The town of Bloomington, situated upon the western bank of the Mississippi between Davenport and Burlington, almost equal to these in size, in January 1841, with a population of about eight hundred persons, had only ten Catholics. On the twenty-fifth of the same month the first Mass was celebrated in the house of a Catholic woman whose husband was Protestant. There were eight Communicants at this Mass. The Missionary considered that he would fulfill the most important part of his ministry towards those outside of the Church, by preaching in a large hall used as a schoolhouse by the village, and where all the ministers of the different sects were accustomed to preach their doctrines.

One who has been trained in the errors and almost incredible prejudices of Protestantism is inclined to laugh at that exterior garb in which the Catholic Priest presents himself before an audience to teach the Gospel truths. This was the case with a few of his Protestant hearers in Bloomington. The cassock, the surplice and the stole seem useless or absurd novelties to those who, familiar with ministers, see them continually preaching the Bible in their secular garb, which they use on all religious occasions. An explanation of the reason and Religious signification of the Priestly vestments served wonderfully to win respect and reverence for that Church which covers the frail humanity of the priest with the Mantle of her Apostolic Mission and with the emblems of her celestial virtues or better with those of her Divine Spouse, humiliated and suffering on earth. The holy Sign of the Cross, which must be called the standard of Redemption upon the brow of the Catholic, is regarded with contempt by nearly all the Protestants of the United States; and for this reason the Priest often has occasion to cite that saying of the Apostle: "We preach Christ Crucified; unto the Jews indeed a stumbling-block, and unto the Gentiles, foolishness." (I Cor. I, 23). An earnest and feeling instruction upon the practice of making the Sign of the Cross always proved a great assistance to the cause of the Faith.

Several times in the years 1841 and 1842, the Missionary preached in the town of Bloomington; with the full liberty of speech enjoyed in that section he undertook to defend publicly the truth of Catholic dogma against the errors of the religious sects. At that time the Mercy of God called to the bosom of His Church, the husband of that good woman in whose home the Divine Mysteries had been celebrated for the first time; he died a few months after his baptism with sentiments of the most tender piety.

The zeal of the Bishop of Dubuque led him to purchase a tract of land in the centre of this flourishing town and, in 1842, to build there a wooden Chapel, dedicated to the Apostle Saint Mathias. This, although the smallest in the Diocese, is well finished and answers perfectly the present needs of the few faithful there; it also offers a home to the Priest when he visits that town. At the same time, a little Church precisely like that at Bloomington was built in the village of Bellevue, upon the western bank of the Mississippi, thirty miles from Dubuque. This little Church was dedicated to the Apostle Saint Andrew. This Mission is under the charge of the devoted Priest, Reverend John Perrodin, who, as stated in Chapter XXVIII makes his principal abode in the Parish of Saint Patrick's. We have judged it well to give an account of these Churches in order to preserve to posterity the memory of them, for there is reason to hope that in the brief course of half a century when these new villages shall have been transformed into populous cities, our holy Religion will there have its splendid Temples where the praises of God will be daily sung. Now, however, the poor, wandering Missionary celebrates there a few times in the year and under the roof of the poor Chapel itself takes his sweet repose; he is in truth, without a country, without a home, without the ordinary necessaries of life, but he is not without a well-grounded hope of soon enjoying the riches of Paradise, his own country that he sighs for, and he can say with Apostle of the Gentiles: "We have not here a lasting city, but we seek one that is to come." (Heb. XIII, 14).

Chapter XXXVII.

THE TEMPERANCE SOCIETY—ITS SALUTARY EFFECTS UPON THE CAUSE OF CATHOLICITY IN AMERICA.

Very few persons in the United States cultivate the vine or make wine to any extent, so this beverage forms one of the objects of commerce with France, Spain and Italy, while the distance, imposition of duties, etc., render it not only costly, but also very scarce. But to supply the lack of the vine in America, extensive use is made of strong spirits extracted from Indian corn, which grows there in prodigious quantities and can be had at a very low price. Many of the people are addicted to the abuse of this strong liquor to such a degree as to fall unhappy victims of intoxication.

A great number of the emigrants from Ireland, notwithstanding the Faith, the generosity, the honesty, the industry and all the other virtues that so eminently distinguish the race, were often too weak upon this one point, giving themselves up in bondage to the vice of intemperance. The more zealous among the Protestants, especially the Presbyterians, took occasion from this to hurl bitterest reproaches and invectives against the Catholic Church, which they accused of being far from the Evangelical sanctity she professed, while she held within her own bosom so many leading scandalous lives. But God who often makes use of His very enemies as instruments to carry out the inscrutable designs of His grace, raised up our far-famed Father Matthew in Ireland to banish the demon of drunkenness from that island, and to enroll millions of his compatriots in the Temperance Societies by virtue of which they pledged themselves to taste no beverage that could intoxicate.

The Irish, who comprise more than half of the Catholics of the United States, followed the example of their brethren in Europe, and Temperance Societies were founded in every city and village of the land. It could be asserted now that these children of that Saint Patrick to whom Ireland owes her conversion to the Faith are now very few exceptions models of temperance. The Catholic Clergy exerted themselves to the utmost in America, to bring about a change so marvelous and so necessary to the advancement of the Faith; the Faith that had retrograded among many Catholics through the vice of intemperance. A number of the Bishops and nearly all of the Priests are zealous members of this Society.

It must be stated here that the sects, the Presbyterians in particular, had Temperance Societies among their followers, but when the Catholics established their own societies the promise not to use intoxicating liquors took on a certain sacredness, because in many Congregations it was made in church, in presence of the Priest. The motives, then, which induced Catholics to inscribe their names in the Society proceeded from an earnest desire to improve their own ways of life and those of their brethren by means of good example, and in this way to remove that occasion of scandal which rendered fruitless so many of the discussions made in defence of the truths contradicted by Protestants.

If the tree is to be judged by its fruits, there is no doubt as to the Religious influence exerted by the Temperance Society,—in truth we must ascribe thereto these wonderful effects, the conversion of a great number of sinners hardened in vice for years, who approached the tribunal of penance only after they had promised to give up entirely the use of intoxicating liquors. From the year 1839 when the Societies had become established in the various Missions recorded in these Memoirs, piety actually made visible progress from day to day, in proportion as the virtue of Temperance won its blessed victories among the people; peace and plenty reigned in the families, Catholicity won the respect and reverence of its very enemies, and the Faith spread among the more sincere of those outside the Church. Many of the Catholic Irish abandoned entirely the dangerous traffic in intoxicating drink and sought more honorable means of subsistence.

The obligations contracted by the members of the Temperance Society consist of a perfect and entire abstinence from the use of liquors capable of producing intoxicating, not excepting wine, beer and such beverages; in case of sickness, however, they can be dispensed by their physician. Such rigorous observance was judged necessary for the removal of all proximate occasions of intemperance. Some bound themselves to observe this abstinence for their lifetime; others limited the promise to a certain number of years. Many of the Protestants preferred to join the Catholic Society rather than those of their own Churches, on account of the greater reverence shown by the people and the much higher degree of influence, to which the virtue of Temperance raised many Irish citizens.

The members of the Society receive a certificate, of which we shall give the formula, a beautiful composition drawn almost entirely from Holy Scripture.

Catholic Total Abstinence Society
IN IOWA, ILLINOIS AND WISCONSIN
"IN THIS SIGN THOU SHALT CONQUER"

It is good not to eat flesh and not to drink wine, nor any thing whereby thy brother is offended, or scandalized or made weak. (Rom. XIV, 21.)

Look not upon the wine when it shineth in the glass: it goeth in pleasantly. But in the end, it will bite like a snake and will spread abroad poison like a basilisk. (Prov. XXIII, 31, 32.)

Be not in the feasts of great drinkers who club together for feasting, for these, sleepers as they are, shall be reduced to rags. (Prov. XXIII, 20, 21.)

Woe to you that are mighty to drink wine, and stout men at drunkenness. (Isaias V, 22.)

Woe to him that giveth drink to his friend, and maketh him drunk. Thou art filled with shame instead of glory. (Hab. II, 15, 16.)

The Fruits of Temperance
The Holy Fear of God, Plenty in Households, Peace,
Health of Body, Good Name, The Grace of God, Eternal Life.

Effects of Intemperance
The Loss of God, Poverty and Shame, Discord in Families,
Sickness, Disgrace, Final Impenitence, Eternal Death.

PROMISE

I, N. N., promise to abstain from any intoxicating drink, unless used medicinally and by order of a physician.

Mr. N. N. has taken the Pledge for _____ years, on the _____ day of the month of _____ in the year 18__ .

REVEREND N.N.
President of the Society in the city of _____

Chapter XXXVIII.

THE BIBLE, THE PROTESTANT REFORMATION OF THE SIXTEENTH CENTURY, AND THE APOSTOLIC MISSION—SUBJECTS OF MANY DISCOURSES IN DEFENCE OF THE CATHOLIC FAITH, ASSAILED BY THE PROTESTANT MINISTERS OF GALENA.

The progress of Catholicity since 1839 is in great measure due to the number and exemplary lives of the different Missionaries, and to the establishment of churches where Divine Worship could be carried on in the chief centres. This very progress, however, gave occasion to several of the sectarian ministers to resort to their usual invectives, calumnies and false accusations against the Holy Church. Galena, in the State of Illinois, wielded considerable influence both religious and political on account of its trade and its importance as the County Seat. In this town, where six different Religious sects were established, a minister of the Anglican Church signalized himself beyond his compeers by declaiming more constantly and more violently against the Faith. It may be of interest to some, therefore, to make mention of the principal subjects, forming the themes of many discussions held by the Missionary in his own church, in 1840, 1841 and 1842; these were always attended by a great number of non-Catholics.

Beside defending the principal dogmas of the Faith, as formerly stated, a simple exposition of the causes or chief sources of this ignorance regarding true Catholic doctrine, was always wonderfully effective in dissipating many false impressions given by the ministers. It is to the absurd harangues of these, to the abuse of printed tracts and to the prejudices of a sectarian training, must mainly be attributed the most erroneous of the wrong ideas of Protestants on this point, and their indifference in seeking after truth.

As the entire fabric of the Protestant system rests upon understanding the Holy Scriptures by the private interpretation of the individual who takes the Bible alone for his guide, independent entirely of any Ecclesiastical authority whatsoever, it became necessary to prove, that unless one supposes an infallible authority, the divinity of the inspiration of the Bible becomes uncertain before the tribunal of private reason. A subject of such importance compelled the Priest in the controversy to a series of discourses wherein he took the position of a questioner desiring to be convinced of the Divine origin of Holy Writ through reason alone. By this help, he was bound to investigate the origin and the particular meaning of each Book in the Bible, the authenticity of the very first manuscript, and the slightest changes therein, a task hardly reassuring to him who does not admit of an infallible authority guarding the Sacred Books. The various translations into modern languages only present new difficulties in understanding the Divine Word, to the unaided reason of the Protestant. From the many mysterious obscurities in which Divine Revelation lies hidden, the speaker argued the impossibility for an individual to penetrate the designs of God and therefore to know the dogmatic and moral truths necessary to salvation.

The ignorance, the passions and the circumstances of the daily life of nine-tenths of the human race, the number of sects, the contradictions, the hatreds, the disputes, the quarrels which divide them, and many other circumstances, offered the Priest an inexhaustible source whence to show the absurdity of the Bible, whose authority and true meaning is not found in reason, but only in the unchanging tradition of the Catholic Church.

Few sectarians are acquainted with the history of the Reformation of the sixteenth century from which their false systems emanated. The utility of this subject is equal to its vastness. In this field of history, the Missionary found most useful matter for many discourses upon the true origin of Protestantism and its chief promoters in Germany and in England. Luther, Melancthon, Bucer, Carlstadt, Munzer, Storck, Calvin, Beza, Zwingli, Aecolampadius, Socinus, Henry VIII of England, Cranmer, the Duke of Somerset, Edward VI, Elizabeth of England, Parker, Knox, Wesley and many other personages famous in the history of religious novelties, were characters often brought forward in order to explain the course of that great revolution that convulsed the half of Europe. In these controversial discourses, it became necessary to speak also of the self-interest, the licentiousness, the ambition, the irreligion, the hatred, the ignorance, all that under the mantle of zeal for evangelical truth were really the hidden motives of the religious upheaval in the days of the Reformation. The sacking of the Religious houses, of hospitals, and colleges, the fanatical demolition of so many precious monuments of antiquity, and destruction of so many manuscripts, the tyranny, intolerance, the depraved customs introduced, the bloody wars and other excesses in which the history of the sixteenth century abounds, furnished the speaker ample proofs to disclose the origin and true character of the new religious creeds.

Added proofs were found in the record of the irreconcilable dogmatic wars among the leaders of the Reformation; their mutual excommunications, their pretended revelations, their false prophecies, the extravagances of many of the fanatics making their appearance upon the theatre of the new creeds, all based as they pretended, upon the sacred words of the Bible. The American Republic also offers grave arguments against these religionaries, for these, availing themselves of their political freedom, were not content to simply change the doctrine of the European sects; but they even created so many new, absurd systems of religion, as to force many to despite all religions and live in complete indifference. All this set face to face with the grand unity of dogmas, of worship and of the divinely ordained Catholic Hierarchy, could not but lower Protestantism in the estimation of the hearers and exalt that Church against which so many of her children rebelled in this unhappy sixteenth century.

Another important subject of controversy furnished the Priest themes for several discourses; this was the Apostolic Mission of which Protestants are deprived. The indifference of most of the sectarians in the United States as well as in Europe leaves them in deepest darkness upon this point, — a point which alone can show us with absolute certainty the true religion of Jesus Christ. To bring conviction to the minds of his hearers, he argued from both the Old Law and the New, the absolute necessity of a Divine Mission to him who calls himself a minister of the Gospel; then he set forth from the sacred pages the anathemas fulminated against the false prophets and teachers who preach without divine authority, and for which they are called thieves and murderers by the Saviour Himself. The speaker investigated the

Mission of the Reformers, showed their inconsistent pretenses to the extraordinary prophetic mission claimed by Luther and the Anabaptists and that these, unable to maintain their claim, drove the other heretics to imagine an invisible Church prior to the Reformation,—and from this invisible Church they affirmed that they had received ordinary mission to preach the Gospel. The absurdity of this subterfuge of Calvin's was so glaring as to force his disciple Beza and many others to seek in a connection with the Albigensian and Waldensian sects of the twelfth and thirteenth centuries a proof of the divinity of their own ministry. The Anglican Church, however, holding the ministry of all continental Protestants as a sacrilegious usurpation, were claiming the Apostolic Mission of their Bishops and Priests through Holy Orders which they pretended to have received from the Catholic Church. In the midst of the confusion other systems sprang up to prove the authority of the heterodox ministers, for these desired that the people themselves, that is the laity, might be able to grant the faculty of preaching the Gospel, while yet other Protestants were asserting that the right of conferring Ordination belongs solely to the ministers of their churches, yet without examining whether or not these were true or false.

So many varieties and contradictions in the religions of the Reformers, for the purpose of proving that their preachers have that mission from the Messiah, according to the words: "as the Father sent me, I also send you" (John XX, 21); and for the purpose of answering the question of Saint Paul: "How shall they preach unless they be sent?" led the mass of modern religionaries into the foolish belief that those are the true ministers of Jesus Christ who declare that they are interiorly called to preach by the Holy Ghost. Thus, by rejecting ecclesiastical order and the Hierarchy, the majority of Protestants in the United States, in the western sections especially, have given themselves up to all the errors taught by a multitude of fanatics, who have the audacity to declare themselves commissioned by the Holy Spirit to preach the Word of God.

A clear, strong, impartial series of arguments upon these subjects, as given above, accompanied by the defence of the Catholic doctrine upon the same, although it required a series of discourses, preached on many occasions, yet was of immense service in confirming Catholics in the Faith and silencing the opponents of the Faith. God mad use of these words to call to the observance of Christian duties many souls who had become cold and almost indifferent to Truth; moreover other souls left the path of error to find the unity of the Faith.

The compiler of the Memoirs would have wished to give a more detailed account of the controversial discussions; but to present clearly the arguments of Protestants against the Faith and then give a satisfactory reply, would necessitate a very long digression entirely foreign to his subject. One who is familiar with controversy sees at once that confuting their arguments upon one sole point of doctrine requires a treatise, and this, if not preceded by certain preliminary theological truths, can be well comprehended by a few readers only. If circumstances permitted, the writer had intended to publish a controversial work embracing those Catholic dogmas which are most opposed by Protestants; citations from Holy Writ, and arguments drawn from reason, set forth in a familiar style and accompanied by practical reflections suggested by the truths of Faith, would present the doctrines of the Church under an aspect more interesting and more attractive even to the eye of those not accustomed to reasoning upon such subjects.

Chapter XXXIX.

CONVERSION OF A YOUNG PROTESTANT TO THE CHURCH IN 1842.

The conversion of certain Protestants to the Catholic Church was accompanied by circumstances which may serve to be edification of others. For this reason we will give a brief account here of the means through which Divine Goodness called a non-Catholic to the light of Faith.

A young merchant who had settled for many years in the city of Galena had been attending the Anglican Church to which he and his associates belonged. His minister's reiterated invectives against the Catholic Faith could in no way impress his heart, too honest to be led astray by false reasonings, by bare assertions, and by the pretended wisdom of the self-styled prophet. Sunday after Sunday had the Anglican preacher wearied and disgusted his hearers, by his continual discoursing upon Antichrist, and as if he were akin to that spirit of lies and blasphemy, had often displayed his eloquence by describing the powers infernal, and pretending that this enemy of Jesus Christ was the Pope and the Catholic Religion. But what availed these declamations? What availed this mania to make people believe that he comprehended the mysterious meaning of the Apocalypse? In a country where error has full liberty to discharge its venom in public, it becomes so frantic and so blind as to reveal its full deformity, and instead of convincing succeeds only in repelling. This is a great truth founded upon experience! The preaching of the angry minister roused in his hearers the determination to listen to the controversies then taking place in the Catholic Church, so vilified and attacked by him.

Among the sincere sectarians was the young man just mentioned. Endowed with keen intelligence as he was, he began to read controversial works, to attend Catholic worship, and to implore the light needed from the Giver of all grace. Several months were spent in these preparatory studies, without any tendency to those sudden impulses and hasty decisions which are too often unhappily followed by tepidity and indifference. He was not content with examining by himself into those dogmatic doctrines which distinguish the Protestant from the Catholic, but he held many familiar conferences with the same rabid Anglican minister himself, in order to convince the latter of his own sincerity in the search for the truth, before bidding farewell to his former belief. Heavenly grace had already met a powerful ally in the zeal with which the young soul sought for the spotless Bride of Christ, and so more strongly did it urge him day by day to present himself to the Priest for Baptism. And at last he prepared his soul for this by the observance of the Lenten Fast.

On the holy day of the Resurrection of our Lord and Saviour Jesus Christ, the neophyte knelt at the sanctuary rail, that he might also rise again in the Sacrament of Regeneration to that life of Faith which the Christian lives. As on such occasions there is always a throng of persons present and among them not a few Protestants, the Priest usually begins with an Instruction upon the necessity of Baptism, and the meaning of the ceremonies thereof, and with an earnest exhortation for the purpose of rousing Faith in every revealed Truth, as well as sincere contrition for all the sins of one's life. The devout, humble and penitent demeanor of the youth bore witness to that inner Light shining from the holy Truths of Religion and illumining his whole being, and bore witness also to that sincere sorrow for sins that flooded his eyes with tears and mingled them with the Baptismal Waters and cleansed his soul from every stain. As a child of the True Church, the youth persevered in the practice of virtue and in the holy fervor that characterizes converts in the United States.

Should any reader be tempted to suspect that these conversions are at least in part brought about by lack of mental power, or through motives of self-interest, by the influence of parents and friends or by any human motive whatever, it is only a matter of justice to state that the conversion of this young man in question as well as of many others, was consummated only after long continued study and research, without one shade of earthly profit, and in direct opposition to his parents who were zealous Protestants. Moreover his familiar intercourse and frequent colloquies with the Anglican minister, who was openly hostile to Catholicity, is a fact strongly supporting the assertion that he abandoned the doctrine of the Reformers because convinced that it did not possess the Truth of the Gospel.

For the sake of living in peace in their various sects, many non-Catholics persuade themselves that they are obliged to live in the religious belief in which they were born. But this is a false doctrine, equally applicable to pagans and Turks, but so far from serving as an excuse for these persons, it actually condemns the very first arch-heretics themselves, who educated in the true Church changed their belief by becoming Protestants. He who returns to the Church of Christ only throws himself into the arms of that tenderest of mothers, from whom he once fled at the risk of his eternal salvation; for the Messias declared: "If he will not hear the Church, let him be to thee as the heathen and publican" (Matt. XVIII, 17), that is, as an unbeliever and a sinner.

Chapter XL.

MISSIONS AMONG THE INDIANS IN THE DIOCESE OF DUBUQUE.

The diocese of Dubuque comprises the vast Territory of Iowa, only a thirtieth part of which is occupied by civilized people who are of European descent, — the diocese comprehends therefore within its limits about fifty thousand Indians, of the tribes of Iowas, Sacs and Foxes, some Winnebagoes in the south, Sioux and Chippewas in the north. Now the preaching of the Gospel among the first four tribes has encountered obstacles almost insuperable by reason of the precarious conditions of the tribes, for within the course of only a few years, they have many times sold the land on which they were living to the Government, and so have often changed their abodes; moreover, even on the very soil which they at present occupy, they consider themselves strangers, knowing too well that they must soon leave it, and pass on elsewhere. The gross sum yearly paid to them by the Government brings with it such an excess of demoralization that they are rendered utterly to devoting themselves to Religion, while the vices of drunkenness, domestic discord and the diseases caused by their miserable environments making irreparable havoc among them, have reduced them to a mere remnant of once numerous tribes. Several attempts were made to encourage some religious fervor among the united tribes of the Sacs and Foxes, but to little purpose. When the Reverend R. Petiot, now of Galena, by the advice of Bishop Loras went among the Winnebagoes in 1842, his ministrations brought great consolation to those few Christians who had been converted previous to the year 1835 and had persevered in the path of rectitude; but as his experience convinced him of the almost entire impossibility of helping the others, he remained there only for several months.

The numerous tribe of the Sioux and many also of the Chippewas occupying an immense tract in the northern part of Iowa, a section not so eagerly coveted by the Government as the more southern portion possessed a more secure abode, less frequented by the throng of traders, for which reason they are less contaminated and more open to the influence of Christianity. Bishop Loras, with his usual zeal, did not fail to consecrate to their needs a portion of the funds contributed by the Propaganda, with the hope of obtaining the conversion of these tribes. Before the autumn of 1839, the Bishop had sent the Reverend S. Galtier in his quality of Missionary to that famous point on the Mississippi, generally called Saint Peter's. This place, which now marks the head of navigation on the great River on account of a cascade there called the Falls of Saint Anthony, is about three hundred and sixty miles from Dubuque and at the juncture of the Saint Peter River with the Mississippi. There at the upper extremity of an elevated tongue of land separating the two rivers, the Government has established a Fort for the defense of the Republic against the Indian tribes. The Priest aforesaid found there a few Canadians without a vestige of Catholicity; however, his zeal, aided by the assistance of his Bishop, built a frame Church dedicated to Saint Peter, instructed the people, baptized Indians as well as some children of Canadian fathers and Indian mothers. He exercised his ministry with abundant fruit and established the Faith in the northern regions of Wisconsin near his Mission.

In 1841, the Bishop of the diocese sent the Reverend Louis Ravoux to evangelize the Indians of the Sioux tribe. This devoted Priest pushed on more than six hundred miles from Dubuque, that is, to a distance of about two hundred and fifty miles above the Falls of Saint Anthony, in the firm hope of gaining these poor souls to Christ. It would not be easy to describe the virtues of this Missionary, in whom a perfect contempt for the world, charity the most ardent, humility, modesty, patience, the spirit of prayer and penance render him dear and precious in the sight of the Lord. Always joyous and content in the direst poverty and affliction, he busied himself in learning the language of the Sioux, among who he had fixed his abode; he translated the prayers and the Catechism into that dialect and taught the truths of the Gospel to the Indians. Having no record or direct information as to the present state of his Mission, we cannot report its progress, but from the fact that the Reverend Anthony Godfert, who was ordained by Bishop Loras in the autumn of 1842, was appointed assistant the next year to Reverend

Louis Ravoux, we may conclude that his labor of converting the Sioux, is taking on a favorable appearance and encouraging us to hope that a great number have been regenerated in holy Baptism and are sharing in the inheritance of the children of God.

There is no doubt that the Sioux and the Chippewas could easily be converted to the Faith if we may judge from the moral and political condition of these tribes in the Territories of Iowa and Wisconsin, for these do not present the same obstacle to conversion that are actually encountered in all the other tribes who live nearest to the whites. Yet to carry on this grand work of salvation to successful issue, humanly speaking, the vocation and the zeal of the Priests alone would not suffice, for experience has shown that it is not the labors of isolated individuals, but those of an organization well disciplined and provided with means for founding the necessary establishments, which give permanence and vigor to the Missions.

The reader of this chapter should not content himself with admiring and praising the zeal and the virtues of the Missionaries among the savages, or with simply desiring the conversion of those pagans; he ought also to strive, both by prayers and by alms to propagate that Faith which, God knows costs what sweat and what sufferings on the part of him who preaches that Faith! By this we would not intimate that the Religion of Christ has need of human assistance in diffusing itself among the infidels, but we do mean to simply counsel this as a most excellent work of charity; that is, to contribute to the expenses connected with exterior worship and to lessen the sufferings of him who preaches the Faith, by furnishing him the bare necessaries of life, and in this way cooperating in the fulfillment of those Heavenly missions which made Isaias cry out: "How beautiful upon the mountains are the feet of him that bringeth good tidings, and that preacheth peace; of him that sheweth forth good, that preacheth salvation, that saith to Sion 'Thy God shall reign.'" (Isaias II, 7).

Chapter XLI.

CHURCH OF SAINT AUGUSTINE AT SINSINAWA, WISCONSIN — ACCOUNT OF SAINT MICHAEL'S CHURCH, GALENA, 1842.

In Wisconsin Territory, nine miles from the city of Galena, and seven miles from Dubuque there is an isolated Mount rising about three hundred English feet above the rich, high lands surrounding it. The American gentleman who first owned this most beautiful place a few years ago named it Sinsinawa from a little stream near by which empties into the Mississippi. The discovery of rich lead mines in the earth surrounding induced many families to settle there in 1839 as miners or farmers, among whom are many Irish and German Catholics. These procure means of subsistence by cultivating the lands and laboring in the mines, but as it was very difficult for their families to attend the churches in the cities, the Missionary in 1842 determined that it was the most advantageous thing for the cause of Religion to build a Church near the Mound. The faithful and also several Protestants contributed a considerable portion of the necessary funds. The Priest, as usual in such enterprises, superintending the work, the Lord's House, under the patronage of Saint Augustine, was in the course of the summer erected upon a beautiful eminence. At present, although still unfinished in the interior, it yet serves its purpose for the many Catholics who attend it. Its dimensions are twenty-five feet in width by forty in length; it is but entirely of timber, and finished with much taste, presenting a pleasing and regular appearance. Thirteen hundred dollars were spent upon this building, of which sum, however, the Priest still owes six hundred dollars. These simple details will be of service to those who wish to trace the origin of the first Catholic establishments in the new sections of America, and will be useful historical records to posterity, for the beginnings of Catholic worship in many cities of the United States are now buried in oblivion for want of such historical records.

The work most useful to the cause of Religion in the regions just referred to, was completed in this year, 1842; I mean the Church of Saint Michael at Galena. This building is of stone, was begun in 1835, and the work interrupted several times from lack of funds. In 1841 it had a loan of three thousand dollars, with which the work was brought to completion. In its order of architecture, it is superior to any other of that quarter of the country. It may not be out of place to observe that the church cost fourteen thousand dollars, the voluntary contributions of the faithful of that parish from 1835 to 1842; the disinterestedness economy and indefatigable attention of him who had charge had this result: all the people, among them not a few Protestants, annually contributed according to their means. The parish of Saint Michael extends entirely over Jo Daviess county, about twenty-four miles square, and contains more than two thousand Catholics. From the autumn of 1839 they were almost always attended by two Priests who were often absent, however, for several days, in order to visit the faithful of various stations for a distance of thirty and forty miles. Monsignore Peter Kenrick, the coadjutor of the Right Reverend Joseph Rosati, Bishop of Saint Louis, in July, had the kindness to visit the congregation of Catholics of Galena to bless their church and to preach twice a day during the course of a week. His eloquent moral and dogmatic discourses conduced to the spiritual advancement of many of his hearers.

Chapter XLII.

THE REASON FOR THE PRIEST'S DECISION TO VISIT HIS NATIVE LAND — PREACHING AND CONVERSIONS IN BURLINGTON IN 1843.

The frequent journeys during the summer of 1842 in fulfilment of the various obligations of his missions, in the autumn, brought on a severe illness which threatened the life of the Priest, then staying in Iowa City. In that distant corner of the American Republic, so lately settled, it was not always easy to find physicians endowed with necessary skill in administering suitable remedies; in this case, however, a kind Providence willed that the patient should find one who understood the case and gave the suitable remedies and slowly rescued him from his apparently hopeless condition. During many months of convalescing, it was decided, following the advice of friends, that he should make a visit to his old home, persuaded that this was the Will of God, for the good of himself and others.

With strength partly restored, the Missionary in accordance with the Bishop's desire occupied himself during the winter in organizing the parish of Saint Paul, in Burlington, which had been increased by the arrival of a number of Catholic families from foreign countries. The most respectable and well educated Protestant citizens, among whom were lawyers and sectarian ministers, thronged to the Church every Sunday evening to listen to the discourses on dogma freely preached in defence of the Truth and against error. And though the Priest had signified to his hearers his desire to enter upon a public controversy with any minister, no one appeared to take advantage of such an opportunity of defending the main negative principles upon which their particular doctrines rest.

One result of this Mission was the conversion of an American gentleman to the Faith; he had been a member of the Methodist set. The arguments drawn from Holy Writ, from reason and from ecclesiastical History upon the obligation of Sacramental Confession and upon the Divine Power of remitting sin conferred upon the Church by Jesus Christ, had wrought so powerfully upon this will-disposed soul, that on that very evening, on leaving the Church, he declared himself a Catholic and promised to go to Confession. With the assistance of this grace, he had the consolation at last of receiving the most holy Eucharist in the first Monday of Lent, and the practice of all the duties of a Christian obtained for him that fervor, through which he is now led to the practice of the works of mercy.

A woman who had been a member of the Reformed Lutheran Church, whose children had been baptized in the Catholic Church a few months before, came to be regenerated in that Sacrament. After the administering of Sacramental Absolution (conferred in case the Baptism received in her infancy had been valid) she received with edifying fervor the Bread of Angels, no more to be separated from that loving Jesus Who had called her to Himself. Such spiritual consolations always turn to the edification of the Minister of the Altar, for they are accompanied by the sweet hope that he may have contributed in some way, like an instrument in God's Hand, to increasing the number of the elect.

Bishop Loras in that year appointed as Pastor over the parish of Saint Paul, the Reverend J. Healy, an Irishman who had come to the diocese of Dubuque the preceding year; his edifying life assisted by his eloquence will carry on propagation of the faith in Burlington and the surrounding country, where but a few months ago, it had been almost unknown, and it is to be hoped that after error has been unmasked, the Faith will reign there supreme.

Chapter XLIII.

THE FALSE PROPHET, JOSEPH SMITH, GOLDEN BOOK OF MORMON—SECT OF THE LATTER-DAY SAINTS AND THEIR ABSURD DOCTRINES.

It was in February 1843, that the Missionary determined to see and speak with a heresiarch notorious for years, in every quarter of the Republic and in England, also. With this object, the Priest left Burlington for a few days, and betook himself to the town of Fort Madison where the Reverend J. Alleman was exercising his holy ministry. Descending the Mississippi on the ice for ten miles, he arrived at Nauvoo, the famous city of the Mormons. There the famous "Prophet" Joseph Smith, founder of the sect, has his residence.

In order to awake in the devout reader's soul, sentiments of lasting gratitude to God, to Whose mercy he owes the priceless gift of Faith, we will give here an idea of the new religion of the Mormons. This belief, though founded upon the most extreme imposture and professing the most extravagant and absurd doctrines, nevertheless has found a great number of followers in the blind credulity and fanaticism of those upon whom the light of Catholic Truth does not shine.

The false prophet and heresiarch, Joseph Smith, founder of the sect of Mormons, or "Latter-Day Saints" is a man of thirty-nine years, tall, well-proportioned; his countenance manifests neither amiability nor good judgment, his expression indicates anything but piety, his manners are rather rude. Born of poor parents, he did not have the advantages of an ordinary education. He has a wife and children. His influence over the sect is almost unbounded, and he seeks by every means to hold the Mormons to the belief that he is a prophet of the Most High, with Whom he declares he has frequent colloquies and by Whose inspiration he directs and governs the new church of the "Latter-Day Saints." On the occasion of the Missionary's visit to him, he solemnly declared that he had many times seen Almighty God, face to face, and had received many revelations from the Apostle Saint Paul, to whom he asserted that he was not inferior in goodness. So great was his imposture and effrontery that in one harangue he proclaimed himself great as Moses, and as Jesus Christ. There was much comment of his immorality even among his own followers. The false prophet owes the propagation of his false doctrines to the cooperation of several interested associates, among whom are distinguished, Sidney Rigdon, Parley P. Pratt, and John Taylor. The religious ignorance of the Protestant people also contributed to this result.

    The history of this great impostor of our century dates from 1823, when he was only seventeen years old. Joseph Smith assures us that on the twenty-second day of September in that year, as angel appeared to him from Heaven to assure him his sins were forgiven and to reveal to him where he would find an ancient book written on plates of gold and entitled "The Book of Mormon," written by a certain Moroni, the last of the tribe of the Nephites of the race of Israel, and fourteen hundred years ago deposited in a stone chest upon the bill Camorah in the State of New York. Joseph Smith's desire to enrich himself by the acquisition of this golden book had this result, however, that when he set about removing it from the spot indicated, the Angel would not let him secure it. On September 22, 1827, the Angel of the Lord appeared a second time to the "prophet," consigned to him "The Book of Mormon" together with two stones called Urim and Thummim* looking

---

   * "Urim" and "Thummim" are two Hebrew words meaning "Doctrine and Truth" and were affixed to that part of the Pontifical robes of Aaron, called the Rational, which was the High Priest's breast-plate.

through which he would be enabled to translate from the Egyptian language into English what was written upon the golden plates. After various vicissitudes, Joseph Smith, assisted by two companions employed as writers, finished the translation in 1830. This done, the Angel again appeared and carried away those wonderful plates of portent.

"The Book of Mormon" or "The Records of the Nephites" forms a volume of five hundred pages in octavo, containing fifteen different books, assuming to be the works of the different authors whose names they bear. The history of these books extends over a period of a thousand years, that is, from the time of Sedecias, King of Juda, to the year 420 A. D. In these ill-written records, which might be called rude religious romances, it is pretended that the true history is given of the aborigines or the Indians of the American Continent, who there emigrated from Jerusalem about six hundred years before the Christian era under the leadership of a certain Judaeus Lehi; on their arrival in these regions his children separated into two peoples, one faithful to the Law of Moses, the other wicked and barbarous; the former were called Nephites, the latter went under the name of Lamanites. Thence the book goes on to relate their apostasies, journeys, vicissitudes and wars which disturbed these nations for a thousand years. Different prophets were sent by God to both the Nephites and Lamanites during that period; the Messiah of the world Himself appeared to them after His resurrection in Jerusalem; He also chose out of the tribes of America, twelve apostles to preach His doctrine. But after many years these people delivered themselves up to irreligion and sin, for which reason the Lord roused the most wicked of the two nations to destroy His own people, so that according to the history of the prophet Moroni, two hundred and thirty thousand people were killed in the last battle near the hill Camorah; he alone survived of all his tribe to record the fact by means of the history of the vicissitudes of the Nephites on the aforementioned plates of gold, which he hid by Divine inspiration upon the hill Camorah.

There are documents in existence sufficient to prove that the so-called Book of Mormon was written by a certain minister, Spaulding, who entitled it "The Manuscript Found." After his death in 1816, it fell into the hands of Joseph Smith, an ignorant man, but cunning enough to make a bad use of it by publishing it as a miraculous work of divine inspiration. In spite of the gross imposture on which the book was based, the prophet with several companions whom he declared to have been chosen by Divine inspiration, began to preach and soon gathered about him a number of disciples, whom he baptized by immersion, under the name of the Latter-Day Saints, more commonly known as Mormons.

In 1835, they built a temple in the State of Ohio at a cost of forty thousand dollars, but finding themselves deeply in debt and in distress, many of them emigrated to Missouri and there by God's command to the prophet were to build the eternal City and temple of Zion. But in place of this, in 1838 they were driven out of the State by the united forces of the Missourians on account of their pernicious doctrines in opposition to the Government, and for their insubordination to the laws. At last, early in 1839, they took refuge in the State of Illinois on the bank of the Mississippi; there they commenced the city of Nauvoo upon a most beautiful plain, a town which now contains from eight to ten thousand inhabitants. The Mormons have been occupied for several years in building a great temple of a unique style of architecture; the false prophet declared to his followers that he had conceived the plan for this by Divine inspiration. According to their own estimate the number of these fanatics is not less than a hundred thousand, many of whom are in England and Canada.

The reader may perhaps be anxious to know what points in their doctrines distinguish the Mormons from the other sects. We will, therefore, give here a synopsis full enough to satisfy his reasonable desire.

In the first place, the Mormons believe in the Divine origin of the Holy Scriptures and profess an equal reverence for the Book of Mormon, which is also called the Bible of the Mormons. They affirm that the Redemption of Jesus Christ has already saved the entire human race, therefore children dying before attaining the use of reason, go to Paradise, Baptism not being a necessity for them. Baptism by immersion of the whole body is a necessary condition for the remission of sins committed by adults. This Sacrament, according to their theology, is applicable to the souls of their parents and friends dying at an adult age without having received it. Consequently some Mormons have themselves baptized many times. Through the imposition of hands by their apostles and ministers in the name of Jesus Christ, they believe that they receive the gift of revelation, of prophecy, of visions, of apparitions of the Angels, of curing the sick, of working miracles; in short all the gifts mentioned in the Bible. Moreover, they believe that Apostles and prophets like those of the New Testament should always be in the Church. The Mormons accuse the Catholic Church and also all the Protestant sects of apostatizing from the teaching of the Gospel, and for this reason that the whole world for more than fourteen hundred years has been without the true Church. They pretend that this sect of fanatics has been raised up by Almighty God for the purpose of preparing for the second advent of the Messias who will come in the clouds of Heaven in great power and glory. They assert that this even will be preceded by universal destruction and by judgment upon all the kingdoms of the earth, and that it is already close at hand. In the midst of these calamities the Kingdom of God upon earth will remain unharmed and triumphant.

The theology of the Mormons is for the most part the work of a certain Parley Parker Pratt. This man teaches that all the prophecies of the Bible are purely literal; of these many have been fulfilled, others are approaching fulfillment. The deluded writer, to rouse enthusiasm among his ignorant followers, gives a description of the beauty and perfection of the world before the Fall of Adam, then deplores its present state, and quoting many prophecies literally, predicts that on the second Coming of Christ, this world will be re-established in its original perfect state. The various divisions of the globe with the islands will be united into one continent; there will be neither hill nor valley nor crooked paths; the deserts shall blossom and all nature shall be changed into one delightful garden, the wild beasts grown tame shall live together; the just shall inhabit the earth, enjoying its fruits in perfect peace, all clad in white linen, as becomes immortality.

Among the most remarkable dreams of this man may be considered this that all the Jews will rise to return to the land of Israel, will rebuild the Old Jerusalem, will have David as King; that Adam with locks white as wool, seated in state shall salute all his sons who died in the faith of the Messias. Moreover, in this Mormon Paradise all the Patriarchs, the

Prophets, the Apostles and all the just shall salute each other while the Messias Himself shall offer them bread and wine. This will be the Nuptials of the Lamb.

The Mormon belief teaches also that before the Second Coming of Christ, there shall be built the great City of Sion, sanctuary of the Lord, where gold will take the place of brass, silver of iron, brass of wood, and iron of stone. They predict that the New Jerusalem, as told in the Scripture, will be built in America, conformable to the ancient plan, and that it will serve for the descendants of the Patriarch Joseph, that is, for the Indians of America and for those who shall join them.

The Old and the New Jerusalem and the City of Sion, according to the predictions of Ezechiel and other prophets of the Bible and of "The Book of Mormon," shall continue in peace and prosperity for the space of one thousand years, called the Millennium, but, later, when the heavens and the earth shall be renewed, these cities shall be raised on high with their inhabitants, where changed and made new, they shall descend after the catastrophe, one, upon the land of America, the other upon the site which it first occupied and there they will remain for all eternity. Such is the beautiful paradise of these fanatics.

The Mormon idea of Divinity is a thoroughly material one. Their theologian, Parley Pratt, as quoted by his associate, John Taylor, hints in his writings that as God created man to His own Image, He himself has a material body like ours,—He defends this absurd statement, by quoting expressions of Holy Writ, wherein, in speaking of Almighty God, are employed the words, face, hand, arm, ear, finger, foot, etc. Not only do they attribute a material body to the Divinity, but they believe Him to be subject to the passions, the anger, hatred, fury, revenge, etc., in the same sense as these words have when spoken of men. The Mormon's Deity may justly be termed a new Jupiter.

We may observe here that any system of religion, however extravagant and absurd in its teachings, will always find followers among non-Catholics, whenever the authors of the system know how to quote many passages from the Bible in its defence. The Mormon preachers had so thoroughly studied the Bible as to stand ready to convince their hearers that these dogmas were a commingling of the prophecies and the Gospel; in this way they converted a great number of people, among them not a few minsters of the sects. It seems almost incredible that a people can be so intelligent, so keen-sighted in the business of this world, so enterprising and so fond of reading as are the Americans of the United States, and at the same time so ready to believe every error invented by cunning and religious fanaticism. But of what are not men capable outside of the Catholic Church? Will they be able to find the Truth without it? Will they be able to hold fast to any belief? Will they find any foundation whereon to build? The great apostle of the Gentiles answers us in his letter to Timothy, that they are "ever learning, and never attaining to the knowledge of Truth" (II, III, 7), and writing to the Ephesians he calls them children tossed to and fro, and carried about with every wind of doctrine by the wickedness of men, by cunning craftiness whereby there is any foundation of true doctrine outside the House that there is any foundation of true doctrine outside the House of God, which he declares "is the church of the living God, the pillar and ground of Truth" (I Tim. III, 15).

From this digression let the Catholic learn to be forever grateful to God for the Heavenly gift of Faith which has been granted to him in preference to so many others, who have become the victims of error and religious fanaticism. Let the non-Catholic then, beholding the sad consequences and excesses into which the private interpretation of the Bible carries the sectarians, abandon the false system of the Reformation, by professing obedience to the Church, outside of which are found only the false teachings of those men of whom the Messias prophesied when he said: "And many false prophets shall rise and shall seduce many" (Matt. XXIV, 11).

Returning to the city of Burlington after this visit to the false prophet, the Missionary remained there until the first week of Lent, when he departed for Galena, one hundred and eighty miles distant. He made a portion of this journey on the icy surface of the Mississippi River, a most agreeable mode of traveling with horse and sleigh; but the cold was more intense than on previous years, the temperature being ten degrees below the freezing point for the greater part of the month of March.

Chapter XLIV.

DEPARTURE OF THE MISSIONARY FROM GALENA—HE ASSISTS AT THE COUNCIL OF BALTIMORE — CROSSES THE OCEAN AND FINALLY ARRIVES IN MILAN.

The Christian who recognizes his own inability to understand what tends to his own greater spiritual good is always disposed to abandon himself to the guidance of the invisible Hand of the God, in Whom, speaking with Saint Paul, "we live and move and are" (Acts XVII, 28). Renouncing self and sacrificing his own will to the inscrutable designs of God, he loses nothing and gains everything, according to the Apostle's teaching to the Romans: "We know that to them that love God all things work together unto good." (VIII, 28.)

The many circumstances which led the Missionary to absent himself for a time from his American Mission and to visit his native country, forced themselves upon his attention, under such an aspect as almost to compel him to undertake the long, journey. Serious failure in health, the necessity of a rest, the pressing needs of his different Missions, adding to these the most kindly agreement of the Bishop of Dubuque, with a few other reasons of lesser importance determined his departure. After Easter, 1843, he left the city of Galena, state of Illinois, for Milan in Italy. As he was entirely destitute of money, he relied on Providence for his expenses. The people, convinced that the motive for the journey was not for merely human ideas, but was undertaken for their greater benefit, believed that they were bound in duty to assist in its accomplishment, by contributing money. Bishop Loras, finding himself obliged to go to Baltimore in order to attend the Triennial Council of the Bishops of the United States, took his Vicar to serve as his theologian at that solemn Assembly,—and thus did it come about that he was sped upon his voyage.

On the sixteenth of April after receiving into the bosom of the Church two Protestant of the Anglican Church, the Missionary left the little city of Galena in a steamboat to go down the majestic Mississippi, and four days later landed at the city of Saint Louis. Favored by the delightful breezes of a beautiful spring, he found the deepest delight in contemplating the visible works of God, which always lead the Christian's heart to sigh after a blessed eternity. In truth, the rapid motion of the boat, accelerated by the current, made the view of the hills and valleys, the meadows, the woods, the vast solitudes, the numberless islands, and at intervals, the new rising towns, glide before the eye with swift disappearance to lose themselves in the distance; and all in their silence seemed to say to the traveller, "We are not for thee, thou art travelling towards another land." Yet when Nature is ready to don her green mantle she renders spontaneous that loving cry from the heart of the Prophet David: "Praise ye Him, ye mountains and all hills; fruitful trees and all cedars" (Psalms, CXLVIII). The magnificent starry vault of the sky alone could give one a picture of the glorious eternity according to those words of the Prophet: "The heavens declare the glory of God; and the firmament showeth the works of His Hands" (Psalms, XVIII). Going swiftly down the river, while everything flits back, the sky alone seems immovable to the gaze and offers to the traveler in the dark night of this world a sure pledge of that splendor, the glory and the immutability of Paradise. But until the longed-for Kingdom comes to us, we must continue our journey in this vale of tears.

On reaching Saint Louis, where is established the See of the Most Reverend Peter Kenrick, the two travelers embarked on a beautiful steamboat that was to go down the Mississippi and then up the Ohio, against the current, as far as Cincinnati. On this journey of four days and four nights, the Priest had many times occasion to speak of the Truths of Faith to many of the numerous companies of American ladies and gentlemen.

Unless one has had a long experience, it is not possible to conceive an idea of the false method of reasoning, and the false religious principles of the majority of Protestants, notwithstanding with which Religion in America is treated in familiar freedom with which Religion in America is treated in familiar conversation kept the Missionary busily occupied in complying with the demands of those who either through curiosity or desire for instruction were anxious to know something about the true doctrine of the Church. The city of Cincinnati was very different from the same place as he first saw it in 1828. It then contained only twenty thousand inhabitants; now it numbers more than fifty thousand. Another steamer carried us to the town of Wheeling, whence we traveled by stage one hundred and twenty miles in twenty-two hours to take the railway, at Cumberland. This mode of travelling seems to have attained the last limit in speed, for in eight hours, including the stoppages at the different stations, we reached the city of Baltimore, a distance of one hundred and seventy-five miles. Baltimore contains about one hundred and sixty thousand inhabitants, of whom the claim there are forty or fifty thousand Catholics; there are then churches besides the Cathedral, the latter is not entirely finished.

The Provincial Council of 1843 was opened on the fourteenth of May; the procession of about forty Priests, fourteen Bishops and the Archbishop, all vested in their sacred garb according to rank, proceeded from the Archbishop's House, made a circuit of the exterior of the Church, entered by the great door and took up their position as arrange in the sanctuary. A Pontifical Mass was celebrated, and after the Veni Creator the Council was solemnly announced. The Bishops held private sessions every morning for a week in the Archbishop's house; in the afternoon they assembled in the sanctuary of the Cathedral, where their Theologians were also present, and also the Superiors of the Regular Orders in America. The points proposed on the first day to the Theologians grouped in committee of five to each point, were passed from hand to hand, cited by the Bishop Promoter of the Council; then that member to whom was assigned the point last cited presented his answer written, on which, before passing to the next member, reach was free to express what he thought best. In this manner the various points of Ecclesiastical Discipline were publicly discussed by the Theologians in presence of the Prelates who were in their private councils framing the decrees of the Council. On the fifth Sunday after Easter, May twenty-first, the procession of the opening Sunday was repeated. After the celebration of the Pontifical Mass, the Bishops in cope and mitre, each in turn beginning with the oldest in the episcopacy, singed the Decrees with his own had, on the Altar at the Gospel side. Then the "Te Deum" was chanted. The creation of the new Episcopal Sees and the election of the Bishops now formed the subjects of most interest to the Triennial Council of Baltimore. All these Acts, however, are subject always to Pontifical Authority.

King Providence for our Missionary a rare traveling companion across the sea, in the person of Monsignore J. Chabrat, coadjutor Bishop of Kentucky, who was going to France. Bidding farewell to Monsignore Loras, the Right Reverend Bishop of Dubuque, the Priest set out from Baltimore on the twenty-second of May, traveling by rail to Philadelphia and the following day to New York. At three o'clock on the afternoon of the twenty-fifth, in the Feast of the Ascension, Bishop Chabrat and his companion left the land in the steamer, the "Great Western" (Which signifies "Il Grande Occidentale") and before night the shores of America disappeared from our view.

Here we are on the vast sea, but not tossed by the fury of the winds as in our voyage of 1828, when we could have said with the Prophet David: "The waves mount up to the heavens, and they go down to the depths; their soul pined away with evils." (Psalms, CVI.) But now the soft breath of May helped on the swift course of the splendid ship. By the power of steam made almost independent of the winds with the never-ending whirling of its huge wheels, the ship ploughed the immense waste of waters, seeming to verify the words of the Royal Prophet: "This great sea which stretcheth wide its arms; there are creeping things without numbers. There the shops shall go." (Psalms, CIII.) The immense fires always kept alive, the trail of dense smoke which it left in the air made one think of those horses described by Saint John in the Apocalypse whose "heads were as the heads of lions; and from their mouths proceeded fire, and smoke, and brimstone." (IX, 17.) All the passengers to the number of one hundred and twenty-four were served several times a day at the same table. There were people from many parts, among them more than thirty ladies. The times was spent in conversation, reading and even in amusements according to each one's inclination. Associating with a company of this kind for several days greatly assists the attentive observer in his study of the many characters which make up human society.

On the morning of the fifth of June the experienced captain had told the passengers that the coast of Ireland would be in sight at evening, which proved true, and at six o'clock in the morning of the seventh, Bishop Chabrat and the Missionary landed at Liverpool. On the same day, traveling by rail, two hundred and ten miles they reached London, a place where material wealth rises to the highest side by side with the very extremity of misery. They took up their journey again for Calais, reaching Paris on June eleventh. Here it came to light that the Bishop, as if he had discovered that the funds of his companion were insufficient to take him to his home, had paid all expenses from Liverpool, and now took leave of the Priest to pursue his journey in another direction. After a brief delay at Paris, Lyons and Turin, the Missionary at last entered the city of Milan on the Feast Day of Saints Peter and Paul.

If for the sake of recovering one's health of revisiting parents, friends and native land after many years' absence the world deems it necessary to journey across the continent of America for sixteen hundred miles by rivers, for one hundred and thirty by stage, of four hundred by rail, then crossing the ocean, to travel across Europe two hundred and sixty miles by rail, thirty by water and another seven hundred and eighty-six by stage, what will not the Christian do that the may "come to Mount Sion, to the city of the living God, the heavenly Jerusalem and to the company of many thousand of Angels?" (Heb. XII, 22.) Until we reach that city beheld by Saint John, which "hath no need of the sun, nor of the moon, to shine in it; for the glory of God hath enlightened it and the Lamb is the light thereof" (Apoc. XXI, 23), we exiles upon this earth as says David of the Israelites in the Babylonian Captivity, "shall sit and weep, when we remember Sion." (Psalms, CXXXVI.) However far one travels, whatever riches he possess, the heart is never satisfied, it can always say with King Solomon: "I have seen all things that are done under the sun, and behold all is vanity and vexation of spirit." (Eccles. I, 14.) And so, intent only on persevering in the way that leads to a happy eternity, that country that we long to see, we must needs again forsake parents, friends and earthly home, that we may one day enter our heavenly home. O, the consolation of that well founded hope that makes us cry out with the Royal Prophet:

"In a strange land, if I forget thee, O Jerusalem, let my right hand be forgotten, Let my l tongue cleave to my jaws, if I do not remember thee; If I make not Jerusalem the beginning of my joy." (Psalms, CXXXVI.)

Part III

Chapter I

THE SPIRIT OF PROTESTANTISM.

For the purpose of showing the actual condition of our holy Religion in America, in relation to that majority of sixteen millions of non-Catholics, over two millions of those belonging to the Faith, the editor of these Memoirs has decided that it may be of use to the reader to explain the particular spirit of Protestantism, its sects, and the weapons it employs in combating Catholic principles. Afterwards we will explain how interesting is the mission of the Church, how thoroughly fitted to the situation are her clergy, of how great utility are the Sister of Charity in the United States. Lastly we will give a table of the ecclesiastic statistics of this Great Republic which will be a source of consolation to souls filled with zeal, when they see how deeply the Apostolic Hierarchy has taken root in every quarter of the country, so deeply as to fill us with hope that one day it will bring forth abundant fruit.

In the first place for the better understanding of the spirit of Protestantism, it should be stated that perfect freedom of worship, guaranteed by law, has had the result of developing the true character of the Religious sects in America. These of their nature disposed to division and novelty by the fundamental principle of the Reformation, that is, private interpretation of the Bible, found in that country favorable conditions for displaying themselves in all their deformity. Protestantism having degenerated into a purely negative doctrine and with only individual caprice and intelligence for a foundation, which is influenced by every human passion and frailty, it follows, that in America where the spirit of personal independence is carried to the extreme, sectarians are yet more disposed to deny what others believe, in order to give loose rein to the suggestions of pride, malice, self-interest, the passions, fanaticism, personal delusions. Not only the ministers but even every individual is imbued with a spirit of all-directed religious independence which leads them to consider themselves sole and absolute masters and competent judges of the truths to be believed and of the morality to be practised. The haughty cry, "I am a free man!" seeks to put down every authority and the teachings of all the ages before the shallow, fallacious reasoning of every sectarian. It follows from this, that, generally speaking, in America, the opinion of him who teaches is considered no more worthy of belief than that of his pupil, the interpretation of the hearer is held to be of equal authority with that of the preacher, and the acceptations of the Holy Scriptures are such and so many as to make it impossible to give an account of them. Belonging to a sect does not mean a firm belief in all its teachings, — but rather to go to one Church rather than to another, to attend the sermons of one preacher oftener than those of another, and in many cases it means only that one's father or mother, wife or husband, is a follower of that sect. Few study the history of their own sect, and still fewer its true doctrine.

Every human institution naturally is influenced in some degree by the character of the society and times in which it finds itself, and in the United States, less than elsewhere, does Protestantism depend upon the authority either of history or of its own theologians; the freedom of the individual decides everything. In the sectarian councils, regardless of the beliefs of their predecessors, the points wherein they differ are decided with the utmost freedom not to say, indifference. The idea of a constant, unwavering interpretation of the Bible can have no weight in their decisions and any argument whatever resting upon tradition would be rejected with contempt. In fine, the political principle that the majority ought to rule, is the same as that which regulates in religious matters. To perceive clearly the position of all the sects in this country, the reader must apply these facts to all the Protestant denominations and to all the local associations that compose them, and lastly, must recognize in each individual the unlimited exercise of that maxim. "I am free" in a much wider sense than in its political signification. So strange an individual freedom is the source of innumerable intellectual vagaries, which are indirectly protected by the civil laws, for these never put any hindrance to the public preaching of the most extravagant religious doctrines.

But notwithstanding what has been said on this point, there are principles in the Republic which arrest the progress of any sectarian excesses or least mitigate them to the extent of making them endurable. When a thing is pushed to the height of extravagance it must necessarily fall back; now the press and free preaching carry the religious novelties to the last extremity in the beginning and the people who reach and who grasp everything through the medium of the newspapers soon grow indifferent and laugh at the follies of other people. Besides, there are many ready writers both Catholics and Protestants, whose pens are never idle. These pounce at once upon fanaticism in its various forms from every direction, and so weaken it by reducing the ranks of its followers. The good sense of the masses, the wide spread intelligence and educational training, added to indifferentism, form a powerful force against the innate tendency to non-Catholic principles and the creation of new doctrines.

The constant doctrinal dissensions between sect and sect, with unrestrained liberty of writing and speaking contributes greatly to open the eyes of the sincere Protestants; I will even say, whenever such disputes arouse animosity, hatred, calumnies, many of them not seldom decide to forsake their errors and join the Catholic Church; others end in despising all religions, and professing none of them.

A long residence among a Protestant people has taught the attentive observer that there are many individuals among them trained in prejudice against Catholicity and utterly ignorant of the true spirit of Christianity or else persuaded of the holiness of their own sect who seem to live in invincible ignorance of the true Religion. On the other hand, one often finds among the members of the separated churches a notable degree of piety, of charity, of love of one's neighbor, all united to an earnest desire to believe in all the Truths revealed by Jesus Christ and with the practice of the different works of mercy. Therefore that Catholic would be wanting in wisdom who would condemn indiscriminately and without regard to circumstances or to the inscrutable judgments of God, that person who is found apparently outside the Church.

The political equality that exists in America has completely deprived Protestantism of the possibility of obtaining that dominion over Catholicity that it holds in several states in Europe. Besides the great number of sects, their dependence upon one another for the sake of preserving the mutual freedom of worship obliges each to concede to any other religious belief the same privileges desired by its own followers. In like manner just upon this principle rests the case of Catholicity. But the primary cause which forbids any political superiority whatever of one religious denominations over another rests in the suffrage of the people, whose vote decides the bestowal of almost every public office. The result is that it seldom happens that religious fanatics through the influences of their own sect alone, as also open and declared enemies of Christianity, succeed in securing the vote of the people in general. When Catholicity has many followers in any section, it not only wins the respect of Government officials, but is often able, by its influence to place its numbers in the most important positions of the nation. Therefore considering that there are only two millions of Catholics, intermingled with a population of sixteen millions partly Protestant, and partly without any religion, the present political relations existing between the Church and the non-Catholics in America may be considered as privileges never accorded to her in any other quarter of the word under like circumstances.

Chapter II.

PRINCIPAL PROTESTANT SECTS IN THE UNITED STATES.

The sects in United States numbering the most members are those of the Methodists and Baptists; these are, however, subdivided into various branches differing one from another in some particular method of understanding the Bible or in some different form of government. Although the sects mentioned above publish the statement that they number about seven million followers, there is reason to doubt the truth of their calculation.

In fanaticism and extravagant manifestations of their worship, the Methodists surpass their brethren in Protestantism; the number of their ministers is very great, so that assemblies are always well provided with these preachers, whose special virtue consists in talking much, and as if moved by the Spirit of God,—in raising their voices in shouts, prayers and tears so as to affect their hearers. But the Methodists are distinguished yet more from the other sects by what is called their "Camp Meeting," that is "Campo di adunanza," held twice a year, but principally in the autumn. Thither assemble entire families — fathers, mothers, sons, daughters — of all ages, leaving their dwellings and daily occupations, carrying with them provisions and tents for the purpose of dwelling three or four days and nights in the woods. There, five, six and seven ten thousand of the sect pass the greater part of the day and night in listening to the ministers, in singing hymns and in prying, believing that thus they will obtain an immediate, direct influx of the Spirit of God. Many of the people, of the women especially, at such times become so agitated, so excited and carried away by religious fanaticism as to fall in convulsions, in fainting fits, with trembling of the whole body; transported by their fancies, believing that they see the Messias, they weep, laugh, dance, sing and pray, accompanying all this with violent bodily contortions and convulsions. Our Divine Saviour seemed to indicate this sect where He says: "If any man shall say to you; Lo here is Christ or there, do not believe him. If they shall say to you; Behold He is in the desert, go ye not out; Behold, He is in the closet, believe it not" (Matt. XXXIV, 23, 26).

When the spirit of darkness enters into some of these victims of his, he throws them upon the ground, and causes very strange happenings among them. It is said in the State of Kentucky in 1800, and for many years after, an epidemic of convulsions spread among the assemblies of the religious fanatics; some so convulsed that head and feet met, rolled like a wheel along the earth; others rolled horizontally along, groveling in the mud; some underwent violent contortions all over the body as if pierced with hot irons, sometimes constantly twisting the head round, and throwing the face from one shoulder to the other so violently so as to hideously disguise the form. There were women whose hair rose upon the head at such times, and who seemed to hiss; others jumped around like frogs, assuming grotesque and horrible attitudes; others moved on all fours like a dog, and looking up into the face of the minister barked like those animals.[*] At present, these extravagances are not common in the sect, yet there are still a great number of these fanatics especially among the women who at the "Camp Meetings" adjust the hair and garments as if they were about to endure

---

[*] The particular circumstances referred to were recently printed by Mr. J. B. Turner, the Protestant Professor in Jacksonville College, Illinois, in a work entitled "Mormonism of all Ages."

a struggle, because during the prevalence of this religious excitement they are not themselves conscious of their own actions. The Methodists do not all approve of the "Camp Meetings" on account of the disorders orders and immorality which often accompany such large assemblies.

The Baptists are not behind the sect just described in their enthusiasm and manner of preaching. Their special point of doctrine is the baptism of adults by immersion of the whole body under the water. Very often they argue upon this practice of theirs, condemning the other religions as destitute of true baptism. The minister with the candidate who is clothed in a white garment goes down into a river or lake until the water is up to his waist, then submerges him under the surface of baptism. As a sign of the faith that animates formula of baptism. As a sign of the faith that animates them, not seldom in the cold winter, they break an opening into the ice for this great ceremony without regard to age or sex, much less for the harmful results of so imprudent a proceeding, through which many persons have ruined their health, and even lost their lives.

We may call the reader's attention here to this fact, that the Methodists and Baptist comprise almost one-third of the Protestants of these United States and assimilate the least intelligent class of the people, especially in section outside of the city, and where religious mania finds more abundant pasturage. It is these two sects which appeal most to the feelings, upon which they work by the rapid and extravagant manner of preaching, praying and singing.

The various sects of Presbyterians or Calvinists come next. For several years they lost that influence which they appeared to exercise over public opinion. Their ministers are generally endowed with moderate education, and they heartily detest the Church of Jesus Christ, they are most zealous in the war against the truths which the Church teaches, and are ever foremost in publishing far and wide anything that can possibly appear as a dishonor and serve as a reproach against the Catholics. Judging by the exterior aspect of the Presbyterians, they might be said to be saints upon earth; Sunday is most scrupulously observed by avoiding even those occupations or comforts, which in our day are considered lawful by the whole Christian world. In truth, the Lord's Day is to a pious Calvinist the most gloomy day of the whole week. Indeed, one might be induced to believe in the sanctity of Presbyterianism, had not the Messias said: "Wo to you, Scribes and Pharisees, hypocrites; because you are like to whited sepulchres, which outwardly appear to men beautiful, but within are full of dead men's bones and of all filthiness. So you also outwardly appear to men just, but inwardly you are full of hypocrisy and iniquity" (Matt. XXIII, 27, 28).

To the Calvinists succeeds the Episcopalian sect, which as it was less affected by the Reformation, truly ought to be less hostile to the Catholic Church. It is divided into the Puseyites, the High Church and the Low Church, which follow more or less closely the teachings of the Anglican Church as it was established by the authority of the king and the Parliament of England. The Episcopalian ministers are for the most part educated to the ecclesiastic career. With few exceptions they bear less religious aversion for the Catholics whom, however, they believe to be in error, but still in the preservation of the truths necessary to salvation. And yet on this point, the body of the clergy of the Low Church is rather Calvinistic. The Episcopalian churches are rarely frequented by the poor or by the uncultured people.

The Universalists by their announcement of eternal salvation to all men have obtained many followers, but they are met by violent opposition on the part of the Methodist and the Presbyterians.

Socinianism or Unitarianism, which denies the Divinity of Jesus Christ, has also its supporters, especially in that class that believes itself the most independent and sensible. The ministers of this heresy indulge in the most vain-glorious mode of oratory.

Luther has not much to boast of in America; his adherents generally assume the title of "The Reformed Lutherans," and a good number of the German Lutherans, who are immigrants, give up the sect in which they were trained but which they never have understood, to follow others more after the manner of the present day.

In addition to those already enumerated, various other sects are to be found in the United States, such as the Trinitarians, the Quakers, the Campbellites, the Mormons, the Millerites and many others, who, however taken separately, do not form large communities, nor are they found in every part of the Republic. The divisions existing in all the Protestant sects have also served to increase the confusion: there are the Methodist Protestants, the Methodist-Episcopalians, the Independent Methodists, the Presbyterians of the Old School, the Presbyterians of the New School, the Baptist Protestant, the Baptist Episcopalian, and so on. No religious whatsoever, when supported and promulgated by Biblical fanaticism or by secret pecuniary or political interests of any expert hypocrites, will ever fail to make proselytes. The people like a flock without a shepherd go here and there to listen to him who can offer them agreeable speeches. The famous Miller who was preaching in 1842 that the world would come to an end the following year, everywhere drew crowds to hear him. The soul outside the Church of Jesus Christ is at the mercy of all the wild fancies of false prophets, and that appears to verify the prophetic words of Saint Paul to Timothy: "There shall be a time when they will not endure sound doctrine, but according to their own desires they will heap to themselves teachers, having itching ears. And will indeed turn away their hearing from the truth, but will be turned unto fables." (II Tim. IV, 3–4).

One, who with the help of long experience, has studied the predominating spirit in America, knows that one-third of its inhabitants do not profess and do not believe in any particular creed but are satisfied simply with attending a Church whenever circumstances require and with living as far as possible in an absolute religious indifference, not even in the false supposition that simple natural goodness destitute of all the helps of Faith suffice to secure for him future happiness.

The clergy employed by the many Baptist sects is composed of persons of all classes of society, and it would seem almost an impossibility for the Protestant people to supply their needs and those of the large families by which they are usually surrounded. Those of their ministers who preach regularly to one congregation receive therefrom a salary suited to the place and to the circumstances; those stationed in newly settled sections or who have no fixed abode are commonly considered as missionaries and in that case receive for the most part an annual sum from their respective religious societies.

For propagating the doctrines of each of the sects there are societies founded with considerable endowments—by the voluntary contributions of members of the sect; in this way they provide for the needs of the preachers,—as well as for the printing of Bibles, of various other books and a great number of religious periodicals and lastly for the establishments of their missions in the districts inhabited by the Indians tribes.

In the United States the number of their ministers, including also their wives and children, is at least four times that of the Catholic Clergy in proportion to the number of members of the Protestant and Catholic communities respectively. This is very nearly the relation in which they stand in other countries also where the sectarians are in the majority. The duties of the ministers consist principally in saying prayers and in preaching, while the Priests of the Altar, in addition to preaching must devote almost all their time to visiting the sick, to hearing Confessions, to administering other Sacraments, and to assuming the responsibility of building the Temples of the Lord.

From this we may draw the conclusion that non-Catholics are unjust in finding fault with the great number of Priests and Religious previous to the Reformation, since in their place, a much more numerous clergy with the addition of their families must now be maintained, and from their people receive in return only a number of sermons. A certain Mr. Southey, a Protestant writer, speaking of the Methodists, relates that, in the single county of Middlesex, England, one magistrate in the course of six years granted licenses to one thousand four hundred ministers of that sect; moreover he assures us that "these consist of wandering adventures of all degrees ranging between knavery and madness, and who devoted themselves to preaching a prosperous business." See how Protestantism in general finds itself overburdened with the immense number of its clergy.

Although in the great cities, as New York, Philadelphia, Baltimore, Boston, Cincinnati and others, the sectarians possess some vast, costly edifices, yet the Protestant Houses of Worship are in general far inferior to the Catholic Churches. This results from the difference in worship: the Church of the non-Catholic is a meeting place for the people to listen to preaching, to sing some hymns in English and to say prayers; before and after these functions the structure is only a great empty hall. The Church of the Catholic while serving for the celebration of the Holy Sacrifice, and filled day and night with the adorable Presence of Jesus Christ in the Most Holy Sacrament, is forever the House of Prayer and the Lord's Tabernacle with men. Protestant who are not totally indifferent or not blinded by prejudice against the Faith when entering a Catholic Church cannot help finding there that conviction of the holy and mysterious, sought for in vain in the places of their own religious meetings.

Chapter III.

THE PRESS, PREACHING, EDUCATION OF PROTESTANTS OF THE UNITED STATES IN THEIR RELATION TO THE CATHOLIC CHURCH.

For the better understanding of the relations that Catholicity bears to the various sects in this country, one must keep in mind what has already been said upon this subject in another chapter, namely that the Government is entirely separated from all their forms of religious belief while at the same time it protects individuals in the exercise of the duties prescribed by their particular creeds. From this results that continuous and vigorous defense of the dogmas of all the sects, — carried on by the ministers in their different Churches and also through the medium of the press. Each religious body had its own religious periodicals in many sections of the Republic, which serve as fortresses armed to defend them from the arguments of their enemies. The various works, Biblical, dogmatic, moral, historical and ascetical, published by all these sects, would form an immense library. In America where the whole population speak the English language, and speak it as they write it, without the corruption of different dialects, writers on religious subjects especially are very numerous, and the misunderstood liberty of the press and the passion for reading among the people culminate in the fact that truth and falsehood, praise and calumny, virtue and vice all finds in the press a mighty protector which insinuated itself into every house.

The general aim of Protestant writers in religious works is to set forth their own doctrine and to defend it from arguments in opposition thereto; and herein is a formidable obstacle to Catholicity for it finds the intelligence of the sectarians already possessed by false principles. Then, too, the religious journals and books are not satisfied to confine themselves within the realm of Protestantism, but they fall furiously upon the Catholic Church and accuse her of boundless errors, they cover her with calumnies, with false explanations of her faith, they deride her doctrines, her practices, her ceremonies, her Priests. Not even that is enough to satisfy the anti-Catholic spirit. Every item of scandal that the history of ages past is able to furnish, is employed by the sectarian press to the condemnation of the Church of Jesus; and if peradventure the news of any fault in the Clergy, or eve the suspicion of fault reaches their cars, they are ever on the alert, through the same medium, to give it the widest possible publicity.

Since perfect freedom of worship is inseparable from freedom of the press, the foes of Catholicity constantly avail themselves of the latter to wage against the Church that terrible warfare, which is the spiritual destruction of souls not well grounded in piety, — by making them hard, indifferent, — which confirm many in their errors by destroying any means of finding out the truth. It is the fact that in almost every religious work printed by the Protestants in America, something is found which directly or indirectly, attacks the Catholic Faith, and thus verifies that word spoken by Jesus Christ, "He who is not with Me, is against Me."

The fact that in this country, the faithful are always and everywhere in the closest communication with the sectarians, is the cause of that bitter contest kept alive among them not only in the newspapers, but even by the living voice of their ministers. The majority of these believe that they are rendering a service to Almighty God by preaching against the Catholics, and for this reason there are fanatics both in town and country, in this manner giving full vent to their supreme ignorance, as well as to the religious hatred with which in their blindness they are filled. The Methodists and Baptists distinguish themselves by their enthusiasm in this manner of preaching. The Presbyterians, and some of the Episcopalians with a few others mingle some degree of learning with their anti-catholic harangues. Telling of idolatrous practices of the Catholics, of their aversion to the Bible, of the Pope as Anti-Christ, — predicting the destruction of Catholicity which they term the "Babylon of the Apocalypse," and the life,—all this serve for very many of these false prophets as the salt to season their discourses, and as the profound erudition wherewith to render the same interesting and eloquent. After so many years of this kind of frenzied preaching, the Protestant public seems now to have grown tired of listening to it; the excesses into which many famous ministers have fallen in their controversial discourses have brought about a reaction in favor of Catholicity, and thus many persons of sincere and candid souls are now giving their attention to the study thereof.

The Protestant people in America might be considered as enthusiasts on the subject of sermons,—and for this reason that they consider preaching as the most important and indispensable feature of their religion; for in nearly all their churches there are two sermons on Sunday,—and also on two or three days during the week. There is prayer and singing of hymns both before and after each discourse. Where the Catholics have the Altar, they have a pulpit bearing a large Bible. Some of the ministers read their discourses, others speak out of the fulness of their emotions. Some of these are eloquent, but the greater number lose themselves in a confusion of words, comparisons, repetitions, exclamations, sighs and pointless arguments. In the country places and sparsely populated districts are found the most ignorant preachers, entirely destitute of the knowledge indispensable to the instruction of others; their practice of speaking with extraordinary facility and of extemporizing prayers suffices to keep them busily occupied, here and there, in the people's houses,—in granaries and in open air. There are many engaged in the ministry who at the same time cultivate the land, carry on some trade or even practice medicine, law, follow some business, etc.

None of these sects possesses what the Catholics call the Sacrament of Holy Orders, although in some of their books the word Ordination is found with some prayers attached. The ministers are elected by the people or announce that they have received an interior call to preach, or else after being trained in some institution, they receive a human authorization in various ways from other ministers. All this, however, does not hinder many of them from giving up the ministry whenever they wish, in order to earn their bread by other occupations.

Many of the Protestant prejudices regarding the Church are instilled into the children in the schools, where the tender youth receive from the elementary books, from the authority of the teachers and from perverted use of Holy Scripture those false principles upon which rest their religious beliefs. Here, too, must be noted the fact that children guided by this mistaken idea of civil liberty,—without judgment and discernment, as they are, believe that here, in a special manner, are they free in whatever pertains to religion and they suppose that this is one point concerning which neither parents nor teachers can use any authority,—but that upon themselves rests the entire responsibility of searching for it in the Bible. The outcome of such a fundamental principle is for the most part insubordination towards the parents, and no piety, especially in the boys who form for themselves their own code of morals. All this diametrically opposed as it is to the spirit of Catholicity, gives rise in youth naturally inclined to evil, obstinate hatred for the doctrine of the Church and for her Clergy.

The reader can readily perceive the lamentable consequences of that education that teaches such liberty of thought to the rising generation. The warnings of conscience, are stifled by the spirit of arrogance and absolute independence; contempt for any religious authority carries with it contempt for the Faith and finally indifference and unbelief. This last has never been so triumphant since Christianity was first preached to the world, as it has been since the preaching of Protestantism—a wonderful historical fact. If the world were only wise enough to judge by the fruits, according to the Rule laid down by our Saviour, then casting one glance over the history of the past it would behold the monster of unbelief emerging in the sixteenth century, under the mantle of religious reformation. And when this monster out of its countless contradictory interpretations of the Bible, had built a tower wherein reigns greater confusion than Babel's, it gradually cast away the mask of Faith to raise the standard of deism under which many Catholics themselves, perfidious, took refuge.

Notwithstanding the immense influence of the press, of the preaching and of the training of Protestantism in the United States, the liberty of the Catholic Church is preserved inviolable, and under the eyes of the most fanatical is able to erect temples to the Lord, to practise its worship and spread its own doctrines by the very same mediums, that is by the press, by preaching and by education. For this, it is not the spirit animating most of the sectarians that deserves thanks, but that law granted by a government which guarantees to the Catholics, rights and liberty of conscience.

It would be a serious omission not to record here that at least one third of the citizens in America, from the principle of indifference or interest or rather from the belief that the difference of religions is an affair of little importance, love the Catholics as brethren in Faith. And in consequence they lend themselves to the building of our churches, of our charitable institutions and to supplying the needs of our Priests, to whom they show a religious respect; more than this they prefer to have their sons educated in Catholic Schools and Colleges but especially to have their daughters trained in the Convents.

There is another numerous class of individuals who quite well versed in the truths of Faith from constant reading of the publications that treat of them, or from the fact of associating with eminent and well-instructed Catholics openly declare themselves sincere friends and protectors of the Holy Church, yet without professing her doctrines. These men in their hearts despise Protestantism with all its calumnies and hostility against the Catholics; but influenced by self interest, by the desire to hold the first offices in the Republic, by pride or other motive, live outside the bosom of the Church, yet with a secret determination or lively hope to die Catholics. Divine Mercy often calls these souls to Itself before their passage to eternity, for their deeds of charity practised towards the clergy, towards the Church, towards the maintenance of works of public benevolence.

Chapter IV.

CATHOLIC MISSIONS IN THE UNITED STATES.

After discussing the Spirit of Protestantism, the sects and their various modes of warfare against Catholicity in the United States, it seems fitting to speak here of the Catholic mission in these places, in order to make known the great extent of the duties of its Priesthood in relation to these sects with whom they are in such close contact.

First of all, it must be acknowledged that the most important mission of the Catholic in this great Republic, is not among the Indian tribes, for as we have already seen in the course of this narrative, these tribes have been driven towards the west and in the course of the emigration, by reason of their contact with the Americans, they are gradually becoming decimated by disease, by ill-treatment, by vice and by want, to such a degree that, by the end of another century, the savage will have disappeared from the face of this vast country, extending from the Atlantic to the Pacific, from Canada to Mexico. The increase of the population of the United States (12,852,858 in 1830, and now in 1844 more than 18,000,000), the extent of the land which they have settled and that yet greater extent waiting to be settled, the unity of the government, of language, of customs, of political issues, the unlimited freedom of worship, the universal intelligence among the people, the progress in education, in commerce, in the arts, and in everything that can quickly render a nation great and powerful, — all these are the existing circumstances of the American Republic, now held as one of the foremost nations of the world, with every probability of becoming before the close of this century, the most numerous among the civilized peoples of the world and second to none in intelligence and in power.

From all this it is an easy thing to comprehend of what importance to Catholicity would be an efficacious mission among the commingled mass of different nationalities that compose this young nation. Here, the ministers of Jesus Christ everywhere find great numbers of the faithful who have come from Europe, and who in the midst of general corruption, if not promptly assisted, will lose the right principles imbibed in infancy. Moreover, four-fifths of the inhabitants professing either a false creed or shameful indifference offer a boundless field to the zeal and learning of the clergy. Here is the immense, the laborious, the lasting mission of the Priests of the United States. But, humanly speaking, unless the work of conversion to the Faith, and the fervor and the charity among the Catholics themselves are not reanimated, all will be dragged down to that unbelief which, at this very moment is giving signs of its dominion over a great part of the nation.

In Europe, the Church with the great number of her clergy, with her learning, with her magnificent religious and literary foundations, and with the assistance of the example and influence of powerful families is now, and will be, in a state to oppose this malign spirit; such is not the case, however, in the United States where error has more power in the number of followers, and the financial support it receives. Catholicity, with only a small number scattered over an immense country, with few Priests supported precariously, is hardly yet born, but in the midst of its enemies, it must oppose false creeds, the spirit of self-interest, and the bad example set by Protestants. One in whose heart burns the flame of pure love for Truth, and who understands the position of our holy Religion in America cannot but tremble for its future.

It is true that almost every Priest has received many sectarians into the bosom of the Church, and that these form a considerable number, a consolation to the heart of the true believer, but it is also true that very many Catholics have yielded to the spirit of indifference. Speaking without exaggeration of facts, the number of Catholics compared with the entire population of the country and in spite of the number of converts and of the many faithful who have emigrated from Europe, is no greater than it was many years ago. In a few States and cities the increase is greater than in others, but this fact is balanced throughout the country, by the increase in the number of Protestant inhabitants in places where the faithful are almost unknown.

This situation although it may intimidate souls zealous in propagating the Faith, should stimulate the spirit of prayer and of charity in believing souls, and should animate the ministers of the Sanctuary to greater efforts in their holy and sublime career of preaching the Gospel and adorning it with their example of all virtues.

The Lord Who is rich in mercy, has provided efficacious means for spreading the Truths of the Gospel throughout the United States. The War of Independence in the last century, freeing this country from the domination of England would seem to be in the designs of Divine Wisdom, a means, first, of granting perfect freedom to Religion, and secondly of promoting emigration of many Catholic families from Europe, who have served in a wonderful manner to establish and diffuse the Faith in far distant regions. The civil rights enjoyed by

PART THREE

Catholics equally with Protestants, prevent any and all oppression on the part of the laws, and enable the former as well as the latter to hold the foremost offices of the Republic. This state of affairs was in part the reason why many Priests from Europe were brought to those Missions; moreover it facilitated the erection of Bishoprics, the building of many Churches, the establishment of Seminaries, of Religious Communities, of Religious Schools, of Educational Institutions.

In addition to all this, Catholicity in America has at its disposal, the unlimited use of the same weapons that Protestantism employs to oppose it, and the attentive observer will find that this fact perhaps stands unique in the world. Both Truth and Error have in turn been granted by the world a position most advantageous for their own defence; that is, certain privileges enjoyed by one and denied to the other or perhaps, one of the two has been utterly proscribed or subjected to certain restrictions by the ruling power. But here in this country under a Republican government, Faith and heresy under all possible forms have been set, as it were, on a vast open plain, while the press, liberty of preaching and of teaching, the most powerful weapons employed by Protestantism against the Church, are yet as freely made use of by Christ Himself in order to vanquish error and establish the dominion of Truth.

Catholicity in the United States owes much to the press. The Church has published a great number of works, dogmatic, moral and ascetic, as responded at once to any calumny or reproach made by its enemies, and these enemies although free to print whatever they devise, are in a great measure held in check by the certainty that the Catholics are both ready and effective in their publications. The protestant may preach in the Churches, in the homes, in the open air, whatever, whenever and however it may please him, but the Catholic Priest may if he chooses do likewise in propagating the Truths of a holy Religion. The absolute freedom in educational matters leaves to the Church the superintendence of her own day schools and her colleges, and for the erection of the buildings there is no permission required from the civil power; the subjects to be taught, the books, the teacher, the system of teaching, are matters considered as the exclusive and independent rights of whoever proposes to teach the young.

We see that the Church of Jesus Christ was destined to combat error in its every possible relation to the power of the world. In the first centuries it had for opponent, Paganism supported by all the power of the State; thence in the Middle Ages it had to face the fall of empires, the barbarous nations who were devastating Europe, and all the revolutions and changes of government that succeeded; then, when within her own bosom actual monarchies arose, the Church found herself the living Centre midst the kingdoms of earth;—but these quickly took the ascendency and separated themselves either entirely or partially from her supremacy; from this it happens, that while embracing the whole world, she in her wisdom adapts herself to the various powers of the world.

In the United States, however, the Faith is left alone and without the least assistance or opposition from the government, to fight any Religious error under precisely the same circumstances. Thus the propagation of evangelical truth, depends exclusively upon the force of the truth, the zeal, the learning, and the sanctity of the Clergy, to whom has been entrusted the vast mission of calling the many millions of sectarians to the bosom of Catholic Unity.

It must come to pass that in the struggle between Catholicity and Protestantism under a government where everything is printed, everything preached, everything taught by the two participants, the followers of error must eventually submit and profess the truth, or else reject every system of Religion and abandon themselves to unbelief which is in its results but little removed from paganism. Whenever the majority are reduced to that condition the time will be near when in spite of laws existing regarding liberty of worship, the Church will be subjected even in this Republic to restrictions and probably to persecutions. The reason why this is not the case at present, must be looked for not in the nature of Protestantism but in the number and mutual antagonism of the sects; but unbelief firmly rooted in the majority of the people, would hardly be satisfied to leave to Catholicity the weapons for opposing it, if it had the power of seizing them by force. On the contrary, should the Faith prevail, one cannot easily predict the beneficent influence that it would exercise not only in America,—which before the next century dawns will doubtless be the most powerful nation of the world, but also in other countries by reason of America's commerce over every sea. Who will not pray our Father in Heaven to take away from the eyes of men the veil of that error by which they are being drawn into indifference and unbelief! Who will not sacrifice his time, his knowledge and even his life that he may bring to the Light of the Gospel those who redeemed by the Blood of Jesus Christ have perverted His doctrine!

Chapter V.

THE PRIEST IN AMERICA.

To the Clergy of the United States more than to that of any other country could be applied the prophecy of the venerable Simeon when he blessed the Infant Jesus and Mary, His Mother; "Behold he is set for the fall, and for the resurrection of many in Israel, and for a sign which shall be contradicted." Luke II, 34; for the very small number of Priests and the vital necessity of their ministry render the Catholic Priests' presence in the midst of a non-Catholic population a matter of the greatest importance to Religion. By the faithful, he is regarded as the chief support of Truth and the model of Christian life; by some Protestants he is adjudged to be an impostor, a deceiver, a man faithless and dangerous to society; yet others look at him with respect and approach him in order to receive information of a religious nature. His conduct as regards morality either confounds or delights his enemies; set upon the candlestick of the church he either diffuses the light or else becomes a false deceptive flame; if he is hated by the foes of Catholic truth, when he is an example of virtue, he must not look to them for any compassion towards his faults but he may expect to see them set forth in the public prints. Thus may be to many a cause of spiritual destruction; to others an efficacious means of conversion of sinners and souls outside the Church.

By demeanor, modest, mild and courteous, the Priest may be able to assist in the propagation of the Faith, but a manner frivolous, or of too great exterior coldness that resembles pride will not win confidence. When one Religious body comes face to face with another, the manner of life, the virtues and the faults of the missionaries are compared with the qualities of the Protestant ministers, and the doctrine is often confused with the preacher, by a certain ignorance or habit of the mind, and thus it happens if the latter is held to be good, so also will his doctrine be held good or vice versa. To the clergy in the midst of sectarian the words of the Prophet Isaias are in a special manner directed: "Touch no unclean thing; go ye out of the midst of Babylon, be ye clean, ye that carry the vessels of the Lord." The Priest is often the lone worshipper of the tremendous Mysteries of Redemption, and in secret hears the Most Holy Communion to the sick among his people, and to him may be applied those other words of the same Prophet; "I have spread forth my hands all the day to an unbelieving people who walk in a way that is not good after their own thoughts." (Isaias LXV, 2).

Among the virtues absolutely exacted of the Priest in America, disinterestedness is not the least, for where everything must be done, churches to be built, Seminaries, Religious Houses, Schools, Charitable Institutions, etc., and where the most urgent present needs are far beyond the pecuniary resources of the place, the minister of the Altar must devote his stipend entirely to the fostering of worship. His own wealth lies in the Lord's House which is also his own habitation. Whoever would seek riches elsewhere, will sooner or later bring down upon himself the contempt of Protestants and of Catholics as well, and will become a scandal to men.

Sectarians know or understand absolutely nothing of the spirit of the Religious ceremonies of the Church, so are ever and always inclined to despise them; but respect for Religion, is most surely won by manifesting in one's own exterior, recollection, the liveliest Faith and tenderest piety in the administration of all Sacraments, but in a special manner in the celebration of the tremendous Sacrifice of the Altar, so vilified by Protestants.

There are occasions when, on account of the presence of bystanders, it might become a grievous fault to show any haste in the ceremonies of the Mass, because such a lack of reverence towards the Most Holy Sacrament, might furnish to these bystanders a motive for suspecting that the Priest himself does not believe in the Real Presence.

The building of Churches to establish Catholic Worship constitutes a most important office of the Priesthood; for this object is demanded the highest degree of disinterestedness, together with the zeal which made Saint Paul cry out: "I do all things for the Gospel's sake, that I may be made a partaker thereof" (I Cor. IX, 23). The immense obstacles that interfere with the erection of God's Churches, on account of lack of means or of various difficulties with workmen, are inexhaustible sources of merit for the Priest, who is often humbled and reduced to the last extremity under such conditions, and suffers all things for the cause of diffusing the Faith.

In newly-settled places, the Missionary has no income, and very rarely receives a stipend for the Mass so he is reduced to living on the free alms of the faithful. The happy results of this truly evangelical poverty are a holy confidence in the Lord, and conformity with the life of his Divine Master; from these virtues it comes to pass that nothing needful can be lacking to the Priest. Free from the things of the world, he commands the respect and reverence of the faithful and can say with Saint Peter, "Behold, O, Jesus, we have left all things and have followed Thee." Matt. XIX, 27.

It is fitting that the Priest should be sufficiently informed as to the political affairs of the Republic that he may the better fulfil the duties of his vocation, but the desire of availing himself of his rights as a citizen for the purpose of interfering in elections would be of no advantage to Catholicity except in the case of a necessary defence of Religious liberty, if it should be attacked by cunning political enemies of the Church.

The conversion of unbelievers is to be brought about in a great measure by the good example of the Clergy, who would speak in vain if they did not make the eloquent example of Christian virtues precede their teaching in accordance with that beautiful expression that we read in the first verse of the Acts of the Apostles: "Jesus began to do and to teach", that is, He presented in His life a perfect model of the heavenly doctrines which He taught to His disciples during the last years of His mortal Life.

The preaching of the Priests of irreproachable lives is in the United

States a most powerful means of calling sectarians to the Unity of the Faith. In the case of souls who have been seduced by false principles, and by the insidious arguments of error to become disciples of the most extravagant doctrines, the Missionary should be guided by the tenderest compassion towards the souls who have not the incomparable grace of being born in the bosom of the true Church. Against this spirit of charity which Our Lord Jesus Christ Himself taught us in His Preaching, those transgress who allow themselves to be carried away by ill regulated zeal and set themselves up as judges, condemning with severity the non-Catholics without employing that sweetness and courtesy whose lack only angers instead of converting. In addition to the knowledge of Evangelical Truths, the Priest needs a deep fund of erudition which will enable him to adapt himself to the intelligence of all sectarians, according to their false or limited ideas of Religion. Their education, the varied creeds of these sects, the circumstances of life and the personal character of each individual, necessarily give a varied character to the mental operations in Protestants, their modes of thinking, of reasoning, of allowing themselves to believe in the Divine origin of the dogmas of our holy Religion. Therefore, there is need that the Preacher of the Faith imitate the example of the great Saint Paul: "I became to the Jews as a Jew, that I might gain the Jews:—to them that were without law as if I were without law,—that I might gain them that were without law. To the weak I became weak that I might gain the weak. I became all things to all men, that I might save all."(I Cor. IX, 20, 21, 22)

The arguments best adapted to bring deep conviction to Protestants are drawn from Holy Writ, from reasoning and from the history of the Reformation in the sixteenth century; and to respond to the most common objections against the Church, the Priest should be familiar with that department of the history which records the abuses, the disorders and scandals which dishonored her Sanctity at certain epochs,—that he may be able to direct the censure deserved, to the guilty individuals without allowing the blame to fall upon the Church Herself.

In the Churches, in private houses, in conversation, in the hotels, in journeys by land or sea, everywhere will the Missionary find occasion for defending his Religion because everywhere, regardless of place or time is the subject discussed. Here a gentle cheerfulness, a sweetness and readiness of speech, a modest becoming demeanor, confidence in God, and zeal for the salvation of others, are the irresistible attractions that draw the throng around one who with frank simplicity is vindicating the cause of Catholicity in face of its enemies. Christian prudence also will teach one in the midst of controversial arguments to show reasonable consideration towards political conditions of the United States.

If the saving of a soul is held by ascetics to be a pledge of one's own eternal salvation, oh, what consolation must fill the heart of him who sees at times in the conversion of unbelievers, the sweet fruit of all his toil. Then does Christian hope draw near to the divine certainty of possessing the Infinite Good, God Himself for the extension of whose reign he has cooperated as a happy instrument, by calling those far off to a share in the merits of the Redemption. Here is a divine reward, even in this world, more precious by far than parents, or friends, or native land, or honors, or riches. Such a sweet, well-founded hope of one's salvation may be called "The treasure hidden in a field," of which our Saviour spoke: "Which a man having found, hid it and for joy thereof goeth and selleth all that he hath, and buyeth that field." (Matt. XIII, 44)

In the matter of seminaries the dioceses of America are yet in their infancy; most of the seminaries having been erected very recently, many dioceses have a seminary of only a small number of students, ten or twelve perhaps. The greatest difficulty in the way of establishing them lies in the want of funds for constructing a suitable building for the support of both Professors and clerics. It is much to be desired that the new dioceses of the Western States may find some benefactor to found a seminary in the city of St. Louis, whence the other dioceses could be supplied. At present, the Priests of the United States are for the most part European, as are also the Bishops; France and Ireland are the richest in the vocations. The Irish Clergy especially have always been most helpful to Religion in this country, on account of the language, their political ideas, and their native ardor; often, therefore, those who were priests for many years in their own country, are satisfied to remain in American dioceses.

Chapter VI.

RELIGIOUS ORDERS IN THE UNITED STATES.

The people of the United States, both Catholic and Protestant make little distinction between the simple Priest and one who is a member of a Religious Order, since they recognize in both the vocation to the Priesthood, and vaguely believe them bound to fulfil all the duties belonging to their state; therefore it matters little to the faithful that a Priest is of one Order rather than another, provided only that they devote themselves to the teaching of the truth and to the salvation of souls.

But it is not an entirely indifferent matter to the welfare of the Church that in those places where She is yet young, those Religious Communities which are the work of the Saints, have been established. As we wish to treat this subject only in its relation to America, it will be observed first that the nature of those missions is distinctively adapted to the Regular Orders.

In consequence of the peculiar distractions and perils to which Priests are always exposed near to a society for the most part non-Catholic in the large cities, and by reason also of the spirit of independence, of the difficulty of preserving Ecclesiastical discipline, of the almost secular exterior of the Priest in America, of his constant dealings with worldly persons and of many other circumstances connected with the exercise of his ministry, — on account of all this we consider it a matter of no small importance to have a body of clergy, much more strictly bound to the duties of their vocation by means of the Vows and the discipline of the Religious Orders. In the missions of countries newly settled, where everything is lacking, or among the Indian tribes there is not the least doubt that according to experience a religious body is always more efficacious than a few isolated Priests. No one will deny then that it is the same case where there is lack of means, of everything that can be desired for the establishment of Colleges, of schools, of Religious Houses and of any other Institution directed by many individuals. The Jesuits have the principal colleges in America, and thus render the greatest service to the Catholic Religion and often too convert Protestant youth.

These vast dioceses, destitute of Priests might derive immense benefit from the Religious Orders, whose indefatigable zeal and pastoral disinterestedness are always unfailing sources of whatever is needful to the propagation and beauty of Religion. As the clergy in this country have the entire responsibility of Church buildings, whose needs increase every day, it is easy to see what a Religious body could accomplish in this respect in a very short time.

A certain exterior regularity in the manner of managing temporal, as well as spiritual affairs, besides winning the respect and confidence of the people, would make the Religious Community proceed more cautiously in assuming for Religion's sake those heavy pecuniary responsibilities, which now and then through lack of prudence weigh so heavily upon the most zealous of Priests.

It is a hard lot for one who must live without resources or regular revenue, and depend entirely upon the charity of the people; but if he were a member of a Community he would have a moral certainty of finding assistance in urgent circumstances.

When a Missionary becomes aged or infirm or is in need of a respite from labor, it is not easy for him to find a suitable place of retirement, for he is usually destitute of means; while a Priest of a Regular Order has always a holy refuge when age approaches. Thus personal disinterestedness, and love for the Community of which he is a member, are cherished to the benefit of the salvation of souls, the one object of every Institution founded by a Saint.

Granting as some do, that the Religious Orders are no longer necessary in Catholic countries, where there are a sufficient number of good Priests, yet they are of the greatest advantage in newly-settled countries because there Religion is in its infancy, and in need of everything. But even in America, Monks, Brothers, and the Regular Clergy would be of little help, should they make their Religious life consist in exercises purely ascetic and conventual; with a population just forming, and in great part Protestant we must have the apostolic or at least the active life. The vows, the holy discipline of the cloister must serve to perfect the life which is to be entirely employed afterwards in the sanctification of one's neighbor.

According to the ideas of this republican and enterprising people, it would seem almost a scandal to see a number of Priests shut up in one house, and thinking only of their own souls without making an effort to preach the Word of God throughout the country, or to succor the spiritual needs of the faithful. In the United States, the very necessity of endeavoring to procure the means of subsistence serves to keep our regular clergy also in the active life;—if it were otherwise the faithful would lose their respect for them, and the non-Catholics would seize upon the occasion to censure the Catholics.

It is the general opinion even of the most devout Christians that a Priest is ordained exclusively for fulfilling all the duties pertaining to the care of souls, and that this is the great and divine object of their separation from the world; for according to the words of the great apostle, "Christ had given to them the ministry of reconciliation—making them ambassadors for Christ." II Cor. V, 18, 20.

In the Republic of the United States, the government officials, the military excepted, have no external distinction in the form or color of dress, and it does not at all accord with the taste of the citizens to see an extreme singularity in the clergy, who certainly ought to be distinguished by a certain plainness, uniformity and simplicity of attire, but not to be rendered extravagant by reproducing the costumes of centuries ago. The venerable antiquity of a Religious Habit and the use of it made by the Saints of the Orders carries no conviction to persons in the world, for they would argue that in the case under question, the garb worn by the apostles themselves and by our Saviour Himself ought to have the preference. But without further discussion on the matter, this fact remains, though the perfect liberty of the country and the non-interference of the government in personal matters leaves everyone free to wear whatever garb he chooses, all the Bishops and all the Regular Orders that exist in the United States, as the Dominicans, the Jesuits, the Augustinians, the Redemptorists, and others, conform when in public to the simple garb of the clergy in general, that is boots or high shoes, trousers, a short cassock, or coat with skirt reaching midway between knee and ankle, and a round hat. This costume is convenient, unassuming and is sufficient in this country to distinguish the cleric from the layman and it helps the cause of Religion, which ever seeks to display the beauty of the Spirit of Unity, even outwardly as it appears midst the confusion of the many sects. These latter have already a thousand objections to offer in criticism of the sacerdotal vestments and the many ceremonies of the Church and for this reason many holy and zealous Priests in America as well as in the non-Catholic countries of Europe hold it a matter of prudence not to present new difficulties before the enemies of the Church by introducing among the clergy that singular variety in the matter of habits, remembering that after all, it is not the habits that makes the monk. On this matter it seems that almost all the holy Founders adapted themselves to the times in which they were living; the Religious Orders of the last three centuries give proof of this. If then it is prudent to preserve in Churches and in Religious Houses the use of the garb of the cloister, which by color or form are decidedly singular, it is generally a question of no importance to the propagation of the Faith. The Protestants, however, cannot see why some Priests when at home, dress in so different a manner from what they do in public, and even the faithful seem not to comprehend how in private a singular Habit is able to serve the greater sanctification of Priests on the American Mission.

It is much to be desired that the Religious Orders were more numerous in the United States, where their spirit of disinterestedness, of unity and of consecration to the salvation of the neighbor would be so efficacious an instrument for diffusing and preserving the Faith, no less in the great cities than in the more remote districts. And if there are any Orders unproductive on this point, it is because sometimes being too closely occupied in the purely monastic discipline they seem sometimes to have lost sight of the great aim of their Saintly Founders, which was the salvation of one's neighbor. It is not numerous or wealthy convents that are needed, but active, zealous Priests devoted exclusively to the sublime duties of their ministry; these duties which by means of doctrine, regular observance, fraternal love and detachment from the world are the rule and guide of the faithful amidst a people who oppose virtue and present a thousand opportunities for evil-doing; that is, there are needed Religious Communities consecrated to the obligations of the Priesthood, not Priests consecrated to the Communities. How great detriment to the propagation of the Faith is that want of real charity that unites the members of all the Orders into one single heart, will be easily comprehended by one animated by the true Spirit of Jesus Christ.

Chapter VII.

THE SISTERS OF CHARITY.

Almighty God in His Mercy and Wisdom Infinite provides for the spiritual needs of His people, adapts the means to the circumstances of those upon whom He pours down His graces. Early in the seventeenth century He inspired the glorious Saint Vincent de Paul to found the celebrated Institute of the Sisters of Charity, to succor the countless necessities of our days. The labors of the Saints are "the mustard seed," of which our Lord spoke, "which becometh a tree so that the birds of the air come and dwell in the branches thereof." Matt. XIII, 32. A society so helpful to humanity soon passed beyond the boundaries of France and even of Europe and crossing the sea, spread over the whole world; and America is now feeling the salutary effects of its celestial influence. The first House of the Sisters of Charity in the United States was founded in 1809 by some American ladies in a country place called Saint Joseph's near the little town of Emmitsburg in the State of Maryland, diocese of Baltimore; at present they number more than three hundred and have the direction of many orphanages, schools and hospitals in various parts of the Republic. They are constantly increasing in numbers and are more and more acquiring the esteem and veneration from the whole nation to the great benefit of the Catholic cause.

For a thorough comprehension of the immense utility of this Institute in the United States, we must consider that the people are vivacious and active by nature and they attach little importance to any Institutions whether Religious, literary or political from which the public does not receive considerable advantage. Now the Sisters of

Charity present to the nation a constant example of most indefatigable industry, since they seem to exist solely for the benefit of others; thence arises that lofty and exalted opinion in which they are held by even the Protestant Americans.

As they are bound by a simple annual Vow, they are always contented with their state, being free to leave it without any difficulty or dishonor. In America these Religious receive a good education, to render them fitted to fulfill the many important duties of their vocation. Now their simple Vow, the superior intelligence of the majority of the Sisters and the charitable works to which they consecrate their lives, are circumstances to which the Protestant republican has not yet been able to find an objection.

The modest and simple black robe worn by the Sisters, their appearance when in public (always no less than two together), their facility in working for the interests of the Institute, the cheerfulness and contentment visible in their countenances, and their thoroughly Religious and frank manner of asking for the necessary assistance for the hospitals and the orphans, are just motives for the admiration even of the declared enemy of the Catholic Church.

What heart would not be moved with tenderest compassion, seeing a venerable Sister surrounded by a throng of orphans passing along the street, entering the shops, the business houses of the merchants of all Religious denominations, to ask sometimes for shoes, for wearing material, again for provisions and again for money? It is beautiful then to see this throng of little ones each carrying the donation received from the edifying generosity of American non-Catholics. Protestantism has nothing like it, for, at the most, the needy children will be in the societies founded by the wealthy and benevolent, from whom their own needy receive ready assistance; but Catholicity is the only Religion able to present before the world, the spectacle of the voluntary poor who take it upon themselves to provided for the needs poor orphans, with whom they humble themselves to make common cause for love of Jesus Christ.

The care assumed by the Sisters of Charity for the orphans is a matter of great surprise to one who does not know that in that country there are no houses for such an object endowed with revenues as in

Europe, but that they depend exclusively on precarious beneficence; so that literally they must say to their Heavenly Father: "Give us this day our daily bread." The fervent prayer of so many innocent ones is always heard, for they never want for necessary food and clothing.

In America the Sisters have a number of orphanages for boys and girls whom they sometimes receive at the tender age of a few months; the boys at the age of twelve are placed by the Sisters in Catholic homes for the purpose of learning some trade; at the age of twenty-one these are free to choose their own life; the girls also are provided for almost in the same manner. In connection with the orphan asylums are schools for poor boys and poor girls where without any expense they receive the most necessary elements of education, and what is yet more important they learn the doctrines and practice of the Catholic Religion. The benefits derived from such schools are almost incalculable in a country where the Catholics form only one-ninth of the population; these schools might be considered a most efficacious means in propagating the Faith; and on this account, they deserve all the greater consideration of the many wealthy Catholics of Europe.

Beside the care of the orphans, and the religious schools, the Sisters of Charity are occupied in hospitals where such an enterprise shows itself necessary. According to their Rule, they do not go to the sick in private houses or in public hospitals, which is a matter of prudence in a non-Catholic country, but when circumstances are favorable, they themselves build a house to serve as hospital, and availing themselves of the full liberty guaranteed by law, they become absolute owners of the establishment and introduce therein all the regulations suitable to a Catholic Hospital. If the city and State wish to send patients there, they make an agreement with the Sisters at a certain fixed rate, a rate so low however, as to render it impossible for the other hospitals to receive them at such terms. Many of the invalids who are poor and not at the public charge, are here received in charity. Many persons also who are not poor prefer the Sister's hospital to any other in case if illness, and pay a fixed sum.

These hospitals are like the orphanages, that is without any revenue, and the heavy expenses of buildings and of maintaining them are furnished in part by the patients, as we have said, and in part by the voluntary alms procured by the Sisters themselves. For men as for women, servants of both sexes are employed under the immediate, absolute and independent authority of the Religious, who lend themselves to every work that befits their vocation and their sex. The hospitals as well as the orphanages are the property of the Sisters, and in the matter of administration depend upon no other person, but they themselves hold possession of them.

Among the patients there are always a great many non-Catholics and it is a fact of constant occurrence that many, edified by the exemplary conduct of the Sisters and convinced by their eloquent and holy words, abandon their errors to embrace the Holy Catholic Faith and before death receive the holy Sacraments of Baptism, Holy Communion and Extreme Unction. There are Catholics there who, for what of a Priest, would die without the Sacraments if they had not been received into the Sisters' hospitals. Who could value too highly the services which the Sisters of Charity render in this way to suffering humanity and to the Church?

Blessed are they upon the earth, for in the works of mercy they have a sure pledge of the favorable sentence on that dreadful Day of the Last Judgment, when the Judge as the Shepherd—shall set the sheep on His Right Hand and shall say—"Come ye blessed of my Father; I was hungry and you gave Me to eat; I was thirsty and you gave Me drink; I was a stranger and you took Me in; naked and you covered Me; sick and you visited Me; I was in prison and you came to Me; Amen I say to you, as long as you did it to one of these My brethren, you did it to Me." (Matt. XXV, 34-36, 40)

From what has been it must not be inferred that the Congregation of the Sisters of Charity is the only female Institute adapted to the needs of the American Missions. There are Religious of other Orders who are of the very greatest utility to the edification of the Church in their several vocations: The Dominican Sisters of the Third Order, the Sisters of the Visitation, The Ladies of the Sacred Heart and others. The education of young girls and the conversion to the Faith of many non-Catholics among them is due in great easure to the zeal and exemplary lives of these Communities.

Chapter VIII.

FOUNDATION OF ALL THE DIOCESES OF THE UNITED STATES OF AMERICA—THE SUCCESSION OF THEIR BISHOPS.

I DIOCESE OF BALTIMORE

Comprises the State of Maryland and the District of Columbia (see note 1); erected by Pius VI in the year 1789; raised by Pius VII to Archiepiscopal dignity in 1808.

First Archbishop, Monsignore John Carroll, consecrated in 1790.

Monsignore Dominic Graessel, coadjutor in 1793.

Second, Monsignore Leonard Neale, formerly coadjutor, consecrated in 1795.

Third, Monsignore Ambrose Marechal, formerly coadjutor, consecrated in 1817.

Fourth, Monsignore James Whitfield, formerly coadjutor, consecrated in 1828.

Fifth, Monsignore Samuel Eccleston, consecrated in 1834.

Sixty-nine Priest and 5 Churches (see note 2).

II DIOCESE OF NEW ORLEANS

Comprises the State of Louisiana, was erected by Pius VI in the year 1793.

First Bishop, Monsignore Charles Nerick, Administrator at pleasure of the Archbishop of Baltimore, consecrated in 1808.

Second, Monsignore William Dubourg, consecrated in 1815. Monsignore Joseph Rosati, coadjutor, consecrated in 1823.

Third, Monsignore Leo de Neckere, consecrated in 1830. The Right Reverend Auguste Jean-Jean declined the Episcopacy in 1834.

Fourth, Monsignore Antoine Blanc, consecrated in 1835.

Fifty-two Priests and 42 Churches.

PART THREE

III DIOCESE OF NEW YORK

Comprises the State of New York and eastern half of the State of New Jersey, erected by Pius VII in the year 1808.

First Bishop, Monsignore Richard Luke Concanen, Order of Preachers, consecrated in 1808.

Second, Monsignore John Connolly, of the Order of Preachers, consecrated in 1814.

Third, Monsignore John Dubois, consecrated in 1826.

Fourth, Monsignore John Hughes, consecrated in 1838.

Monsignore John McCloskey, elected coadjutor in 1844.

Seventy-one Priests and 83 Churches.

IV DIOCESE OF BOSTON

Comprises the States of Massachusetts, Vermont, New Hampshire and Maine, erected by Pius VII in the year 1808.

First Bishop, Monsignore John Cheverus, consecrated in 1810.

Second, Monsignore Benedict Fenwick consecrated in 1825.

Monsignore John Fitzpatrick, elected coadjutor in 1846.

Twenty-seven Priests and 25 Churches.

V DIOCESE OF PHILADELPHIA

Comprises the eastern half of Pennsylvania, the State of Delaware, and the western half of the State of New Jersey, erected by Pius VII in the year 1808.

First Bishop, Monsignore Michael Egan, Order of St. Francis, consecrated in 1810.

Monsignore Ambrose Marechal elected in 1815; resigned, and afterwards became Archbishop of Baltimore.

Second, Monsignore Louis de Barth, consecrated in 1817.

Third, Monsignore Henry Conwell, consecrated in 1820.

Fourth, Monsignore Francis Kenrick, coadjutor, consecrated in 1830.

Fifty Priests and 60 Churches.

VI DIOCESE OF LOUISVILLE

Comprises the State of Kentucky; until 1841 the Episcopal See was in the little city of Bardstown, erected by Pious VII in the year 1810.

First Bishop, Right Rev. Benedict Joseph Flaget, consecrated in 1810.
Right Rev. John Baptist David, coadjutor, consecrated in 1818.
Right Rev. Guy Ignatius Chabrat, coadjutor.
Fifty Priests and 40 Churches.

VII DIOCESE OF CHARLESTON

Comprises the three States of South Carolina, North Carolina and Georgia erected by Pius VII in the year 1820.

First Bishop, Right Rev. John England, consecrated in 1820.
Second Bishop, Right Rev. Ignatius A. Reynolds, elected in 1843.
Nineteen Priests and 16 Churches.

VIII DIOCESE OF CINCINNATI

Comprises the State of Ohio, erected by Pius VII in the year 1821.

First Bishop, Right Rev. Edward D. Fenwick, Order of Preachers, consecrated in 1822.
Second, Right Rev. John Baptist Purcell, consecrated in 1833.
Forty-seven Priests and 50 Churches.

IX DIOCESE OF ST. LOUIS

Comprises the State of Missouri, erected by Leo XII in 1826.

First Bishop, Right Rev. Joseph Rosati, administrator of the diocese of New Orleans, consecrated in 1823.
Second, Right Rev. Peter Richard Kenrick, coadjutor, consecrated in 1841.
Forty-five Priests and 50 Churches.

X DIOCESE OF MOBILE

Comprises the State of Alabama and the Territory of Florida, erected by Leo XII in the year 1826.

First Bishop, Right Rev. Michael Portier, consecrated in 1826.
Twelve Priests and 7 Churches.

XI DIOCESE OF VINCENNES

Comprises the State of Indiana, erected by Gregory XVI in the year 1834.

First Bishop, Right Rev. Simon William Gabriel Bruté de Remur, consecrated in 1834.

Second, Right Rev. Celestine de la Hailandiere, consecrated in 1839.

Twenty-seven Priests and 30 Churches.

XII DIOCESE OF DETROIT

Comprises the State of Michigan, erected by Gregory XVI in the year 1833.

First Bishop, Right Rev. Frederic Rèsè, consecrated in 1833.

Second, Right Rev. Peter Paul Lefevre, administrator, consecrated in 1841.

Fourteen Priests and 20 Churches.

XIII DIOCESE OF DUBUQUE

Comprises the Territory of Iowa, erected by Gregory XVI in 1837.

First Bishop, Right Rev. Mathias Loras, consecrated by Gregory XVI in 1837.

Twelve Priests and 10 Churches.

XIV DIOCESE OF NASHVILLE

Comprises the State of Tennessee, erected by Gregory XVI. First Bishop, Right Rev. Richard Pius Miles, O.P., consecrated in 1838.

Seven Priests and 5 Churches.

XV DIOCESE OF NATCHEZ

Comprises the State of Mississippi, erected by Gregory XVI in 1837.

The Very Rev. Thomas Heyden refused the Bishopric in 1837.

First Bishop, Right Rev. John J. Chanche, consecrated in 1841.

Four Priests and only 1 Church.

XVI DIOCESE OF RICHMOND

Comprises the State of Virginia, erected by Pius VII and administered by the Archbishop of Baltimore until the year 1841.

First Bishop, Right Rev. Patrick Kelly, consecrated in 1820.

Bishop, Right Rev. Richard Vincent Whelan, consecrated in 1841.

Seven Priests and 10 Churches.

XVII DIOCESE OF PITTSBURG

Comprises the State of Pennsylvania, erected by Gregory XVI, in the year 1843.

    First Bishop, Right Rev. Michael O'Connor, consecrated in 1843.
    Thirty Priests and 25 Churches.

XVIII DIOCESE OF HARTFORD

Comprises the State of Connecticut and Rhode Island, erected by Gregory XVI in the year 1843.

    First Bishop, Right Rev. William Tyler, elected in 1844.
    Seven Priests and 8 Churches.

XIX DIOCESE OF MILWAUKEE

Comprises the Territory of Wisconsin, erected by Gregory XVI in the year of 1843.

    First Bishop, Right Rev. Martin Henni, elected in 1843.
    Five Priests and 10 Churches.

XX DIOCESE OF CHICAGO

Comprises the State of Illinois, erected by Gregory XVI in the year 1843.

    First Bishop, Right Rev. William Quarter, elected in 1843.
    Twenty-three Priests and 16 Churches.

XXI DIOCESE OF LITTLE ROCK

Comprises the State of Arkansas, erected by Gregory XVI in the year 1843.

    First Bishop, Right Rev. Andrew Byrne, elected in 1844.
    Four Priests and three Churches.

XXII VICARIATE APOSTOLIC OF OREGON

Comprises those vast tracts belonging to the United States which extend from the western boundaries of the Territory of Iowa, the State of Missouri and Arkansas to the Pacific Ocean, erected by Gregory XVI in the year 1843.

    Fist Bishop, Right Rev. Francis N. Blanchet, elected in 1843.
    This Mission probably has ten Priests.

XXIII VICARIATE APOSTOLIC OF TEXAS

Comprises the Republic of Texas, erected by Gregory XVI in the year 1841.

First Bishop, Right Rev. John Baptist Mary Odin, C.M., consecrated in 1842.

Note 1. The extent of many Dioceses in the United States at the time of their erection was much greater than that given in this Chapter; after their creation they had been subdivided into new Dioceses.

Note 2. The number of Priests and of Churches in each Diocese increases year by year; we have given what was considered correct in 1843. Among the Priests are included not only those in charge of souls, but also those in colleges, schools, Religious Communities, etc.

Chapter IX.

PROVINCIAL COUNCILS OF BALTIMORE.

It is an incontrovertible fact, that wherever the Church of Jesus Christ has enjoyed perfect liberty in the exercise of her beneficent influence, to propagate the Faith and maintain her Religious practices, her Bishops have from time assembled in Council in order to fitly govern the flock entrusted to them by the Supreme Pastor of souls. Availing themselves, therefore, of the non-interference by the Government of the Republic of the United States in the matter of Catholicity, the Bishops of those regions held several Provincial Councils.

The first was celebrated in the month of October, 1829. There were present the Archbishop of Baltimore and five Bishops. Thirty-eight Decrees were formulated.

The second was held in the month of October, 1833. The Archbishop and nine Bishops were present. Eleven decrees were drawn up.

The third was held in the month of April, 1837. The Archbishop and nine Bishops were present. Eleven decrees were drawn up, and the Holy See was petitioned for the erection of three new Bishoprics.

The fourth was held in the month of May, 1840. The Archbishop and twelve Bishops were present. Eleven decrees were formulated.

The fifth was held in the month of May, 1843. The Archbishop and fifteen Bishops were present. Eleven decrees were drawn up and also a petition to the Holy See for the erection of five new Sees and one Vicariate Apostolic.

It belongs exclusively to the Prelates assembled in Council to propose for each Bishopric three names from which the Supreme Pontiff selects that one who will occupy the Episcopal See.

THE END.

Biblical References

Acts XVII, 28	246	Luke XIV, 33	3
Apoc. XXI, 23	250	Luke XX, 35	5
Eccles. I, 14	250	Luke XXI, 25, 26	12
Hab. II, 15, 16	225	Luke XXII, 35	176
Heb. VII, 19	24	Mark XVI, 15	99
Heb. XII, 22	250	Matt. VI, 31	4, 169
Heb. XIII, 14	221	Matt. IX, 36, 37	5
I Cor. I, 23	220	Matt. X, 36	6
I Cor. I, 27	4	Matt. XI, 25, 26	41
I Cor. II, 14	25	Matt. XIII, 32	280
I Cor. II, 5	4	Matt. XIII, 44	275
I Cor. III, 6	7	Matt. XVIII, 17	232
I Cor. IX, 20, 21, 22	274	Matt. XVIII, 3	32
I Cor. IX, 23	273	Matt. XIX, 27	5, 273
II Cor. V, 18, 20	278	Matt. XXIII, 27, 28	259
I Tim. III, 15	245	Matt. XXIV, 11	245
II Tim. IV, 2	21	Matt. XXV, 34–36, 40	283
II Tim. IV, 3–4	260	Matt. XXVIII, 19	4
Isaias V, 22	225	Matt. XXXIV, 23, 26	257
John VI, 54	25	Numbers XXIV, 5	2
John VI, 56	24	Phil. II, 21	175
John VI, 67	24	Prov. XXIII, 20, 21	225
John VIII, 21	178	Prov. XXIII, 31, 32	225
John XV, 16	3, 168	Psalms, XVIII	247
John XIX, 26, 27	195	Psalms, CIII	249
John XX, 21	17, 229	Psalms, CXXXVI	250
John XX, 22, 23	26	Psalms, CXLVIII	247
Luke I, 28, 35	195	Rom. V, 3	170
Luke II, 34	271	Rom. X, 15	5
Luke X, 2	7	Rom. XIV, 21	225
Luke X, 7, 8	170	Tob. XII, 3	13
Luke XI, 15	27		
Luke XII, 32	199		

General Index

Adorable Mystery, 178
All Saints Day, 82
Alleman, Reverend J., 239
altar, 10, 29, 38, 54, 58, 69, 74, 83, 93–95, 106, 135, 149, 159, 169, 176, 185, 187, 192, 196, 239, 264, 272
American Churches, 48
American Continent, 241
American Independence, 140
American Indian, 40, 108, 120
American Mission, 246, 279
American Republic, 47, 133, 143, 162, 210, 228, 237, 267
American Union, 137, 161, 180, 215
American War, 19
Andrew, Saint 221
Anglican Church, 29, 226, 229, 230, 246, 259
Anglican Mission, 96, 97, 101, 102
Anthony, Saint, 102, 234
anti-catholicism, 263
Apostolic Authority, 161
Apostolic Chair, 162
Apostolic Hierarchy, 253
Apostolic Mission, 105, 220, 226, 228, 229
Apostolic See, 161, 162
architecture, 48, 237, 242
Augustine, Saint, 236
Ave Maria, 53, 74, 81, 195

Babylonian Captivity, 250

Badin, Reverend Vincent, 135
Baltimore, 13, 161, 164, 188, 246, 248, 249, 261, 280, 284, 285, 287, 289
Baptism, 26, 33, 38–40, 51, 66, 70, 74, 91, 108, 116, 118, 157, 188, 190, 221, 235, 238, 283
　administered conditionally, 198
　bestowed on children in danger of death, 111
　by immersion of whole body, 258
　daughter of chief of tribe received, 80
　forty Indians underwent, 40
　Indian woman received funeral rites and, 107
　infants go to Paradise without receiving, 242
　instructions prior to, 89
　lawyer, wife and daughter received, 196
　man with two wives received, 79
　meaning of ceremony, 231
　not of absolute necessity, 198
　only a ceremony, 198
　practiced by Protestants might be null and void, 197
　reception of sacrament helped to organize parishes, 188
　sick woman received, 107
　some consider themselves Catholic without, 36
Baptismal Record, 51

Baptismal Waters, 207, 232
Baptists, 156, 159, 190, 207, 217, 256, 258, 263
Baptized Indians, 108, 234
Baraga, Reverend Father, 51, 52, 55, 78
Beloved Apostle, 27
Bible, 23, 26, 31, 123, 156, 196, 206, 217, 254, 256
 Bible Readers, 103, 104
 contradictory interpretations of, 265
 dispute over true sense of words in, 99
 distribution of copies of, 99
 divine origin of, 98
 divinity of the inspiration of, 227
 is full of difficulties in letter and sense, 99
 Mormon preachers have thoroughly studied, 244
 of the Mormons, 242
 preaching of Bible in secular garb, 220
 private interpretation of, 22, 226, 245, 253
 prophecies of Bible are purely literal, 243
 quoting of, 157
 translation approved by King James I, 101
bishoprics, 163, 164, 166, 167, 269, 289
Bishop-Elect of Dubuque, 174
Black Gown, 59
Black Hawk War, 62

Blessed Sacrament, 9, 76, 84, 88, 89, 113, 173, 178
Blessed Virgin, 133, 195, 216
Bloomington, 181, 211, 220, 221
building, types of:
 Frame House (Casa d'ossatura di Travi), 47
 Log House (Casa di Travi), 47
Burlington, 158, 181, 199, 208–216, 220, 237–239, 245

Calvinist Church, 72
Calvinism, 21, 22, 25, 26, 34, 72, 101–103, 136, 168, 259
Camp Meetings, 257, 258
Canadians, 22, 46, 57, 65, 74, 76, 85, 87, 193, 234
canoe, 49, 55, 59, 63, 67, 75, 77, 173, 193
Canon Law, 150
catechism, 83, 91, 93, 94, 107, 234
cathedrals, 15, 82, 134, 146, 167, 188, 189, 192–194, 248
Catholic Bishops, 17, 191
Catholic Church, 2, 13, 17, 22, 25–27, 29, 33, 55, 83, 96–98, 149, 155–158, 165, 175, 185, 195, 197, 209, 210, 222, 227, 229–231, 238, 243, 245, 255, 259, 262, 263, 265, 281
Catholic Church:
 a subject of attack and contempt by Protestants, 195
 Apostolic ministry in, 17
 contamination by holy images in, 29
 enemies of, 25

Faith and practices in, 33
Hierarchy of, 17
infallible testimony of, 98
insult, ridicule and hatred against, 157
liberty enjoyed by, 148, 265
miracles belonging to, 26
principal dogmas of, 22
prophecies against, 27
Protestant accusations of error, 263
Society of Antichrist, 197
true church of Antichrist is, 27
unchanging tradition of, 227
unity of the sacred in, 2
Catholic Churches, 137, 142, 261
Catholic Clergy, 55, 102, 105, 166, 187, 223, 261
Catholic Doctrine, 32, 34, 86, 200, 226, 229
Catholic Faith, 10, 20, 28, 46, 60, 71, 186, 226, 230, 263, 283
Catholic Hierarchy, 190, 191, 228
Catholic Hospital, 282
Catholic Indians, 78, 87, 118
Catholic Irish, 223
Catholic Missionary, 28, 98, 160
Catholic Missions, 96, 97, 115, 116, 123, 129, 266
Catholic Priests, 75, 76, 99, 103, 105, 129, 156, 159, 160, 220, 269
Catholic Profession, 207
Catholic Religion, 21, 27, 30, 101, 104, 117, 123, 137, 171, 202, 205, 217, 231, 277, 282
Catholic Schools, 266

Catholic Society, 224
Catholic Total Abstinence Society, 225
Catholic Truth, 2, 98, 239, 271
Catholic Unity, 16, 56, 270
Catholic Worship, 115, 131, 209, 215–217, 219, 220, 231, 236, 273
Catholicity, 10, 90, 97, 138, 149, 163, 185, 195–197, 202, 211, 212, 215, 222, 223, 232, 234, 275, 281, 289
aversion to, 29
belief in wins respect of Government officials, 256
Calvinistic hatred towards, 101
can in brief time teach all Christian morality, 85
can put itself in harmony with Republican government, 136
consolidates peace and rights of others, 122
conversion to, 46
has same weapons that Protestants use, 269
hostility towards, 232
interfering in elections, 273
obstacles in progress of, 110
owes much to the press in the United States, 269
predicting destruction of, 263
prejudice against, 255
Protestant dominion over in several European states, 255
reasons for progress of, 226
strong opposition to, 22
struggle with Protestantism, 270
Truths of, 81

GENERAL INDEX

Catholicity (*continued*)
   use of freedom of the press against, 263
   warfare against, 266
Causse, Reverend James, 186
celibacy, advantage of Catholic priest over Protestant minister, 160
Chabrat, Bishop, 249, 250
Chief Magistrate, 167
Chippewa Indians, 102, 114
Christ Crucified, 220
Christian Doctrine, 74, 164
Christian Faith, 23, 46, 133
Christian Indians, 53, 83, 91, 96, 106, 110, 115
Christian Religion, 24, 65, 90, 100, 102, 106, 107, 157, 169, 191
churches:
   at Arbre Croche, 52
   at Dubuque, 133
   at Galena, 137
   Church of Mackinac, 51, 58
   Church of Saint Augustine at Sinsinawa, 236
   Church of Saint Matthew at Shullsburg, 218
   Church of Saint Paul at Burlington, 208
   Church of Saint Raphael in Dubuque, 146
   Church of Saint Rose of Bardstown, 14
   Church of the Archangel Gabriel in Prairie du Chien, 208
   civil permission not needed to build, 142
   clergy have entire responsibility for care of, 277
   description of, 48
   difficulty in building in new territories, 10, 47, 161
   European funding of, 194
   important duty for missionary to build, 130, 175, 273
   Iowa Legislature sets lots aside for building, 215
   legal ownership of, 150, 202
   Protestants sometimes contribute to building, 175
   Saint Anthony's, 154
   Saint John the Evangelist, 47
   Saint Michael, 146
   of simple improvised variety, 94
Cincinnati, 7, 9, 10, 13–18, 59–61, 66, 73, 77, 78, 81, 127, 128, 155, 163, 247, 248, 261, 286
civilization, 115, 117–123, 131, 157, 162, 165, 182, 183
Claire, Saint, 82
clergy:
   bishops, 149, 161, 163, 165, 167, 190, 194, 223, 229, 246, 248, 249, 275, 278, 284, 289, 290
   holy orders, 21, 190, 199, 229, 264
   monks, 277
   nuns, 82
   ordination, 11, 14, 17, 18, 21, 60, 229, 264
   priests, 1, 6, 14, 18, 20, 21, 55, 65, 66, 83, 114, 116, 127, 129–131, 134, 143, 144, 147, 156, 163, 167,

GENERAL INDEX

190, 217, 223, 229, 235, 248, 261, 266–269, 271, 275–280, 284–289
coadjutor, 237, 249, 284–286
Columbus, 11
Communion, 1, 20, 31, 33, 36, 40, 58, 59, 72, 77, 82, 83, 88, 115, 190, 207, 272, 283
community, 14, 33, 110, 121, 150, 216, 277
compassion, 5, 13, 31, 52, 91, 113, 158, 271, 274, 281
condemnation, 38, 56, 200, 263
Confession, 21, 25, 30, 31, 35, 56–58, 66, 76, 84–87, 95, 106, 114, 142, 143, 147, 171, 177, 178, 198, 238
Confirmation, 36, 40, 114, 190, 192
congregations, 16, 168, 171, 210, 223
Congress, 6, 123, 142, 148, 179, 205, 212, 213, 215
Consecrated Particle, 178
contempt, 27, 33, 68, 88, 170, 178, 195, 220, 234, 254, 265, 272
contrition, 34, 35, 58, 66, 78, 81, 108, 198, 232
controversy, 22, 28, 29, 32, 33, 196, 210, 227, 228, 230, 238
converts:
    among the Menominees, 93
    among the Ottawas, 69
    among the Winnebagoes, 79
    at Green Bay, 114
    Christian Indians better at making, 91
    from Protestantism baptized a second time, 197
    from Protestantism given a second baptism, 197, 198
    in Iowa City, 218
    not converting due to pressure or selfishness, 232
    not increasing proportion of Catholics in America, 268
    simple preaching effective in making, 100
creed, 66, 103, 138, 139, 142, 260, 267
Cretin, Reverend Joseph, 188, 189, 209

Davenport, 152–155, 171, 181, 199, 200, 210, 218, 220
decrees, 111, 116, 191, 248, 289, 290
Des Moines, 180
destruction, 6, 12, 23, 119, 164, 184, 228, 243, 263, 271
devotion, 35, 38, 51, 53, 56, 79, 83, 88, 95, 110, 128, 134, 145, 195, 206, 217
devotions, 141, 192
Diamond Grove, 171
dioceses, 18, 131, 163, 164, 212, 275, 277, 284, 289
discipline, 8, 44, 190, 248, 276, 279
Divine Bounty, 170
Divine Faith, 70
Divine Goodness, 88, 205, 230
Divine Grace, 20, 31, 32, 70, 73, 76, 78, 197
Divine Institution, 163
Divine Justice, 32, 35, 36, 52, 58, 61, 82
Divine Mercy, 5, 16, 25, 30, 32, 38, 52, 77, 86, 187, 197, 207, 266
Divine Mission, 17, 228

GENERAL INDEX

Divine Munificence, 9, 32
Divine Mysteries, 35, 145, 199, 217
Divine Omnipotence, 24
Divine Providence, 1, 2, 8, 9, 13, 66, 70, 127, 130, 136, 145, 160, 189, 202
Divine Redeemer, 207
Divine Revelation, 227
Divine Service, 38, 72, 83, 96, 146, 171, 201, 216
Divine Spouse, 220
Divine Truths, 107
Divine Victim, 54
Divine Will, 131, 162
Divine Wisdom, 122, 268
Divine Word, 20, 36, 50, 88, 111, 227
Divine Worship, 10, 150, 211, 216, 226
Dodgeville, 171, 209
dogma, 23, 24, 191, 211, 221, 238
Dominic, Saint, 14, 16, 61, 81, 127, 128
Dominicans, 128, 283
Dominican Order, 128
drunkenness, 37, 38, 54, 73, 89, 110, 120, 177, 222, 225, 233
Dubuque, 128, 131-135, 144, 146, 148, 152, 161-164, 166, 168, 172, 174, 181, 186, 188, 189, 192-194, 199-201, 210, 213, 216-218, 221, 233, 234, 236, 239, 246, 249, 287
Dubuque City, 200
Dutch Settlement, 202

Eastern States, 102, 161, 201, 203
ecclesiastical:
    authority, 142, 162, 226
    career, 170
    dignities, 61, 149
    discipline, 248, 276
    hierarchy, 17, 23, 163
    history, 131, 238
    laws, 187
    order, 229
    progress, 162
    property, 150
Ecclesiastical Superior, 163
education, 7, 8, 41, 96, 98, 103, 104, 113, 114, 120, 166, 184, 217, 240, 258, 262, 265-267, 274, 281-283
Educational Institutions, 269
Edward, Right Reverend, 39, 78
eloquence, 12, 15, 17, 92, 157, 190, 231, 239
emigration, 44, 122, 132, 153, 161, 162, 179, 181, 200, 201, 203, 205, 212, 214, 267, 268
English Protestant, 26
Episcopal Seat, 81
Episcopal See, 161, 163, 166, 285, 290
Eternal Life, 1, 8, 32, 56, 65, 66, 111, 116, 225
eternity, 2, 31, 58, 67, 120, 178, 244, 247, 250, 266
Eucharist, 21, 24, 37, 58, 66, 88, 171, 174, 178, 192, 195, 238
Eucharistic Feast, 88
Eucharistic Table, 6
European Churches, 10
Europeans, 38, 42, 54, 102, 121, 122
evangelical:
    charity, 7
    discipline, 190
    laborers, 7, 104, 164, 188, 190
    liberty, 176

GENERAL INDEX

mission, 3
poverty, 68, 273
sanctity, 222
truths, 211, 228, 270, 274
virtues, 137
word is the work of Christ, 4
Everlasting God, 25
Evil Spirit, 45, 73, 90, 92
Extreme Unction, 58, 178, 283

faith:
   drifting away from, 113, 115, 205, 230
   indifference towards, 33, 56, 57, 76, 110, 149, 187, 206, 228, 231, 254, 260, 265–268, 271
   lack of, 24, 29, 88, 110, 139, 199, 208, 265, 267, 270, 271
   profession of, 138, 242, 260, 270
fanatics, 22, 98, 142, 157, 228, 229, 242–244, 256, 257, 263
Feast of the Assumption, 133, 193
Fenwick, Bishop Edward, 14, 15, 39, 78, 114, 127
Fevre River, 134
Flaget, Bishop, 15
Fond du Lac, 102
Fort Madison, 181, 239
Fort Winnebago, 73, 112
Fox River, 36, 102, 116
funds, 104, 135, 165, 177, 194, 234, 236, 237, 250, 275
Fur Company, 19
Fur Trade, 19

Gabriel, Angel 193, 195, 208

Galena, 127, 128, 132, 134, 135, 143–147, 151, 168, 172, 174, 177, 185, 188–190, 192, 194, 195, 197, 199, 205, 210, 216, 218, 219, 226, 230, 233, 236, 237, 245, 246
Galtier, Reverend S., 234
General Government, 149, 166, 215
General Land-Office, 204
generosity, 9, 45, 102, 175, 176, 219, 222, 281
German Catholics, 177, 236
German Lutherans, 259
Godfert, Reverend Anthony, 234
Gospel Truth, 162
Government Agent, 104
Government lands, 203
Gratiot Grove, 171
Great River, 63, 65, 110, 116, 145, 148, 172, 182, 212, 234
Great Spirit, 20, 45, 73–75, 83, 92, 93
Great Waters, 193
Great Western, 249
Green Bay, 18, 20, 36, 37, 39, 47, 59, 62, 63, 66, 73, 81, 82, 84, 90, 91, 93, 96, 101, 104, 105, 114, 150

Healy, Reverend J., 239
Heavenly Bread, 152
Heavenly Father, 1, 4, 282
Heavenly Redeemer, 34
Heavenly Spouse, 29
hierarchy, 17, 23, 163, 190, 191, 228, 229, 253
High Church, 259
Holy Baptism, 40, 93, 107, 111, 116, 207, 235

Holy Books, 99
Holy Catholic Faith, 46, 283
Holy Communion, 20, 31, 40, 58, 59, 72, 77, 82, 88, 115, 207, 272, 283
Holy Days, 71, 75, 83, 231
Holy Eucharist, 21, 58, 66, 178, 238
Holy Faith, 25, 34, 37, 51, 54, 82, 95, 113, 123, 191, 197
Holy Father, 68, 164
Holy Mass, 20, 94
Holy Mysteries, 71, 88, 147, 186
Holy Orders, 21, 190, 199, 229, 264
Holy Redeemer, 66
Holy Sacrament, 39, 40, 56, 83, 85, 88, 95, 261, 272
Holy Sacrifice, 10, 29, 35, 38, 53, 66, 74, 83, 94, 95, 106, 133, 135, 143, 159, 168, 171, 185, 187, 216, 261
Holy Scriptures, 22, 27, 31, 41, 98, 226, 242, 254
Holy See, 81, 289, 290
Holy Spirit, 192, 229
Holy Table, 31, 88, 144, 188
Holy Writ, 5, 227, 230, 238, 244, 274

immorality, 34, 46, 73, 110, 120, 240, 258
Incarnate Wisdom, 1, 24
Independent Methodists, 260
Indian Affairs, 41
Indian Agent, 103
Indian Reservation, 182
Indian Tribes, 37, 39, 41, 100, 104, 108, 117, 118, 120, 131, 181, 202, 203, 215, 234, 267, 276
infallibility, 21–23, 195

Infant Jesus, 271
Infinite Mercy, 35, 77, 87
inspiration, 4, 227, 240–242
institutions, 88, 101, 102, 163, 254, 264, 276, 277
Iowa City, 181, 212, 213, 215–218, 237
Iowa Legislature, 215
Iowa River, 213, 214
Iowa Territory, 134, 172, 220
Ireland, 130, 201, 212, 222, 249, 275
Isaias, Prophet, 272
Island of Mackinac, 18, 28, 34, 36, 62, 67, 71, 100, 113, 116
Italy, 95, 222, 246

Jeremias, Prophet, 3
Jerusalem, 61, 96, 241, 243, 244, 250
Jesuit Fathers, 123
Jesuits, 36, 51–53, 56, 69, 277, 278
Jesus Christ, 4, 22, 46, 61, 79, 88, 89, 99, 107, 117, 123, 152, 160, 175, 191, 195, 206, 207, 228, 229, 231, 238, 240, 242, 243, 255, 258–261, 263, 267, 270, 271, 274, 280, 281, 289
Jesus Crucified, 206
John, Saint, 1, 27, 47, 48, 208, 249, 250
Johnson County, 213
Joseph, Saint, 14, 16, 17
Judaism, 139

Kenrick, Patrick, 15
Kenrick, Peter, 237, 247
kings, 56, 101, 241, 243, 249, 250, 259
King David, 56
King Providence, 249

GENERAL INDEX

King Solomon, 250

La Pointe, 68
laborers, 5, 7, 104, 161, 164, 174, 177, 178, 188, 190
Lake Erie, 18
Lake Genesareth, 173
Lake Huron, 18, 49, 75
Lake Michigan, 18, 20, 36, 51, 53, 66, 69, 90, 116, 148
Lake Superior, 18, 19, 50, 68, 82, 101, 102
Lake Winnebago, 91, 102, 116, 151
Lamanites, 241
language, 10, 11, 13, 14, 17, 19, 23, 29, 41, 52, 53, 55, 56, 68, 73, 74, 78, 79, 81, 84, 85, 98, 101, 102, 111, 121, 144, 188, 234, 241, 262, 267, 275
Last Judgment, 283
Last Supper, 88
Lead Mines, 131–134, 162, 175, 185, 218, 219, 236
Leclaire, Antoine, 152
Lent, 30, 35, 71, 82, 238, 245
Lenten Fast, 231
Light Divine, 89
Living God, 1, 9, 57, 245, 250
Loras, Bishop, 185, 187, 197, 201, 209, 233, 234, 239, 246
Loras, Right Reverend Bishop, 161, 185, 187
Low Church, 259
Lutz, Reverend G., 135
luxury, 41, 118, 129, 155, 176

Mackinac Church, 60

Maquoketa, 200, 201
Master General, 162
Matthew, Saint 219
McMahon, Reverend John, 132, 135
Medicine Man, 46
Menominee Christians, 90
Menominee Indians, 59, 84, 151
Methodist Church, 199, 211
Methodist Episcopalians, 215
Methodist Protestants, 260
Michael, Saint, 146, 237
Michigan, 18, 20, 36, 39, 41, 43, 51, 53, 55, 66, 69, 81, 82, 90, 116, 148, 179, 287
Middle Ages, 270
Mineral Point, 127, 171, 209
Missionary Clergy, 163
Mississippi River, 62, 102, 122, 128, 145, 168, 172, 181, 185, 192, 245
Missouri River, 116, 179
Monarchical Government, 141
Montreal, Canada, 113
morality, 37, 85, 86, 117, 120, 123, 157, 253, 271
Mormon Paradise, 243
Mormons, 239, 240, 242, 243, 259
Most Blessed Sacrament, 84, 88
Most Holy Viaticum, 178
Mother Church, 205
Mount Sion, 250
Mystic Bread, 34

New Diggings, 171
New Jerusalem, 244
New Law, 35, 53, 94, 159
New School, 260

GENERAL INDEX

New Testament, 24, 191, 243
New World, 10, 155, 156
New York, 11, 12, 102, 104, 240, 249, 261, 285
North America, 10, 56, 108, 122, 131, 138, 142, 181
North American Indians, 108
Northern Michigan, 116
Northern Mississippi, 43, 45

obedience, 8, 10, 11, 61, 136, 157, 167, 176, 245
obligation, 25, 33, 82, 85, 132, 139, 143, 157, 165, 166, 198, 207, 238
obstinate, 49, 57, 66, 70, 91, 110, 178, 186, 195, 265
Ocangra Aramee Wawakakara (Winnebago Prayer Book), 81
Ohio River, 15, 128, 155, 177
Old Jerusalem, 243
Old Law, 228
Old School, 260
Old Testament, 27, 82, 217
Omnipotent God, 174
ordination, 11, 14, 17, 18, 21, 60, 229, 264
Oregon Territory, 123

Parish Priests, 71, 129
Pater Noster, 74, 81
Patrick, Saint, 200, 201, 222
Paul, Saint, 1, 4, 21, 24, 25, 100, 170, 175, 208, 210, 218, 229, 238–240, 246, 260, 273, 274
Pelamourgues, Reverend Anthony, 188, 189, 199

penitent, 35, 57, 84, 85, 232
Perrodin, Reverend J.C., 201
perseverance, 12, 60, 67, 103, 115, 146, 167, 173, 175
Peter, Saint, 3–5, 23, 180, 193, 234, 273
Petiot, Reverend Remigio, 199, 233
Point Saint Ignace, 55, 113
polygamy, 79, 109
Pontifical Authority, 249
Pontifical High Mass, 60, 248
Portier, Michael, 161, 286
Postal System, 154, 214
Prairie du Chien, 62, 63, 65, 66, 102, 103, 109, 112, 127, 144, 193, 208, 209
Pratt, Parley, 244
preachers, 7, 14, 102, 103, 128, 157, 162, 168, 229, 244, 256, 260, 264, 285, 286
Precious Blood, 111
prejudices, 16, 32, 33, 136, 137, 166, 188, 191, 210, 217, 220, 226, 265
Presbyterian Church, 22, 197
Presbyterian Mission School, 101
Presbyterians, 21, 158, 190, 198, 215, 222, 223, 258–260, 263
priesthood, 3, 7, 11, 14–17, 34, 86, 137, 191, 267, 273, 276, 280
Propaganda Association, 217
Protestant Americans, 281
Protestant Bible, 196
Protestant criticism:
    causes many to fall into skepticism, 144
    of Church superstition, 168
    denying Real Presence of Christ

GENERAL INDEX

in the Eucharist, 24
rouses curiosity, 28
in the sectarian press, 263
Protestant Houses, 261
Protestant methods of conversion:
fail with Chippewa Indians, 102
focus on young, 105
inferior to that used by Catholics, 100
utilize histrionics during sermons, 157
weakened by lack of education among ministers, 157
Protestant Missions, 96, 100
Protestant Reformation, 157, 226
Protestant Societies, 22, 101, 104
Public Treasury, 205
Purcell, Bishop John, 128
Purgatory, 21, 26, 195

Quesnel, Edward, 11
Quickenberg, Reverend Van, 135

Raphael, Saint, 146
Ravoux, Reverend Louis, 234, 235
Real Presence, 21, 24, 88, 89, 273
reconciliation, 32, 57, 86, 113, 211, 278
redemption, 1, 17, 24, 39, 53, 77, 88, 110, 117, 198, 220, 242, 272, 275
Redemptorist Fathers, 73, 82, 84, 104, 114
reformation, 157, 226–229, 245, 253, 259, 261, 265, 274
Reformed Lutheran Church, 238
regeneration, 33, 38, 48, 54, 59, 107, 110, 197, 206, 207, 231

Regular Clergy, 277, 278
Regular Orders, 248, 276, 277, 278
Religious Associations, 122
religious celebration:
at the altar, 10, 29, 38, 54, 58, 69, 74, 83, 93–95, 106, 135, 143, 149, 159, 169, 172, 173, 176, 185, 187, 189, 192, 196, 239, 248, 261, 264, 272
centred on the Eucharist, 21, 24, 37, 58, 66, 88, 171, 174, 178, 192, 195, 238
through use of the Chalice, 159
Communion, 1, 20, 31, 33, 36, 40, 58, 59, 72, 77, 82, 83, 88, 115, 190, 207, 272, 283
consecration, 80, 136, 193, 279
Viaticum, 16, 178
Vespers, 56, 82, 83
wearing of vestments, 83, 95, 220, 279
Religious Communities, 269, 276, 279, 289
Religious Habit, 278
Religious Houses, 228, 272, 276, 279
religious instruction:
using catechism, 83, 91, 93, 94, 107, 234
and doctrines, 23, 39, 100, 139, 141, 220, 230, 231, 238–240, 242, 254, 255, 263, 266, 273, 274, 282
using dogma, 23, 24, 191, 211, 221, 238
with general teachings, 21, 40, 42, 101, 113, 159, 196, 244, 245, 253, 254, 259

GENERAL INDEX

religious instruction (*continued*)
  no limitations on , 269
  through study of Bible, 22, 23, 26, 31, 98, 99, 101–104, 123, 156, 157, 196, 206, 217, 220, 226–228, 242–245, 253, 254, 256, 263–265
Religious Memoirs, 217
Religious Orders, 150, 276
Religious Schools, 269, 282
Republican Government, 136, 139, 269
Rèsè, Right Reverend Frederic, 81
Rigdon, Sidney, 240
rites, 10, 46, 107, 108, 189, 207, 217
Rock Island, 145, 147, 152
Rocky Mountains, 123
Roman Pontiffs, 150
Roman Rituals, 207
Rosati, Bishop Joseph, 189
Rosati, Guiseppe, 128
Rose, Saint, 14
Royal Prophet, 249, 250

Sacrament of Regeneration, 59, 110, 197, 206, 207, 231
Sacramental, 25, 30, 31, 56, 58, 66, 85, 86, 88, 198, 238
Sacramental Absolution, 198, 238
Sacramental Grace, 58
Sacraments, 21, 24, 39, 75, 112, 164, 168, 169, 171, 177, 185, 187, 188, 200, 210, 219, 261, 272, 283
Sacred Books, 227
Sacred Heart, 283
Sacred Text, 23, 32
Saint Louis, 65, 128, 132, 135, 143, 145, 147, 161, 171, 188, 189, 237, 247
Saint Michael's Church, 174, 236
Saintly Founders, 279
Samuel, Prophet, 30
sanctity, 46, 68, 92, 108, 132, 136, 142, 145, 191, 222, 259, 270, 274
Sault Sainte Marie, 49, 50, 61, 62, 101, 114
Saviour Jesus Christ, 231
sciences, 40, 41, 53, 85, 117, 118, 123
Second Coming, 243, 244
sectarianism, 75, 97, 104, 110, 144, 196, 226, 238, 253, 254, 263, 272
Sioux Indians, 103
Six Nations, 102
Smith, Joseph, 239–241
Snake Hollow, 185
Snow Shoes, 67–69
South America, 121
Sovereign State, 212, 215
Spiritual Exercises, 39, 59, 60
Stabilimento Irlandese, 202
Stabilimento Tedesco, 202
State Government, 215
steamboats, 128, 145, 147, 189, 211, 246, 247
Sunday Vespers, 56
Superior General, 128
superstitiousness, 20, 26, 39, 45, 46, 73, 83, 86, 89, 90, 107, 109, 117, 207
Supreme Court, 213
Supreme Pontiff, 27, 136, 150, 290
Supreme Ruler, 12
Surveyor General, 204

Te Deum, 248

GENERAL INDEX

temperance, 106, 222–225
Temperance Societies, 222, 223
temples, 27, 56, 83, 96, 136, 176, 217, 242
Ten Commandments, 81
Territorial Council, 213
Territorial Government, 148, 179, 199, 212–215, 217
territories, 41, 130, 149, 163, 166, 168, 203, 235
theologians, 25, 31, 32, 244, 246
Thomas, Saint, 185
Three Divine Persons, 73
Total Immersion, 207, 217
tribes, 19, 31, 37, 39, 41–44, 54, 56, 57, 60, 62, 65, 73, 79, 85, 99, 100, 102–106, 108, 111, 113–118, 120–123, 131, 145, 152, 162, 180–184, 202, 203, 212, 214, 215, 217, 233–235, 241, 261, 267, 276
tribunal, 31, 58, 60, 66, 143, 223, 227
Triennial Council, 161, 246, 249
True Church, 25, 27, 159, 232, 243, 274
True Faith, 28, 29, 86, 108, 109, 164, 173, 197
Two French Preachers, 103

Uncreated Wisdom, 54
United Colonies, 138
United States Government, 41, 62, 96, 121, 123, 145, 152, 212, 214
unorthodoxy:
　fanatical, 22, 98, 142, 157, 228, 229, 242–244, 256, 257, 263
　heretical, 4, 6, 195, 259, 269

sectarian, 16, 23, 28, 30, 33, 120, 132, 137, 149, 156–159, 168, 190, 215, 217, 220, 221, 223, 232, 242, 243, 245, 266, 267, 274, 279
Upper Mississippi, 128
Ursuline Convent, 142

Veiled Divinity, 173
Veni Creator, 248
Vicar General, 66, 161, 162
Vicar Provincial, 81
vices, 43, 54, 73, 80, 89, 100, 110, 120, 131, 233
Vincent, Saint, 280

wealth, 48, 102, 118, 129, 130, 132, 144, 152, 175, 201, 250, 272
Western States, 47, 152, 156, 160, 163, 166, 180, 182, 201, 212, 275
Winnebago Indians, 78, 103, 105
Winnebago Prayer Book, 81
Winnebago Tribe, 73
Wisconsin, 18, 36, 41, 43, 56, 59, 62, 63, 65, 68, 73, 78, 80, 100, 102, 106, 110, 114–117, 127, 134, 148, 150, 168, 179, 185, 208, 209, 218, 219, 225, 234–236, 288
Wisconsin River, 65, 73, 78, 80, 106, 110, 112
Wisconsin Territory, 56, 62, 68, 73, 100, 116, 117, 134, 148, 150, 218, 219, 236
Wisdom Incarnate, 37
Wisdom Infinite, 280
Word Divine, 40
Word Incarnate, 2

www.ingramcontent.com/pod-product-compliance
Lightning Source LLC
Chambersburg PA
CBHW022050160426
43198CB00008B/182